Social Interaction and Cognitive Development in Children

This is a volume in
EUROPEAN MONOGRAPHS IN SOCIAL PSYCHOLOGY

Series Editor: Henri Tajfel

A complete list of titles in this series appears at the end of this volume.

EUROPEAN MONOGRAPHS IN SOCIAL PSYCHOLOGY 19
Series Editor: HENRI TAJFEL

Social Interaction and Cognitive Development in Children

ANNE-NELLY PERRET-CLERMONT

*Faculté de Psychologie et des Sciences de l'Education,
Université de Genève, Genève*

Translated from the French by Carol Sherrard

1980

Published in cooperation with
EUROPEAN ASSOCIATION OF EXPERIMENTAL
SOCIAL PSYCHOLOGY
by
ACADEMIC PRESS
A Subsidiary of Harcourt Brace Jovanovich, Publishers
London New York Toronto Sydney San Francisco

ACADEMIC PRESS INC. (LONDON) LTD.
24/28 Oval Road
London NW1

United States Edition published by
ACADEMIC PRESS INC.
111 Fifth Avenue
New York, New York 10003

British Library Cataloguing in Publication Data

Perret-Clermont, Anne-Nelly
　Social interaction and cognitive development in
　children. – (European monographs in social
　psychology; no. 19).
　1. Cognition in children　2. Social psychology
　I. Title　II. Series
　155.4'13　　　　BF723.C5　　　　70–41523

ISBN 0–12–551950–8

Film set in 11/13 point Baskerville
Printed and bound in Great Britain
by W & J Mackay Limited, Chatham

Foreword

Psychologists of the Genevan school have set themselves the task of explaining the regularity, the necessity even, which characterizes individual cognitive development. Using the famous tests of conservation, for example, they are able to show how individual children, each starting from the same initial uncoordinated centrations, usually manage to construct for themselves the same operations of reversibility, identity and compensation. This orderly acquisition of progressively more complex operations is supposed to ensure that each child attains, without too much difficulty, a level of competency required for success at school.

At this point the sociologists step in and remind us of another regularity which characterizes our school systems: the fact that many children, especially those from certain underprivileged environments, do not pass through these school systems without a great deal of trouble. There is a certain irony in the fact that our schools, which are founded on the most egalitarian of principles, manage to reproduce the social order with the very means they use to activate the cognitive competencies of the children entrusted to them.

All kinds of speculations have attempted to link up these two sorts of regularity: the elegant lawfulness of Piagetian genetic epistemology, and the apparent iron inevitability pointed out by the sociologists. Determinisms are then invoked, which some claim to find at the level of hereditary biological factors, others at the level of social environments which may be more, or less, able to enhance the cognitive yield of their children. After this come risky attempts at a complete picture, which are enthusiastically welcomed by some ideological groups, and even more energetically rejected by others. It takes courage, therefore, to enter into this debate.

Anne-Nelly Perret-Clermont has had the courage. Her work in Piagetian psychology at Geneva, and her work in sociology with Bernstein in London, have placed her at the centre of the controversy. In order to chart her way, she has become a social psychologist. The title*

---

* The title of the book in the original French edition is "La Construction de l'Intelligence dans l'Interaction Sociale" (Translator's note).

of her book clearly indicates that it no longer considers cognitive coordinations to be exclusively individual, but studies them in the context of social interaction. The thesis of this book is that it is cognitive coordinations *between individuals* which are the foundation of *individual* cognitive coordinations. To illustrate this thesis, A-N. Perret-Clermont took as her point of departure our research with G. Mugny which showed how, at certain levels of cognitive development, collective performances are superior to individual ones. She shows convincingly how participation in these structuring social interactions plays a part in subsequent individual structuring, and how the social conflict of centrations has an important role in the elaboration of new cognitive coordinations.

This is an important contribution to the debate on the link between cognitive processes and social processes, because it introduces a psychosociological conception of intelligence. This conception of intelligence allows the author of this book to reconsider the import of many studies of the notorious "socio-cultural handicap". These studies are most often based on individual performances in school tests and tasks. But this handicap seems to fall away, at least for performances on Piagetian tasks, when children work together. Of course there is need for more research in this field, but it seems already that the results which A-N. Perret-Clermont presents at the end of her book raise the question of how well-founded purely individualist conceptions of intelligence are.

The research contained in this book ties up with a tradition of the 1930s which culminated in G. H. Mead's "Mind, Self, and Society", Piaget's "Moral Judgment in the Child" and Vygotsky's "Thought and Language". In these classic books, conversation by gesture, interaction among peers, and inner speech are so many forms of social interaction considered essential for the development of the individual. Until now, research in this direction has barely begun. We dare to hope that A-N. Perret-Clermont's book will encourage many others to relate to this important tradition, which remains a very innovating one even today.

February, 1980   **WILLEM DOISE**

Contents

1

Cognitive Development and Social Variables: The Problem

Failure at the beginning of school life: The problem of relating psychological and social factors

That children's chances of success at school vary according to their social origin has been demonstrated many times: Coleman (1966), and Jencks (1972) have shown this in the United States, and Girod (1963), Haramein (1965), Perrenoud (1970), and Gonvers (1974) in Switzerland, to cite only a few examples. In England, Douglas (1964) has shown how early in life the process of selection begins to operate. The C.R.E.S.A.S. (1974) report that 50% of children in French primary schools have had one or more experiences of scholastic failure, that this is already true of 20% of the children by the time they reach the age of 6, and that there is a strong correlation between the scholastic failure of children and the socio-professional standing of their parents from the beginning of school life.

THE PSYCHOLOGICAL APPROACH

Parallel with the findings, there is a series of correlations between school success and verbal and intellectual aptitudes. Jencks (1972) has shown the determining effect of variables related to cognitive aptitudes in school achievement (p. 159), but indicates in the same study how these variables are themselves linked with social class (e.g. p. 78). Such a description suggests an interdependence, but gives no clue as to the nature of any casual relations.

The link between I.Q. and socio-professional category has in fact been known since the time of Binet, and has been the subject of many studies which have systematically added to the picture of such a link existing at the start of education, and becoming stronger with age (see Tort, 1974, p. 22 ff.).

How are these psychological and educational variables related to the sociological variable—social origin, which is of such a very different nature? What mechanisms cause the social status of children to be reflected in their school behaviour and in their performance on psychological tests in such a way that systematic links are found between social disadvantage, intellectual "handicap" and school failure?

If, as Labov (1972a) in particular has asserted, these links exist right at the beginning of school life, what we should examine are, firstly, the processes at work in the psychological development of the child who is first starting school, and secondly the nature and resources of the institution into which the child is being placed.

It has been the aim of some programmes of "compensatory education" to modify school resources so as to give all children an equal chance of success, regardless of their social provenance (see, eg, Little and Smith, 1971 for a review). The relative lack of success of these programmes reveals the inadequacy of a merely pedagogical response to a problem which is educational, psychological and social. Does this force us to the conclusion that it is an impossibility for schools to contribute to the creation of greater social justice, even, following Illich, to the kind of solution which involves the abolition of schools? Or should these failures be attributed to the inadequacy of the psychological science itself to understand properly the psycho*social* processes at work in the development of an individual and their interaction with the teaching institution?

THE SOCIOLOGICAL APPROACH

The contribution of sociologists, as we have indicated elsewhere (Doise *et al.*, 1976), has been to show the links which exist between the teaching institution and the social system, and the way in which, by means of its syllabuses, structure and selection criteria, the school participates in the perpetuation of the existing social classes. This analysis has been the rationale behind the adoption of certain administrative or institutional measures (reform of syllabuses and streaming systems, allocation of grants and bursaries, etc. including in some socialist East European countries and the United States the use of quota admissions, e.g. for black students) which have aimed at a democratization of education. But these reforms have fared no better than those based on a pedagogical rationale in producing measurable results. Western countries are far from having achieved a full democratization of education.

As for the countries of Eastern Europe, "It has been demonstrated statistically . . . that the children of urban working class parents are represented in higher education in proportion to their number in the general population. This is not yet the case for the children of agricultural workers, even though democratisation is in general more advanced in these countries than in the other countries of Europe" (Rapport de la Conférence des Ministres de l'Education d'Europe, UNESCO, 1967, p. 66.). The problem, therefore, still exists for the Eastern European countries. Some authors have interpreted the limits on the success of measures taken in these countries as being due to the impossibility of adopting educational policies which would place at risk the privileged position of the dominant classes* (implying that the same problem is merely posed in different terms in the East and the West). It is possible, however, that the limits imposed are those of sociological analysis, which has been unable to provide any adequate solutions. There is, in fact, a whole area which has been relatively little explored: that of the *mechanisms* by which children are assimilated into society as a whole, and into the groups to which they will belong as adults, in different social contexts—the school being one of these contexts.

This process of assimilation begins very early. As we have seen, right from the beginning of school life, the chances of success are correlated with children's social origins. In parallel, both psychological testing (Tort, 1974) and Piagetian methods of assessment (e.g. Coll Salvador *et al.*, 1974) result in hierarchical classifications of children which reflect their social status. What are the mechanisms underlying the assimilation process we have pointed out? More particularly, how can social contexts be related to developmental levels of cognitive functioning, even to the extent of *determining* them?

TOWARDS A PSYCHOSOCIOLOGICAL EXPLANATION

Several authors have recently put forward hypotheses about the psychosocial conditions in which children are called upon to actualize

---

*"There are good reasons for thinking that a real democratisation of education would be against the interests of the dominant classes, either in eroding their numbers with succeeding generations, or in threatening their dominance in the system of production . . ." (Perrenoud, 1974, p. 35). Even though this author is still hopeful that "with a relatively autonomous educational system, radical and irreversible changes could take place with the help of those who attach more importance to the idea of equality than to their class privileges" (p. 36).

their potentialities. They have seen, either in the content of a test or an examination, or in the psychosocial context of the taking of a test or an examination, factors leading to the differentiation of children. Accordingly, C.R.E.S.A.S. (Vial *et al.*, 1974) have made a new departure in research relevant to this problem, in which "the methodological approach is modified by setting up experimental situations, or types of observation, which permit the investigation of *every* (my italics) child's modes of expression, and which it is hoped will lead to the development of theoretical tools which will integrate the analysis of the different situations in which children are studied, including the social class affiiliations of both researchers and children" (Vial *et al.*, 1974, p. 46). A similar attempt has been made by Marion *et al.* (1974), following their previous finding, between two populations of children from different socio-cultural backgrounds of "clear differences in the manifestation of the children's potentialities . . . particularly in the manner in which a child conducts itself during an examination, in verbal answers, in periods of silence, in argument, and also in the manner of the examiner toward the child, in short in the total adult-child interaction" (Marion *et al.*, 1974, p. 83). For Tort (1974) "the test situation, which comprises the psychologist, the test, and the child, is not an experimental situation but a social relationship whose meaning is not the same for children of different social classes". Eells (1951) has also called into question not only the cultural bias of tests, but also their social bias, arising from their academic and competitive character. Katz (1973) has given a similar analysis. Labov (1972a) makes an analogous criticism of verbal tests, as follows: "The child is in an asymmetrical situation where anything he says can literally be held against him. He has learned a number of devices to *avoid* saying anything in this situation, and he works very hard to achieve this end. One may observe the intonation patterns which Negro children often use when they are asked a question to which the answer is obvious. The answer may be read as 'Will this satisfy you?' If one takes this interview as a measure of the verbal capacity of the child, it must be as his capacity to defend himself in a hostile and threatening situation." (p. 184). Haroche and Pêcheux (1972) consider that the social bias of a test resides, above and beyond the norms of which it is the vehicle, in the relationship between those being tested and the content of the test. The evaluation of intelligence cannot be independent of the ideology implicit in experimental situations.

It seems, then, that certain psychosocial factors could be at the origin of differences in the way in which children manifest their intellectual activity. Do these psychosocial factors merely interfere with the overt *expression* of cognitive aptitudes, or do they rather determine the *course of development* of cognitive processes throughout childhood?

This latter thesis will be explored in the present research, which will look at the interactional processes leading to the genesis of cognitive structures.

The limitations of separate psychological and sociological analyses of the problem seem to reveal a specific *psychosocial* domain of inquiry, which includes in particular the study of the *interactional* processes involved in the course of development. It is interesting to note that it has been with a similar approach—neither simply psychological nor sociological, but "educational"—that a research team at the National Centre for Scientific Research in Rome has arrived at a thesis very similar to ours, namely that childrens' cognitive development is enhanced if they are allowed more social interaction with other children.

AN EDUCATIONAL EXPERIMENT; THE EFFECT OF INTENSIFYING SOCIAL INTERACTION

What was found in Italy in a study of the school system during the decade 1960–1970 (Cecchini and Tonucci *et al.*, 1972) was the persisting existence of a high percentage of educationally retarded children, and also a gap between rich and poor regions, and between higher and lower social classes.* This situation persisted in spite of programmes instituted by the State in order to correct it. These programmes included: financial help for children of poor parents, reduction of class sizes, increased contact hours, the systematic introducion of audiovisual and other technical equipment into schools, in-service training for teachers, special classes for children with specific disabilities (physical, mental and emotional handicaps), and socially mixed classes. However, the intended result was not attained. Cecchini and Tonucci single out for particular notice the failure of the special classes which aimed to integrate into the normal school system children with mild

---

* Such a situation is not confined to Italy. Similar findings in Britain, for example, led the Plowden Committee to recommend measures comparable to those adopted in Italy, in their report "Children and their primary schools" (1967).

intellectual defects. They point out that intellectual defects generally correlate with "cultural deprivation" in terms of social and geographical provenance. Nor has the construction of new school buildings, though, like the other programmes, an essential prerequisite for the creation of favourable school environments, been the remedy for the failure of the other programmes. Cecchini and Tonucci regard the failure of the measures taken, to be due to the fact that they have been confined to particular teaching conditions, and have not affected teacher training, or the orientation of teachers to the teaching situation. They have therefore turned their attention to changing the approach to teaching, which requires in the first place, identifying the mechanisms mediating the correlations between school failure and social class. Starting from the work of Bernstein (1961), Whiteman and Deutsch (1968), and Hunt (1968) they have set up hypotheses regarding the importance of *communication* and *motivation* in the existence of correlations between social class and intellectual development. The work of all these authors, in fact, implies that it is not social class in itself which retards intellectual development, but a kind of "social deficiency" which is closely related to it. This "social deficiency" makes its appearance in several ways. Firstly, in the fact that the child engages in frequent and complex interactions in his own milieu without being aware of whether it is the time taken up by exchanges, or their degree of elaboration, which is the important thing about them. In their educational implications, however, these two variables are equivalent, since in order to augment either, children must be led to communicate on subjects appropriate to their level of cognitive development—i.e. on progressively more complex subjects, otherwise the motive to communicate will be absent. Other ways in which "social deficiency" is manifested are in parents' level of aspiration for their children, and in housing conditions.*

From their study on levels of aspiration, Cecchini and Piperno (in press) conclude that "there is a conflict between the norms of the teachers, whose expectations are calibrated by the pupils of the higher social classes, and the performance of the lower-class children; the removal of the conflict should increase the motivation of lower-class children, as well as their self-esteem and cognitive ability, as a result of

---

* See Lautrey (1974) for a possible explanation (though still unverified) of the role of material conditions in the genesis of cognitive and social structures within the family environment.

removing the gap between their actual and their ideally desired abilities". In order to bring about the transition from teacher-centred norms to child-centred norms on the pedagogical level, and so to resolve this conflict, they recommend changing the directions of communication within the classroom—abandoning the classic exchange *between teacher and pupil* and replacing it with a network of interactions *between pupils*, the role of the teacher then being one of suggesting to the group or groups of pupils motivating, (and therefore interesting) problems. Freinet has already attempted this.

This approach is additionally justified on the grounds that it creates a situation in which the child is led toward self-expression, creativity and exploration through the confrontation with differing points of view. This is in keeping with the importance attached by Piaget's theory of the development of intelligence to the activity of the child, and in particular to exploratory behaviours, and also to the interrelationship of language and thought, and to the growing capacity to coordinate different points of view.

Cecchini and Tonucci's hypothesis is then, that differences in performance between children of different social classes will be removed, and the performance of all improved, by changing teaching methods.

They insist that any method permitting the full development of all children must be based on the construction of knowledge (in the Piagetian sense) on intrinsic motivation toward the task, and on an intensification of interaction and communication between children, with the consequence entailed by all this: the transformation of the relationship between teacher and pupil. I have described elsewhere (Perret-Clermont, 1976) how the type of activity they recommend is related to the familiar world of the child, and forms a link between social relations and school life. School life should no longer centre on a monolithic bloc of children, but rather on the children as an autonomous social group with its own dynamic.

These researchers have carried out a number of experiments, in close collaboration with teachers, which have extended over months or years. Their first results, comparing school performance of lower-class children in their experiment with the performance of children in different types of traditional schools, indicate a measure of success in achieving their aims (Cecchini *et al.*, 1972; Pazienti *et al.*, 1972; Cecchini and Tonucci, 1973). In particular, comparisons of the linguistic production of children of different groups indicate "that the possible linguistic handicaps stemming from socio-economic origins can be easily averted even by the end of the second year in primary school, if an adequate teaching method is used". Children who were taught by this method produced linguistic output which was "of greater length, syntactically more complex, and more 'elaborated' than that of children who were matched for socio-economic status but taught by a traditional method". It was even the case, in these authors' research, that the written language of higher socio-economic status children was relatively inhibited by traditional teaching methods, since the written language of low socio-economic status children receiving an adequate teaching method was superior to that of higher socio-economic status children receiving a traditional teaching method. The question arises whether the same result would be obtained if groups of different socio-economic status received the same adequate teaching method. Would the privileged children keep their advantage? The research done by Cecchini and his colleagues does not answer this particular question, but two such groups were given tests "of cognitive and perceptual performance which indicate that the difference between the groups had considerably diminished by the end of the second year in primary school". The two groups were even "equivalent on Piagetian tests of logic".*

However, detailed comparisons of this kind are not at issue here, even though the evaluation of a teaching programme—which is unavoidably a global matter—creates a number of methodological problems in so far as the demonstration of results is concerned. The authors themselves were less concerned to show the effect of a single mechanism than to demonstrate the fruitfulness of a teaching method which is effective for all kinds of children and which simultaneously takes into

---

* These results should be compared with others coming from research done by the Department of Psychology in Barcelona, which illustrates the role of the teaching method in the acquisition of concepts. Villaronda, *et al.*, (1974) studied the classification behaviour of children from a poor area, and found differences in favour of those who attended a "progressive" school in comparison with others who attended a traditional school. Ciutat Montserrat and Udina Abello (1974) report similar results for the conservation of quantity: "differences in performance on this test which are due to social class tend to diminish, without however disappearing completely, with the introduction of a teaching method which is appropriate to the genetic development of the child" (pp. 132–133). The authors describe this teaching method as "active", but unfortunately give no further information about it. It is however quite likely that a school described as "active" will be one influenced by Freinet and Decroly, and therefore run along lines similar to those recommended by Cecchini and Tonucci.

account fundamental processes of development; processes which are, according to their analysis: the construction of knowledge, intrinsic motivation and communication. The originality of their approach lies in the particular attention they have paid to stimulating communication, and especially interaction, between children.

Problems of education suggest the existence of psychosocial processes. What knowledge do we currently have of these interaction processes, and more generally about the role of social factors in development?

The role of social factors in development

Various theoretical or experimental approaches have attempted to specify the role of social factors in development. They have frequently led to contradictory hypotheses.

THE MACRO APPROACH: CROSS-CULTURAL DIFFERENCES

Some studies have approached the effects of social factors by looking at cross-cultural differences in intellectual development. Representative studies taking this approach are those of Bovet (1968), Inhelder *et al.* (1974, Chapter V), and Bovet and Othenin-Girard (1975). But these authors' emphasis is solely on the internal capacity of the subject for equilibration. Social factors are not seen as causally affecting development, nor at the level of influencing mechanisms, but are rather seen as modulating the course of development differently in different cultures. Some of the work of Bruner *et al.* (1966) is also at this level of definition of the object of study. However, while stating that "although the order of succession (of stages) is constant—each stage is necessary for the construction of the following one—the mean age at which children attain each stage can vary considerably from one social environment to another or from one country to another". Reporting an example from some research in Iran which shows "notable differences between children from the city of Tehran and illiterate children from the villages" Piaget (1972, p. 7) formulates some hypotheses concerning the possible mechanisms: "these different rates (of development) would be due to the quality and frequency of intellectual stimulation received from adults, or via the possibilities for the children to act spontaneously in their environment", and later (p. 8) "the formation and completion of cognitive structures imply a whole series of exchanges and a stimulating environment; the formation of operations always requires an environment favourable to 'cooperation', i.e. to shared activities (consider the role of discussion, of mutual criticism, of the problems raised by the exchange of information, of curiosity sharpened by the cultural influence of a social group, etc. . . .)''. Such hypotheses are higly relevant to the characteristics making up the richness of an environment, but, because they do not form the principal object of study, experimental work in this tradition does not systematically investigate psychosocial features of the environment, and therefore does not provide us with information as to their mode of operation.

Taking a similar global approach to social reality, first in Norway (Hollos and Cowan, 1973) and later in Hungary, Hollos (1975) compared the behaviour of children from environments differing in terms of "the quantity of social and verbal exchanges in which the children are involved". They found that these children differed not so much in logical operations, but in their role-taking skills (the ability to take the role of another person, or to consider points of view different from one's own). Farm children living in a socially isolated environment did less well than village and town children on tests relevant to role-taking, but their performance in logical operations was superior. These results lead the authors to consider that, beyond a certain threshold, language and schooling do not have such an important role in concept-formation as Bruner's theory would claim. They consider their "threshold hypothesis" confirmed: "a minimal level of verbal and social interaction seems to be sufficient for the development of logical operations. In contrast, role-taking behaviours require a higher level" (1975). Their work therefore touches on several of the problems we have already raised, and they themselves pose the question: "what verbal, social and physical aspects of the environment affect what specific aspects of cognitive development has only begun to be given serious attention" (1973, p. 640).

THE MICRO APPROACH: FROM THE SOCIALIZATION OF INDIVIDUAL
THOUGHT TO THE INTERDEPENDENCE OF STRUCTURES OF THOUGHT AND
THE FORMS OF SOCIAL RELATIONS

The Piagetian Approach

In contrast to studies taking a global approach to social reality, some of Piaget's early research includes observations which concern the social development of the individual, but which start from a viewpoint centred exclusively on the individual. Thus Piaget (1923) describes the development of the child out of a primitive egocentrism. This viewpoint leads Piaget, particularly in his book "La Psychologie de l'Intelligence" (1947) to write of "the socialization of individual intelligence" (p. 169, 1956 edition). The terminology alone implies that thought is individual in origin, and becomes progressively more socially determined: "according to the level of development of the individual, the exchanges with the social environment will be very different, and these will in turn modify individual mental structures in equally different ways" (ibid., p. 169). Piaget describes the development of these relations between the individual and the environment: "during the sensori-motor period the baby is naturally already the object of multiple social influences . . . but there is no exchange of thought, since the infant at this level is ignorant of thought; consequently there is no profound modification of intellectual structures by the surrounding social life. With the acquisition of language, however, i.e. in the symbolic and intuitive periods, new social relations occur which enrich and transform the thought of the individual" (ibid., pp. 169–170). Then, at the pre-operational levels, "the structures peculiar to nascent thought preclude the formation of cooperative social relations, which alone can bring about the establishment of logic: oscillating between distorting egocentrism and the passive acceptance of intellectual constraints, the child is not yet subject to a socialization of the intelligence, a process which could profoundly change the mechanisms of intelligence. The problem of the respective roles of social exchange and of individual structures in the development of thought does not arise until the level of the construction of groups of concrete operations, and becomes particularly acute at the level of formal operations" (ibid., p. 173). Following this genetic analysis, Piaget shows how the ability to cooperate would be linked with the development of operations, but he still insists on the simultaneously social *and* individual nature of logic. "As the child's intuitions become articulated and are finally grouped operationally, so it becomes more able to behave in cooperation with others, a social relationship which is different from constraint in so far as it presupposes a reciprocity between individuals who know how to differentiate their respective viewpoints" (ibid., p. 173). "On the other hand, logic itself is not simply a system of free operations—at least, from the psychological point of view, which is the one we are interested in here.

Logic is manifested through states of consciousness, which are charac-
terised by certain constraints to which it is difficult to deny a social
nature, whether this be primary or derivative."

From this text, then, it would appear that it is only that expression of
intelligence which Piaget calls "true thought", i.e. operational, which
can be considered *socialized*. This is a notion which seems reductivist
both of intelligence and of socialization. Piaget himself provides the
possibility, in his other studies, of introducing a much clearer distinction between, on the one hand, the *nature* of intelligence, with its
developmental origins, and, on the other hand, the *forms* which intelligence may adopt. Is it not precisely these forms which may be more or
less socialized, in the sense of being behaviours which are more or less
regulated by the system of relations which Piaget represents as being
optimal and rational: i.e. "cooperation"? To set up, as Piaget does, a
structural isomorphism between operational intelligence and cooperative behaviours should not imply that the social factor, which indeed is
described elsewhere (Piaget and Inhelder, 1966, pp. 122–123) as "the
third fundamental factor in mental growth" has no role to play in other
stages of development. Nor does it entail the absence of isomorphisms
at other levels (this point is developed for the case of categorial differentiation by Deschamps *et al.*, 1976).

Piaget himself has described such isomorphisms between the structure of social interaction and the cognitive structures of individuals at
different levels of development in his sociological (1965) and
psychosociological (1958–1960) approaches. For although, as we have
just pointed out, the problem which Piaget poses is: "the respective
roles of social exchange and individual structures in the development of
thinking", the problem of the interdependence between the structures
of thought and the forms taken by social relations is equally at the
centre of his concerns. Thus Piaget perceives a structural analogy
between the three levels of psychological development—sensori-motor
activity, intuitive thought and operational thought—and the technical,
ideological and scientific activities which constitute social development. In particular, at the level of relationships between social interactions and cognitive operations, he describes how relations of
exchange—intellectual as well as economic—bear witness to a logic
identical with that which is seen in individual operations: ". . . social
relations, when in a state of balance and cooperation, constitute 'group-
ings' of operations exactly like all those logical actions performed by the

individual on the external world, and the laws of grouping define the form of ideal balance common to both" (1965, p. 159). For intellectual cooperation, Piaget specifies the nature of its activities by designating technology and scientific thinking as its special domain (1958, p. 235). At the opposite pole are to be found "collective representations", "the ensemble of non-controlled opinions, obligatory beliefs, myths and ideologies, about which it may be supposed that their formation is intimately linked to their mode of transmission in so far as the prestige of the elders who transmit them plays a role in the formation of concepts in the young people who receive them. The product of the transmission therefore constitutes a form of thought which is more symbolic than objective" (Piaget, 1958, p. 235). This seems to imply, more generally, that since logic presupposes equality in exchange, cooperation permits the full transmission of a notion, while this is not the case for interactions which are rendered asymmetrical by relations of prestige, authority or coercion. In fact, for a concept to be fully acquired, it must be "recreated" by the subject. Short of this, it remains an opinion only, consolidated by extra-logical factors, and arising from non-operational thought.

It is clear that Piaget has concentrated on the role of cooperation, as a *social* factor in cognitive growth. But does not the social factor operate in other situations, and, we may also ask, what are the cognitive consequences of other forms of social interactions? In particular, do interactions which occur earlier than cooperation have any importance in development? Piaget condemns "forms of school organisation which place priority on the authority of the teacher and on primarily verbal transmission, and which lead to perversions of the scientific spirit in the direction of simple, collective, obligatory beliefs" (1958), p. 235). But is the case similar for all forms of interaction which do not arise from cooperation? Are there not some forms of relationship and exchange which prepare the way for cooperation, because they are involved in the genesis of structures of operations from which cooperation arises?

Experimental Investigations

We have so far considered the theoretical aspects of Piagetian views. What research efforts have these given rise to? We can distinguish two currents of research. The first one is based on the hypothesis of a correspondence between the structures which regulate the cognitive activities of the individual and those structures which underlie social interactions. The other current is concerned with the notion of "childhood egocentrism".

In the first category must be included first of all Piaget's own work on language (conversations between children, explanations made by one child to another), on the development of moral judgment, and in particular his study of the development of the game of marbles. This work hypothesized a correspondence between structures involved in individual cognition and in social interaction.

The same framework was adopted by Nielsen (1951), who studied the behaviour of children in situations where they could either act alone, or in collaboration. Techniques were selected which should lead to a cooperative strategy. For instance, two children are asked to produce drawings using pencils which are tied together with a string; this obliges them to coordinate their actions. The aim of this research was to see how the social life of the child is constructed as an "intellectual activity with several participants" (Nielsen, 1951, p. 139). All the techniques she has used show a progression from egocentricity to cooperation, and she writes that, in comparing her results with those of Piaget "we were astonished to find an almost perfect correspondence between his experiments and ours, which demonstrate a complete turning point in social development between the ages of 7 and 8" (Nielsen, 1951, p. 159)—note that this is at the time of appearance of concrete operations. Although Nielsen found the expected isomorphism, it nevertheless appears that understanding was not the only factor involved in these tasks. The social rapport which is established between the partners also has a role: thus, in the example we have already cited, strong competition would oppose the accomplishment of the task, which is to complete the drawing simultaneously.

Dami (1975) has studied the development of children's cognitive strategies in cooperative games for pairs of children. The results indicate development as a function of age, but the line of development is not always that expected theoretically. Children do not necessarily adopt the most rational strategy when they become capable of doing so. The presence of a competitor can have two types of effect on a child's behaviour: "on the one hand it exerts a positive and constructive influence, by allowing the subject to perceive the situation in a more diversified manner, and with greater flexibility (arising from the need to change tactic frequently as a result of the competitor's moves); on the other hand, it exerts a negative and inhibitory influence, since the competitor's activities are constantly opposed to those of the subject, who is prevented from attaining the end in view" (Dami, 1975, p. 209).

Moessinger (1974, 1975) has approached the question from the viewpoint of sharing behaviour, and found that, although very young children do not attempt to appropriate to themselves the goods of both parties, this egalitarian behaviour precedes the appearance of another, very elaborate type of *social*, though not *sociable*, behaviour—blackmail, which is shown by children at the stage of formal thought.

The fact that experiments do not always produce expected behaviours in older children probably indicates that, among "socialized" behaviours, the more "sociable" are not necessarily the most elaborate. Thus, behaviours which do not seem very sociable may nevertheless presuppose a high degree of social intelligence. It seems, then, that the above-mentioned authors probably observed children at the stage where they are capable of cooperating, and in fact cooperating—in the sense of coordinating their actions and operations—but without this being a collaboration in the sense of a rational joining of the resources of the two partners toward the same goal. The system of interpersonal relations implied by cooperation does not seem to be the only one to engender a level of intellectual elaboration. This possibility should be studied by examining in more detail the different types of social interaction, and their relationship to the cognitive resources of subjects.

The work of Flavell (1968) and his colleagues has also been concerned with the correspondence between the development of cognitive activities and certain forms of social interaction. Flavell has not hypothesized any causal relationships between these aspects of development, but has attempted to describe the growth of communicative abilities and role-taking skills. His technique is to set up situations in which the child must coordinate its actions with those of the experimenter, and such situations are used to study the cognitive mechanisms entering into social interaction. Thus he observes, for instance, in very simple games, how the child gradually comes to take into account the intentions of the experimenter. In other tasks, inspired by Piaget and Inhelder's (1948) perspective problem (or three-mountain test). Flavell has traced the development, as a function of age, of the ability to discover the point of view of another person. In another experiment, a set of seven drawings is presented to the subject, who is asked to tell a story about them. Three of the drawings are then removed from the set, and the child is asked what story might be made up by the newcomer who had seen only the four remaining drawings. Decentering in relation to the original story appears around 9–10 years of age. Other tests are concerned with the child's developing ability to take account of the characteristics of a listener, and with the behaviours—and in particular the arguments—used by a child in persuading an interlocutor in role-playing games. This work as a whole demonstrates how the child becomes progressively more able to distinguish between, construct, and take active account of different points of view. While it is clear that this development is tied to that of cognitive structures, we have no precise indication of which intellectual operations are involved in the behaviours which have been studied. This, together with the fact pointed out by Doise (1976b, p. 8) "that social interaction is rarely the expression of a single cognitive structure" no doubt partially explains why neither Rubin (1974) in a study of egocentrism in the spatial domain and in communication, nor Turnure (1975) in research which examined cognitive and role-taking behaviour, found any correlation between the two domains of behaviour of the type that Flavell's descriptions would indicate. Selman (1971), has however found such a correlation between moral judgment and role-taking behaviour which is taken to indicate an "ability to see the interaction between oneself and others from the point of view of others".

In fact, the level that a child appears to have attained for a given concept depends, in part, on the type of task performed. This emerges, for example, from the work of Hoy (1974) which demonstrates that children's success on tasks involving spatial perspective depends on the type of task chosen. Hoy found that the ability of 6, 8 or 10-year-old children to predict the point of view of another person depended most notably on the type and number of characteristics of the object concerned, and the technique used to elicit the response. Similarly, Cox (1975) showed that the age at which children make responses which are no longer egocentric on Piaget and Inhelder's (1948) three-mountain test varies as a function of the experimental procedure. This experiment used two groups of children. The subjects in the first group are asked to indicate the perspective from the viewpoint of a doll which is placed in different positions around the display. For the second group, the procedure is the same except that it is the experimenter who takes up the different positions. Cox obtained better performances (more correct responses and fewer egocentric responses) in the condition where the child had to predict the viewpoint of an adult, rather than a doll.

Appropriately enough, differentiation of the notion of "egocentrism" has been the aim of a second line of research stemming from Piagetian theory. Starting from Piaget's statements about child egocentrism, and his findings on the interdependence between cognitive operations and the ability to coordinate different points of view in 7–8-year-old children, workers in this field have questioned whether egocentrism can really be a useful concept in understanding the nature of children's thought, and whether the socialized behaviours of cooperation might not occur earlier in development than some Piagetian approaches would predict. Thus Borke (1975) has modified the three-mountain test so that it can be used with younger children, and has succeeded in demonstrating that children as young as 3–4 years can appreciate a point of view different from their own.

Flavell and his co-workers (Masangkay *et al*, 1974) used very simple tasks to find out whether children between 2 and 5 years could infer the visual viewpoint of a person in a different position. This ability emerged between 2 and 3 years of age—at least, this is inferred by these workers, since the subjects at this age were capable of "non-egocentric" behaviours such as realizing that another person could see an object which was hidden from them. It is clear, though, that this ability is not of the same order of complexity as that required in dealing with visual perspective, as in the three-mountain test; "if then we say that very young children are capable of representing to themselves something concerning the visual perception of other people, what in fact is being represented? . . . Young children understand that another person can or cannot see the same object as themselves by virtue of certain variables which can be globally characterized as the orientation of the head and eyes of the observer in relation to the object observed. However, this does not mean that the perspective of the object is also understood. In other words, it is possible that no distinction is made between the observer's merely seeing an object—as opposed to not seeing it—and the observer's having a specific perspective on it" (Masangkay *et al.*, 1974, p. 360).

Garvey and Hogan (1973) and Garvey (1974) have observed verbal and play interactions between children of 3–5, which have led them to conclude that there are certain social competences which are prerequisites for these behaviours, and that the concept of egocentrism is not in keeping with them.

The problem remains of the status of the behaviours and social interactions observed. In regard to the interactions in particular, do they arise from some form of "co-action" which precedes true coopera- tion? Are they dependent on a certain level of cognitive development? Or are they rather the basis of a type of development which is simul- taneously social and cognitive? In this case, cooperation would be only one of the forms taken by these interactions as they evolve and develop. In the present state of research, such questions are entirely open.

While we have attempted to show the possible contributions to theoretical debate in psychology of a knowledge of the psychosocial mechanisms operative in child development, and the role of these mechanisms in educational and sociological problems, particularly in poor performance at school, it is clear that such knowledge is still very limited. Piaget's contribution has been mainly to hypothesize an interdependence between cognitive structures and the forms of sociali- zation—on the level of behaviour as well as of judgement or representa- tion. His followers have, firstly, shown how different sociocultural environments can modulate development, and secondly they have attempted to describe with precision the simultaneous development of behaviours at the levels specified by Piaget. This latter approach has shown the precocity of social interaction behaviours, but has not thrown any light on their origin. It is an approach which tends to consider exclusively the subject's actions on the physical environment, and the subject's processes of internal equilibration, as the sources of mental growth.

Such a concentration on the individual considered in isolation, with- out any parallel study of the role of transactions between the subject and the social environment, may lead to the mistaken implication that the "epistemic" subject can be studied in a social vacuum. Whereas other authors present evidence that social factors are operative very early in infancy: "the new-born's gaze follows objects more readily if they are held by someone who imparts a 'teasing' movement to the object—i.e. a movement which takes account of the baby's responses. This fact demonstrates the new-born's extraordinary sensitivity to persons in the environment." (Trevarthen *et al*., 1975, p. 452). Further, these authors have described how the social environment affects the development of the infant from birth, their observations leading them to ascribe a primary role to social factors in the acquisition of con- sciousness and voluntary action: "Just as the visual exploration of detail develops within a context of innate visual orientation movements, so the smile becomes differentiated as a single element out of an innate global communicative activity. Mothers are sensitive to the total communicative activity, not only to the smile: even when the baby cannot produce a very recognizable smile, the mother nevertheless recognizes its sociability. At two months, babies respond to those around them with a whole repertoire of actions which prefigure adult conversation. We are now convinced that, without neglecting the importance of culture in the development of language, whether it be gestural or verbal, the foundation of interpersonal communication exists at birth. Towards eight weeks, this communication is already remarkably developed, while cognitive and memory processes have hardly begun to be manifested. It is tempting to suggest that human intelligence develops, from the start, as an interpersonal process and that the development of consciousness and the capacity to act voluntarily in controlling the physical environment are the result, and not merely a part of, this process." (ibid., pp. 456–457).

Research perspectives

STUDY OF THE EMERGENCE OF CONCRETE OPERATIONS

The research reported here is designed to demonstrate the effect of social interaction on certain aspects of cognitive development. There are several reasons for electing to study development at the time of the emergence of concrete operations.

Educational Relevance

This stage in the mental development of the child corresponds roughly with the first years at school. As we have already indicated, there are certain problems which can arise at this time, of which failure at school is one symptom, and whose solution most probably calls for changes in teaching methods. The most promising innovation would seem to be that of changing pupil-teacher relations, and relations between pupils themselves—a means not only of improving the social and emotional climate of the classroom, but also of improving learning at the same time. At the practical level, educationalists such as Cecchini *et al.* (1972) and De Vries and Kamii (1974) have followed Piaget (1969) in recommending cooperation between children and the use of team work (or games): "from the intellectual point of view, it is this factor (co-operation) which is most likely to encourage the real exchange of thought and discussion, i.e. all those behaviours able to educate critic-ism, objectivity, and discursive reflection" (Piaget, 1969, p. 263). This statement rests essentially on the fact of the simultaneous appearance of operational behaviours and cooperation, and on a structural analysis of their interdependence: "each grouping internal to the individuals is a system of operations, and cooperation constitutes a system of opera-tions held in common, in the proper sense of 'co-operations'. This type of equilibrium cannot really be considered either as the sole result of individual thought, nor as an exclusively social product: internal operational activity and external cooperation are only, and in the most precise sense of the words, the two complementary aspects of a single entity, since the equilibrium of each depends on that of the other" (Piaget, 1947, p. 177). But this analysis does not make explicit any causal mechanisms. On the practical level, the result of this is a lack of precision as to the conditions which should be provided in order for cooperative interaction to take place with the expected beneficial results.

What, then, are these conditions? Two certainties, at least within the Piagetian approach, are that the partners should have attained a particular level of development in order to be capable of cooperation, and that they should be grouped as peers so that their interpersonal relations are not determined by authority or hierarchy, for instance. "In an egalitarian relationship, cooperation is founded on mutual respect between equals. In contrast, in an unequal relationship, 'coop-eration' signifies obedience to the one who holds authority." (Kamii and De Vries, 1974, p. 30). "Relations between adults and children can never be relations between equals, no matter how hard we try. In contrast, relationships between peers are relationships between equals (this equality stems from the fact that all children are children in relation to adults. No child can have the power of an adult)" (Kamii and De Vries, 1974, p. 33–34).

These, however, are theoretical statements which cannot be accepted before we have answers to the following questions: what level of development must be reached before "cooperation" is possible? Does the child require mastery of the notions involved in exchange, or is some pre-operational level of competence sufficient? What has been claimed for partner relationships needs to be verified by determining whether all collaboration between children is in fact collaboration between peers; is it not possible that one of the partners takes on, either explicitly or implicitly, an adult-like position of power? It would be interesting to look at the role of the child's perception of the other child as a peer, as distinct from the role of actual equality. What would happen in the case of an interaction between children who consider themselves as equals, but whose levels of intellectual development are different? The answers to these questions dictate the choice of teaching method: can we recommend "tutoring" (in which a more advanced child takes charge of a less advanced one), or other forms of mutual teaching? Should team-work participants be at the same level of development? Would all benefit in an interaction between children at different levels, or would this amount to an instance of the much-feared levelling to the lowest common denominator? Only experimental studies can help here, and the studies reported later have been directed at these questions.

It is also important to clarify the nature of the tasks used in cooperative work, if we are to identify the conditions which lead to beneficial interactions between children. Such a study can make use of the concepts and methods developed within the framework of social psychological studies of group work in adults (Moscovici and Paicheler, 1973). Although these studies were first focussed on a comparison between individual and collective performance, and led to very varied conclusions (according to criteria and type of task, groups were better, equal to, or less good than individuals) definite gains were made in knowledge about the interaction within groups as affected by the type of task. It seems very likely that similar effects will be found in the case of children, and that a developmental perspective on this subject will help us to define better the conditions of cognitive growth and activity.

The Psychological Contribution

Although the elucidation of the links existing between social interaction and the emergence of cognitive structures at the stage of concrete operations is particularly interesting from the pedagogical point of view, there is another reason why this period of development should be of interest to social psychology. The reason is that this stage in the mental development of the child has been given great attention, not only within the behaviourist framework of research, but above all within the tradition of genetic psychology, which has accumulated a great deal of precise knowledge on this particular subject. Furthermore, it is at this stage of development that intelligence tests appear to reveal most unequivocally the presence of cognitive structures and the extent of their maturity. There are of course similar tests designed to show the operations of formal intelligence, but as we have indicated elsewhere (Doise *et al.*, 1976, pp. 16–18 and 35–40), the contents of these tests are likely to affect the likelihood of subjects' recourse to formal reasoning according to their familiarity, their perceived relevance, or the images they invoke (Haroche and Pêcheux, 1972). We suspect that these problems are more acute at the formal operational than at the concrete operational level. Piaget has commented in a similar vein that adolescents "reach this stage (of formal operations) in different domains as a function of their aptitudes and vocational specialisations: yet the way in which these formal structures are utilised is not necessarily the same in all cases. In our research on formal structures, we have often used experimental situations of a type specific to physics, logic or mathematics, because these seemed to us to be understood by the children (we interviewed). However, it is debatable whether these situations are basically generalizable and capable of application in any school or professional environment" (Piaget, 1972, p.10). "We can keep the notion that formal operations are independent of their specific content, but it must be added that this is only true in so far as the experimental situation appeals to the same aptitudes or to comparable motivations" (ibid., p. 11). If the "social" variable is thus capable of intervening at the level of content, it seems important to us, at least at the beginning of our research, not to take simultaneously as objects of study the effects on cognitive functioning of social interactions, *and* the social significance carried by different contents. An ambiguity on this level would seem to be more easily avoided at the concrete operational level than at the formal operational level. The problem remains, however, and it is necessary to attempt to ensure, perhaps by using a sociological perspective, that the type of interaction situation proposed does not already, of itself, influence the course of the intellectual processes we wish to study.

Epistemological Significance

Finally, while the study of the role of social interactions at the stage of concrete operations is relevant to psychological and educational interests, it also has epistemological significance. From the interactionist point of view, Inhelder, Sinclair, and Bovet, close collaborators of Piaget, consider "knowledge as a relationship of interdependence between the knowing subject and the object known, and not as the juxtaposition of two dissociable entities" (1974, p. 18). We believe that this point of view should be widened to include the interdependence between the knowing subject and *other* knowing subjects, as well as between these and the object of knowledge.

Piaget has demonstrated structural isomorphism which exists between operations and "cooperation", a particular form of social interaction which is characteristic of nascent operational thought. But we believe that approaching the question of *causality* at this level should permit greater clarification of the interactionist and constructivist conception of intelligence.

In his study of Moral Judgement (1932) Piaget does seem to consider cooperation between peers as a causal factor, but he no longer does so in the "Etudes Sociologiques" (1965) and his very plausible hypotheses on cooperation, which ". . . is the most important social relationship for the elaboration of rational norms" (Piaget, 1932, p. 77) remain to be verified experimentally. In the work reported here, we have tried to demonstrate the effect of social interaction on certain aspects of cognitive development, and in particular to see in which conditions the coordinated actions of individuals facilitate the emergence of certain cognitive operations.

The attempt to show that social interaction plays a causal role in cognitive development does not imply an underlying epistemology which conceives of the individual as being passively moulded by external processes. On the contrary, we see the subject as active, in an environment which is always both social and physical, and in which the presence of others obliges the child to coordinate its own actions with theirs. We believe, and attempt to show, that it is through these coordinations with others that the child comes to formulate systems of organization of its actions on the world. The child first seeks to master the surrounding environment of interacting and coordinating individuals, then within this environment will develop its own cognitive structures by a mechanism of abstraction.* In turn, the cognitive development attained will permit the child to participate in novel social interactions, which will again modify the structure of the child's thought. The causal link is circular, and its progression corresponds to the spiral that Piaget traces to describe the direction of development.

What are the links between social interaction and cognitive development? To point out the relationship between the collective and the individual does not commit us to the idea of a simple projection of either one of these on the other, nor to seeing the origins of cognition in the passive appropriation by the individual of a "social heritage", or in a scheme of development determined by external conditions. Our conception is rather interactionist and constructivist: at precise times, which depend on the accumulation of preceding development, certain social interactions in the course of which the individual coordinates actions on the world with those of others, induce the formulation of new cognitive organizations. The coordination of actions between individuals precedes the individual cognitive coordination of certain actions, while being based on competencies which must have been previously acquired or inherited. Thus coordination participates in the dynamic of mental growth without being the only causal factor. The foundations of psychological development are rooted in the conditions of life—in the biological sense of the term—of an organism which is born into an environment which is both physical and social, and which seeks to progressively interact with and master this environment.

Piaget has debated whether "intellectual operations . . . were the product of life in society (as opposed to the egocentric illusions endogenous to the individual), or were the result of nervous or organic activity used by the individual in the coordination of actions" (Piaget, 1966, p. 248) and has concluded that "society . . . is, like all organizations, a system of interactions in which each individual constitutes a small sector which is both biological and social. In this case, the development of the child takes place through continual interactions,

---

* We are referring here to the process of reflective abstraction which "converts . . . the organisation of action schemes into an organisation of logico-mathematical operations in the strictest sense, which appears at around 7 to 8 years. These operations are interiorisable and reversible actions, coordinated in a general system" (Mounoud, 1970, p. 22). "Reflective abstraction draws its information from the coordination of actions which the subject performs on the object. Neither the actions, nor their coordination, have their origin in the object, which merely plays a supporting role" (Inhelder *et al.*, 1974, p. 19).

and it is much too simplistic to see this as the simple response to the educative activity of parents or teachers. Here, as everywhere, there is a dialectical relationship, and the child only assimilates social nourishment to the extent that it is active and engaged in real interactions, not passive or purely receptive" (ibid., pp. 248–249). We would like to be more explicit and, using these very concepts of Piaget's, insist on the role of a social factor which does not merely provide *"social nourishment"* to be *assimilated*, but which calls for an *accommodation* from the subject, an accommodation which in itself creates novelty and is a causal factor in mental growth.

SOCIAL INTERACTION: A CAUSAL FACTOR IN MENTAL GROWTH

"To arrive at the causal mechanism of a development requires in the first place the reconstruction of the pre-existing acquisitions (for no development takes place unless it is from a starting-point of existing structures which are thereby completed and differentiated), and secondly the demonstration of how, and by what factors the existing structures are transformed into those we are primarily interested in" (Piaget and Inhelder, 1959, p. 9).

Piaget and his colleagues have made well-known attempts to reconstruct the different stages through which the development of cognitive structures passes, using logico-mathematical models. The way in which the more developed structures transform out of the lower ones is also an object of research in Geneva (Inhelder *et al.*, 1974). It should be pointed out that the work reported here does not aspire to continue or refine the work of Piaget and his colleagues. Our aim is rather to contribute to the experimental exploration of just one of the factors which influences the development of the child's mental structures. Alongside maturation, the role of experience in acting upon physical objects, and equilibration, Piaget and Inhelder distinguish "a fundamental factor—that of social interactions and transmissions" (1966, p. 123), and this is the object of our study.

We will, however, make use of the knowledge of the development of cognitive structures which has been won by the Genevan group. This knowledge seems to us sufficiently precise to enable us to see the effects of different manipulations of the variables relevant to social interactions.

If we succeed in creating the conditions for cognitive development at the level of mental structures, we will have identified some fundamental processes in mental growth, as well as in social relations. Our approach is similar to that of Inhelder *et al.* (1974) who, in studying "the integrative nature of development . . . necessary for the creation of novel behaviours" (1974, p. 20) started with "the hypothesis that in certain conditions an acceleration of cognitive development would be possible; such an acceleration would be an important sign that we had engaged with the mechanisms of development" (1974, p. 44). Although our approaches are not entirely dissimilar in this respect, they do differ in the object of research. Inhelder *et al.* were interested in the actual formation of cognitive structures, and the mechanisms at work in all aspects of the subject's learning. Our object is to seek to identify the characteristics of social interactions at this formative time, and the way in which these can affect the subsequent organization of the individual's activity and the organization of cognitive structure.

What specific characteristics of social interaction are likely to lead to mental growth? We would hypothesize that one fundamental process in interaction is that which brings about conflict between opposing centrations, which implies, for its resolution, the construction of systems which can coordinate different centrations. This hypothesis is somewhat analogous to the position of some writers who consider that the relevance of interaction with the world to the growth of knowledge consists in the "production of contradictions between the judgments or predictions of the subject and the observations of fact" (Inhelder *et al.*, 1974, p. 323), and who emphasize "the important role of the confrontation of the subject's actions or planned actions with their results" (ibid., p. 324). However, we situate the first cause of these mechanisms, not at the level of a contradiction which the subject might be in with himself, or with the physical world, but at the level of a confrontation between the subject and the statements or actions of other persons—a confrontation which may well be *about* the physical world, or actions upon it. This does not preclude the possibility that these mechanisms can only affect the child's reasoning in so far as the child is capable of the accommodation necessary to set up new coordinations.

This is the reason for the following thesis, which the research reported here is designed to demonstrate: at certain phases of development, the common action of several individuals depends on the resolution of conflict between their different centrations, and this state of affairs leads to the construction of new coordinations in the individual.

One important consequence follows from this: the child who is already relatively more advanced can progress just as much as the less advanced child, in a situation in which two children are finding ways of coordinating their activities.

The thesis we are putting forward is, therefore, opposed to hypotheses of the "modelling effect" type, according to which all learning which occurs during interaction with a partner is due to imitation of the other's behaviour, and that such learning can only occur through imitation of a superior model. Accordingly, it is for us to show that it is not only subjects at a less advanced level, but also those at a more advanced level, who benefit from the coordinations between individuals which bring about restructurings that the individual child alone would not so early be capable of. It needs therefore to be shown that the "modelling effect" is not sufficient to explain the emergence of certain behaviours.

When we began this research, we had fully in mind the early work, mainly American, which tried to explain concept-formation in children according to the theory of social learning, and which formulated particular hypotheses on the effect of the presentation of a model. Our efforts to counterpose a constructivist and interactionist thesis to this view of concept-formation and learning have guided the course of this investigation. It is therefore appropriate to outline our research here by orienting the account with reference to social learning theory. Although we began the research with certain results flowing from this theory in mind, numerous reports have since been published which are relevant to the argument, and which sometimes led us to modify our research plans. For greater clarity, therefore, the outline of our research is given chronologically. The more recent publications stemming from social learning theory will be discussed with those of our experiments to which they are immediately relevant, whether it is the case that these publications actually stimulated the experiments, or that they report results comparable to ours.

Outline of research

CONCEPT DEVELOPMENT CONTRASTED WITH SOCIAL LEARNING THEORY
AND THE MODELLING EFFECT

So far in this introduction, we have posed the problem under the general heading of "social interaction". However a number of researchers, mainly in the United States, have focussed on a particular type of social interaction: that which involves observing a model. The decision to study this type of interaction stems from an orientation according to the "social learning" type of theory formulated by Bandura (1971a,b).

This model effect was first demonstrated and studied in widely different areas—in motor behaviours, affective and interpersonal behaviours, and in moral judgement. The research of Rosenthal and Zimmerman (1972) was one of the first to explore the influence of "social learning" on the modes of reasoning in young children. Using the classical social learning experimental paradigm, Rosenthal and Zimmerman first did a pre-test to determine the subjects' level of performance on conservation problems (using a method adapted from Goldschmid and Bentler's Concept Assessment Kit, 1968). They then asked the subjects to watch an adult model, giving them the following instruction: "Now let's give this lady a chance to play the games. I want you to watch and listen carefully, and you will have a chance to play the game again later." The woman who acted as model was then questioned by the experimenter, and she systematically gave conservation responses on all items. After this session with the model, the subjects were immediately post-tested using the pre-test items and a parallel form. There was also a control group, who did the same pre- and post-tests, but without the session with the model. The results obtained from these two groups showed that only the subjects in the experimental group showed a marked increase in conservation responses in the post-test.

How can these results be interpreted? Rosenthal and Zimmerman see them as showing that conservation responses are acquired through imitation, and went on to do an analogous inverse experiment, in which subjects who gave numerous conservation responses in the pre-test reduced their number of such responses in the post-test after having watched a non-conserving adult model. The authors conclude that the rapidity and magnitude of the changes in behaviour brought about demonstrate the efficacy of modelling techniques for the transmission of abstract knowledge, and they underline their pedagogical importance.

This thesis is an important one in relation to that we are putting forward. In effect, it says that any development observed in a subject after an interaction with a person at a more advanced level of development must be attributed to the simple fact of having been in the presence of a superior model. Similarly, any regression occurring after an interaction with an inferior partner would be explained as the converse of this. The implication is that the group can only be a locus of transmission of pre-existing behaviours, the acquisition of these behaviours occurring through simple imitation either in a progressive or regressive direction.

This kind of research appears to us to raise to view a number of methodological problems, whose interest goes beyond the implications of this one experiment.

One of these problems concerns the instructions, and the social situation experienced by the children who are the subjects of this experiment. Silverman and Geiringer (1973) have emphasized that the exigencies of this experiment could induce the subjects to modify their responses simply because they interpret the instruction as an invitation to copy the behaviours displayed by the adult model. The subjects therefore modified their responses in the post-test because they thought they had to conform to the behaviours they had observed, and not because their beliefs or their perception of the phenomena had changed. Silverman and Geiringer's criticism is therefore a two-level one: it brings into doubt the cause of the change in the observed behaviour (this could be not the fact of having seen a different type of behaviour, but the understanding of the instructions as a request to imitate the model), and it questions the depth of the apparent modifications in response, which could merely be superficial, not reflecting a change at the level of reasoning. But would a knowledge of the subjects' true interpretation of the instructions add to our understanding of their behaviour? While this question is an interesting one, it is not fundamental, since if the subjects did interpret the instructions in the way suggested by Silverman and Geiringer, it is possible to formulate hypotheses equally plausible as the modelling effect to account for the results. Thus, for example, we could ask whether an eventual cognitive change in the subject could not be brought about by their having played a role. The subject could, through having played the role of the adult model, and therefore imitated the adult's gestures and opinions, have undergone a change in perception. This possibility seems to us to be just as plausible as the one put forward by Rosenthal and Zimmerman, especially as Nuttin (1972) has pointed out phenomena of this kind in other areas, and in particular that emotional role-playing can change the affective, conative and cognitive aspects of attitudes—not merely overt behaviour. It seems, in any case, important to be able to specify precisely the consequences of the behavioural changes observed, and therefore to identify the level at which they are produced. It is only on this basis, as Smedslund observes, that it is possible to construct a solid theoretical analysis: "the validity of identification of mental processes is a prerequisite for fruitful theorising at a higher level" (Smedslund, 1969, p. 248).

It is this problem, then, which seems to us fundamental in the interpretation of Rosenthal and Zimmerman's experiment; were sufficient precautions taken in even the identification of the subjects' conservation behaviours? Interesting as this study is, it is difficult to separate the subjects' responses of compliance from any "structural" responses (one cause for suspicion is that the effects of the inferior model appeared particularly on items said to have been "imitated", and less on tests of generalization, suggesting the presence of pseudoregressions). Without a more detailed study of the understanding of instructions, and the coherence of responses, it hardly seems possible to evaluate the significance of the changes observed by these authors. We may indeed ask whether the real object of their research has not been the possibility of changing the verbal behaviour of the child as a function of the more or less implicit demands of the adult experimenter, rather than of changes at the level of reasoning in the child. The psychosociological and pedagogical implications of these two possibilities are very different, only the second offering access to the mechanisms of development.

Rosenthal and Zimmerman's hypotheses therefore require careful examination. If modifications at the level of cognitive structure can be shown, and we think this is possible given an appropriate social situation, it still needs to be established that this is not due to simple imitation. Chapters 2 and 3 are concerned with the demonstration of cognitive changes, and a first attempt to deal with the imitation thesis.

In chapter 4 we look at one of the important aspects of the possibility of certain structural cognitive changes—the developmental level of the experimental subjects at the start of the experiment. On this point, in a sense we meet up with Cowan et al. (1969) who have shown in experiments on moral judgment that an effect which they themselves impute to a model is partly due to the developmental level of the subject in the pre-test. This study of the differential effect of the subject's initial competence permits us to situate any observed progress within the overall framework of development, and at the same time to increase our understanding of the constructivist aspect of development.

Rosenthal and Zimmerman believe that they have shown that modifications in the behaviour of subjects can be produced equally in terms of progression or regression, as a function of the nature of the model. We are also interested in the role of the developmental level of the partner in interactions. The research of Cowan *et al.* (1969), which replicates and extends that of Bandura and McDonald (1963), seeks to establish the limits of the modelling effect, and shows that the effects are both more general and more stable when the model is at a more advanced level. For obvious ethical reasons, and in view of its lack of pedagogical interest, we have avoided any systematic study of the conditions in which subjects may regress cognitively. However, in order to look at this problem we do consider interactions with less advanced partners in cases where it can be hypothesized that they stimulate development in the subjects. If such cases can be effectively demonstrated, they would constitute strong counter-examples to Rosenthal and Zimmerman's thesis. This is the aim of chapter 5.

In the first chapters, then, our aim is to verify that certain social interactions can induce advance in children at the level of operational structures. At the same time, we examine one of the prerequisites of such advance: the developmental status that the subject needs to have reached in order to be affected by the interaction. We also look at how the developmental status of the partners vis-à-vis each other affects the nature of the interaction between them. In chapter 5 we focus on a mechanism we regard as an explanatory key to these interactive processes: socio-cognitive conflict.

The notion of conflict appears as an essential element in the study of the mechanisms of cognitive development. Recent studies on the genesis of operational structures have operationalized this notion in different, but not opposed, ways. Several different types of conflict have been studied, for instance the conflict between hypotheses and the observations which may disconfirm them or create intellectual dissatisfaction (Inhelder *et al.*, 1974) and the operational conflict in which different schemas are simultaneously brought into play but are contradictory (Lefebvre and Pinard, 1972). The object of our study is a third type of cognitive conflict, socially experienced, in which an individual's strategy is explicitly contradicted by another person's strategy. In chapter 5 we report research which aims to verify experimentally the hypothesis according to which the cognitive conflict created by social interaction is the specific locus of cognitive development. We shall show that this socio-cognitive conflict (which is at the same time cognitive yet socially embodied) cannot be reduced to any simple social expression of the types of conflict mentioned above, nor can it be reduced to the imitation of a model.

The results of the total research programme reported here have given rise to two lines of possible further development. Firstly, within the framework of a developmental social psychology which is only now beginning to be established, we can see a coherent field of study in the articulation between individual development and collective processes. Secondly, there are implications for the theoretical foundations of certain pedagogical practices such as group work, tutoring and reciprocal teaching.

Before entering into these possibilities, however, we attempt in chapter 6 to place our results in a sociological perspective. Unfortunately, this can only be sketched. Although from the start our interests have been within a socio-educational framework, as the beginning of this report makes explicit, we could never hope to arrive through the course of a few experiments at any results which would be significant for problems in this area. For this reason we presently lack the necessary means to carry out a systematic and definitive sociological analysis of our results. Even so, we have some material on which to attempt such a placing in perspective: the possibility appears promising, and calls in particular for investigations which would coordinate variables at the psychological and sociological levels. Such a coordination is of course the aim of social psychology, and a sociological reading of the final results of our research suggest that we have indeed reached truly psychosocial mechanisms.

THE METHOD: CLINICAL AND EXPERIMENTAL

So far we have introduced the object of study, the problems which it involves, and the outline of our research. It remains to specify the method. This is a dual one. Since we intended to trace the course of developing intelligence as described by Piaget, we have used the clinical method progressively elaborated by Piaget and his co-workers. This is a method which respects the complexity of the object under study. As Smedslund (1969, p. 237) points out: "many objectively studied mental processes are not anchored to physically defined stimuli at any point. Furthermore, their anchoring is frequently not to physically defined response categories but to the *meaning* of the subject's acts . . . mental processes have the status of constructs and should not be identified with any set of their behavioural manifestations." The study of such processes, if it is to produce valid results, must therefore involve a series of inferences starting from observing and listening to the child. The experimenter is only in a position to make such inferences if he can verify his interpretative hypotheses immediately with the subject. It is this possibility of "instant verification" which is the special contribution of the clinical method: "instant verification, which has always seemed to us to be one of the special characteristics of our method, therefore proceeds alongside experimentation and questioning of the child and leads to an interpretative analysis of behaviour" (Inhelder *et al.*, 1974, p. 40).

The clinical method therefore offers one of the best ways of access to fundamental cognitive organizations. However, our object of study is the role of different types of social interaction in development. In order to carry this out, we must also make use of comparisons, and thus adopt a more quantitative experimental method.

This dual clinical and experimental approach seems indispensable, given the nature of our research. On the one hand, given the complexity of mental processes, the determination of their level of development calls for a minute analysis; such analysis can only be standardized in the broad lines of procedure. On the other hand, we need to set up standard situations which are going to induce a change in the individual. Plainly, such experimental situations are never the sole source of influences on the subject. Factors outside the experimental sessions could either enhance or limit change in the individual, and therefore we need to use quantitative statistical comparisons in order to validate hypotheses which impute a role to the experimental situations in bringing about these changes.

LIMITATIONS OF THE METHOD

The diversity of methodological approaches implies a multiplication of difficulties. Thus, the use of the clinical method confers a greater theoretical validity on the results, but in some of our research this is achieved at the cost of validity on the quantitative and statistical level.

This is due to the fact that clinical procedures require a large investment of time in the collection of data, but also to the difficulty in matching samples given the multiplication of variables and the methods of detecting them.

The attempt to combine the clinical and experimental approaches is not the only source of methodological difficulties. Experimentation using quantitative methods has to meet the difficulty that *all social situations are ephemeral*. A social psychology experiment does not take place in a social void. The mechanisms which come into play during the experimental session are also operative in the social situations experienced by the subject outside the experiment—this is, of course a fundamental question as to the relevance of laboratory situations. At the same time, it is possible that "relevant" effects brought about by the experimental situation are constrained by the fact that similar, though more important ones, take place elsewhere. Deschamps and Doise (1974) have discussed such limitations, but pointed out that the nature of a process at one level does not affect its nature at another level—this relative to the subject's more permanent social environment. This point allows Doise to conclude that "experimentation which takes place within a social setting is neither more, nor less, artificial than other situations. Of course, in so far as it is a transitory situation, an experiment often creates transitory effects which are rapidly absorbed by more important social considerations . . . However, even if the effects are transitory, the processes which take place in an experimental situation are subject to laws which are general enough to transcend any particular situation . . ." (Doise, 1976a, p. 175). Two incidental observations made during the course of our research illustrate the constraints on the experimental demonstration of processes whose very generality means that they must be operating without the manipulations of the experimenter.

The first concerns a little girl of six who was part of the control group in our first experiment. We gave her pre- and post-tests only, on the conservation of liquids, so that according to our experimental design she would provide us with information as to the "natural" development of a child who had not experienced the experimental aspect of the social interactions set up to bring about a measurable cognitive change. At the time of the post-test she displayed behaviours markedly superior to those in the pre-test, but explained to us that she had been so intrigued by the questions in the pre-test that when she got home she asked her mother for glasses and fruit juice and to watch with her what happened to the liquid in different glasses. This little girl, through her attitude after the pre-test and her experimentation with her mother, had created for herself the conditions of our experiment, and these conditions had produced in her the expected cognitive effects! Adhering strictly to our experimental design, we would have to say that this little girl's results weaken our hypotheses.

Another observation of the same type occurred during our third experiment. In the children's recreation break, we noticed a game being played by a little girl who had just been a subject in a pilot experiment in which the task was to share some chocolate drops between two dolls. This five-year-old little girl was playing in a corner of the playground with the dolls and some pebbles, re-living the experimental situation she had just been in. One of her class-mates was watching her. What is the meaning of this game? Was it the working-out of a thought she had had during the experiment? Or was it more a matter of role-playing, at an affective, rather than cognitive level? In fact the occurrence and the meaning of this game did not directly compromise the aim of our experimental design, but what would have happened if the class-mate who had been watching had joined in the game? On what level would the intervention have been, and how far would it have gone to create a social situation of the type we were aiming to create in our experiments? We have no answers to these questions. As for our subject's responses, they indicated that she had progressed by the time of the post-test.

If we were able to observe such "interfering" factors at work in the case of a control subject and a pilot subject, it is highly likely that such factors affected children in the experimental groups. The independent games of these children should serve to remind us, also, that the social factor is not the only one in development, and that its effects are sometimes supported, but sometimes obscured, by other factors.

Of course the observations we have discussed here are extreme cases which probably do not occur very often. It is nevertheless true that experimental interventions such as ours can only be isolated events in the lives of children, and because of this their effects are not easily detected. In an image, they may be compared to weak sound signals in a background of loud noise. The noise may obscure the signals. At the same time, there may be several transmitters other than the one in which we are interested.

Our experimental approach was to try to induce a change, and then to detect it. If we succeed, we will believe that it is because we have managed to engage with the mechanisms we were looking for. Even so, experimentation is not completely outside the realm of reality. It takes place within the context of a reality which is always more complex than the one envisaged by the theory behind the intervention, and which continues to have its own effects throughout. This why we must discover its effects—in order to know whether we have touched upon the levers we are looking for—yet we must not expect necessarily to find great amplitude in our results.

2

The Conservation of Quantities of Liquids: The Effect of Social Interaction on Individual Conservation Behaviour

Before beginning a study of the role of social factors in the intellectual development of children, it must first be shown that certain social interactions can produce an effect at the level of cognitive structure. What group and individual processes are already known which might support an experimental attempt to induce change at the level of operational structures?

Cognitive structuring in group performance

Piaget (1965) has devised a model which demonstrates the isomorphism between operational structures and the structures underlying the social exchange of ideas or values (pp. 49–53, 90–99, 100–171). Elsewhere (1947), Piaget has shown the close correspondence between individuals' ability to participate in certain social interactions and their level of cognitive development. More specifically, some studies have shown that children or adults who coordinate their actions or judgments produce performances which are cognitively more structured than those produced in an individual situation.

Doise (1973), in a study of collective decision-making, compared judgments made by individuals with those made collectively after a group discussion. In a first experiment he asked 4 subjects to individually describe photographs of people using a Likert type scale, and then to reach a consensus description. Factor analysis showed a clearer structure of dimensions in the case of the collective judgments than in the individual judgments. In two other experiments, the subjects were children. The results showed that when they were asked to make aesthetic judgments by ordering figures according to 3 criteria, the children in groups were more likely to make use of the criteria in a hierarchy than they were as individuals. Finally, when groups of children were asked to choose between 5 professions using the method of paired comparisons, intransitivities of choice were less frequent than when individual children made the choices. Using diverse materials and methods, these experiments converge on the conclusion that cognitive structuring is stronger in groups than in individuals. Doise explains these results as arising naturally from social interaction: "it is the divergence at the level of responses which obliges the subjects to work on the underlying opinions, and to re-organize their cognitive approach to the material" (p. 136) . . . "the group, far from contenting itself with a superficial strategy which would be to seek for the response least unsatisfactory to all, instead carries out a thorough re-working which . . . allows them to opt for positive positions".

Taking up this question in the domain of actions and spatial representations, G. Mugny carried out an experiment, described in detail elsewhere (Doise *et al*., 1975) in which he compared the individual and collective performances of children aged from five to six. The experimental task was derived from Piaget and Inhelder's "Three Mountains" test (1948), which brings into play childrens' spatial representations by requiring them to deal with relations of perspective. A model village of three houses in Lego was constructed on a cardboard base which bore a clearly visible coloured mark, to serve as a point of reference for the orientation of the base board. The subjects are given enough Lego pieces to construct another 3-house village on an indentical base board, but four types of village are to be produced. Two of these are easy, the base board of the copy having the same orientation as the model village's, but two are difficult, the base board in these cases being turned through 180° in relation to the model's. The subjects were asked to build the copy villages either individually or in pairs. The dependant variable was an evaluation of how well the houses were placed, in terms of localization as well as orientation. The results showed that the children working in pairs did better than the children working individually, particularly with the more difficult copies.

Could the better performance produced by social interaction simply be an artefact due to the higher probability in a pair of children that one of them will be sufficiently advanced to produce a good performance, independently of the other? An analysis using a technique of Lorge and Solomon's (1955) rejects this hypothesis in favour of the one according to which social interaction produces effects which are not reducible to a simple addition of the cognitive "capacities" of individuals.

The experiments we have just described show, then, that in certain conditions social interaction leads to more complex cognitive structurings than individual action. But from the developmental point of view, are these differences which favour the group rather than the individual found systematically, or are they a function of individuals' degree of mastery of the task? Another question is whether, when interaction produces an effect on collective performance, this effect will be found in individuals later tested alone.

Doise and Mugny (1975) were concerned with the first of these two questions in an experiment on the coordination of motor activities. The results of this experiment showed that, though the difference between performance of individuals and of pairs was significant in the younger children, it was not in the older children. The group produces better-coordinated actions than individuals, but only at a particular level of development, and this superiority disappears with further development.

This result would appear to support the thesis that operations are formed during interaction, but are only acquired later in individuals. However, to give an adequate answer to the second question above, this thesis must be experimentally verified by looking at individual performances following interaction. This is the aim of our first experiment on the conservation of liquids.

Before reporting this experiment, it should be pointed out that similar hypotheses were being put forward at the same time as this work was in progress, by Maitland and Goldman (1974). They took their departure from Piaget's work on cooperation between children (Piaget, 1923) and from studies of peer influence (Haan et al., 1968) but their concern was specifically with moral judgment. They were able to verify both that groups of adolescents formed more developed moral judgments (according to Kohlberg's criteria) than individual adolescents, and that the same individuals *after* group discussion made superior judgments to those they had made before, but these post-test judgments did not differ significantly from the group judgments.

The effect of interaction on individual cognitive structuring

Following Piaget (1923) and Flavell (1967), F. Murray (1972) hypothesized that a conflict in communication which would oblige a child to take account of the viewpoint of another child would be an effective way of teaching what he called "the behaviour of conservation". He gave children with a mean age of 6·7 a pre-test which consisted of a version of Goldschmid and Bentler's Concept Assessment Kit (1968), with a standardized set of questions on six problems of conservation. Each child was awarded a score on the basis of one point for a correct judgment, and two points for a correct judgment accompanied by an operational argument. The maximum possible score was thus 12 points. Murray considered children scoring from 0 to 4 points "non-conservers", and those scoring between 10 and 12 "conservers". In the second experimental session, Murray grouped the children into trios comprising a non-conserver and two conservers, and gave them all the pre-test problems to solve as a group. A week later, the children did the pre-test items again, together with two parallel versions. The results showed that all the subjects scored significantly higher on the post-test than on the pre-test, on all forms of the test. In the absence of a control group, the post-test performances were compared with Goldschmid and Bentler's norms, and found to be significantly superior. Accordingly Murray rejected the hypothesis of improvement due to maturation, and concluded that the improvement was due to the social interaction. Appearing to have forgotten his original hypothesis concerning a conflict of communication, Murray considers that "It is not clear what the non-conservers learned in the social situations that sustained them in the individual situation" (p. 5), and entertains several explanations: is the effect due to imitation of a model, or to the effectiveness of instruction given by peers? Botvin and Murray's study (1975) indicates equal effectiveness of learning based on the presentation of models, and of learning based on active interaction, thus leaving these questions unanswered.

While Murray's experiment shows that interaction between peers can change operational *behaviours*, the significance of these changes at the level of *cognitive structures* still needs to be evaluated. This cannot be done using Murray's data, because the non-conservers who improved had mean scores of between 5 and 8 only on the post-test. It is not possible to tell whether these are due to real operational argument, or to simple correct judgment, since only scores higher than 6 indicate unequivocally the presence of arguments. A proper evaluation of the effect of the social interaction would require an individual analysis of the change undergone by each subject. Our experiment does this by comparing operational improvement in an experimental interaction condition (between peers) with a control condition without interaction.

Another problem left undecided by Murray's experiment is the nature of the mechanism which led to the changes he demonstrated.

Silverman and Stone (1972) did attempt to find out whether the solving of problems in groups led to lasting and general changes in cognitive functioning. As a pre-test, they gave four problems on the conservation of surfaces to 8-year-old children. Those who responded correctly, and with arguments, to all four problems were classed as "conservers"; children who showed no understanding of conservation were classed as "non-conservers". The remaining children were classed as "intermediates". In the week following the pre-test, they put together a conserving and a non-conserving child, told them that their answers had been different, and asked them to agree on a single answer. A month later, the subjects underwent a post-test which was similar to the pre-test, but included two supplementary items. Silverman and Stone found that, as they had predicted, the response of the conserver was adopted as the consensus, in almost all cases (11 out of 14). They attributed this to a feeling of necessity and coherence engendered in the conservers by their reasoning. However, these results show that the subjects in the experimental group gave significantly better conservation responses in the post-test than control subjects who had not experienced interaction. Were these subjects who had improved by the time of the post-test simply repeating the advice they had been given by the conservers? This is quite a feasible hypothesis, since only one of them offered arguments which had not already been given by their conserving partner at the time of the interaction. Even so, it is remarkable that the subjects produced these arguments a month after the interaction, and were able to generalize them to other items.

Using different conservation tests, Silverman and Geiringer (1973) used the same experimental paradigm with the youngest children in primary school, expecting that these subjects would be less likely to improve than older ones, since, still not having acquired conservation in any domain, they would be less likely to put into practice what could be a simple transfer. They had no hypothesis regarding interaction with a peer, but confined themselves to predicting, from Piaget's model of equilibration, that if changes occurred they would be in the direction of conservation rather than non-conservation. Their results confirmed this, and corroborated those of Silverman and Stone (1972). They concluded that the susceptibility of non-conservers only to change following interaction, could not easily be explained by social learning theories, but was rather a datum in favour of the equilibration model.

But how do the mechanisms of interaction influence the process of equilibration? Before exploring these interaction mechanisms themselves, the effects of interaction found by Silverman and Geiringer must be confirmed, and their operational significance specified. This should let us verify whether the effects are due to simple memory or imitation, or whether they are the sign of mastery of new operations.

The conservation of liquids: Experiment I

In order to study the effects of interaction on operational development, we decided to adapt Piaget's classic test on transferring liquids between different containers (Piaget and Szeminska, 1941), which demonstrates that continuous quantities are not initially considered as constant, but their conservation is constructed progressively according to a precise intellectual mechanism. This test offers several advantages for our purposes. Firstly, the notion of conservation is linked with the emergence of concrete operations, an important milestone in the development of thinking. The intellectual operations involved in the conservation of liquids are relatively well known from a psychogenetic point of view, and the clinical method provides a means of identifying them (Vinh-Bang, 1966; Smedslund, 1969). The conservation of liquids has already been the object of many learning studies (see in particular Sinclair, 1967; Inhelder *et al.*, 1974). Secondly, as we shall show in the methodological section, the conservation of liquids test can easily be made into a collective task of a specific kind: sharing. This kind of activity, of its very nature, produces social interaction which is determined by the situation, and not exclusively by the instructions. It is not perceived by the subjects as having a specifically didactic aim.

Our hypothesis was that if a non-conserving subject was asked to share an amount of fruit juice equally between two conserving subjects, in cases where the conservers' interests were not being served they would lead the non-conserver to understand a "fairer" way of sharing out. Such coordination must affect the non-conserver at the level of organization of operations. Then, it should be shown that the child can give evidence of an extended structural understanding of the notion, beyond simple imitation of the partners' behaviour. Such understanding we expected to be revealed in valid and explicit arguments which the child had not previously heard, and which were operationally relevant.

METHOD AND SUBJECTS

In a preliminary study of three schools in the city of Geneva, we found that most of the children in the nursery school (aged 5) were non-conservers (29 out of 36) whereas in the second year of primary school (aged 7) they were usually conservers (ratio: 6 to 7). Accordingly, we decided to select subjects from the first year of primary school (aged 6), so that both non-conservers and conservers in the collective sessions would be from the same school class.

The experiment was carried out between November, 1972 and May, 1973. For the pre-test, children were selected at random from the class registers, although it was occasionally the availability of a child at the time of asking which determined the choice. Only those children who were willing to follow the experimenter out of the class-room and into the experimental room were accepted as subjects. Although, at the beginning, about 1 in 10 children were unwilling, this problem solved itself in the following weeks. It was probably the fruit juice which led to the experiment's eventual popularity! Only two children had to be sent back into class because they were ill at ease in this unfamiliar situation. By the end of May we had managed to see almost all the children in the classes concerned. Most of these children were foreign, but often claimed to speak French better than their native language. We did, however, have to leave out 4 subjects who had obvious difficulties in expressing themselves in French.

We finally had 100 subjects for the pre-test, their ages ranging from 5·6 years to 7·5 years. (The mean age of the control group was 6·7 years, and of the experimental groups 6·6 years.)

MATERIALS

These were a series of transparent laboratory glassware of different shapes: 3 identical 250ml beakers, A, A' and A"; a glass C wider and shorter than the A glasses; a glass D narrower and taller than the A glasses; an opaque bottle containing fruit juice; and some straws.

INSTRUCTIONS, PROCEDURE AND EXPERIMENTAL CONDITIONS

Pre-test Procedure

This was a conservation of liquids test using glasses A and A′ and C.

The child (S) was seated at the head of a table with the experimenter (E). After a brief conversation to establish rapport, E invited S to "play a game with some juice", after which S could drink the juice if he/she wanted to. Then E gave glass A to the child, took A′ for himself, and poured juice into it from the opaque bottle. After this, E asked S to pour some juice into his own glass, so that "both of us have as much to drink (no more, and no less than each other); then we shall both be as happy as each other". In general, this instruction was immediately understood by S, who then carried out the action. E next asked: "what have you done?" or commented "you've poured some juice into your glass", and then added: "well, tell me now, if I drink all the juice in glass A′, and you drink all the juice in glass A, shall we both have drunk as much as each other, or did one of us drink more, or less, than the other—or what do you think?" (The order of presentation of suggestions "more", "less", "the same" was alternated in order to avoid a response bias.) E made sure that S was quite satisfied with the amounts of juice in the two glasses, or, if S was not at first satisfied, encouraged them to modify the amounts so as to be certain that "both have as much as each other to drink". At this point in the procedure, most subjects evinced a scrupulous concern to equalize the levels of juice in the two glasses.

Once this equality was clearly established, E took glass A′ and said to the child: "watch carefully what I am going to do. I feel like having a different glass. I'm going to put my juice in this glass (C)". E then poured the contents of A′ into C, and asked the child: "now, what have we got? have we got the same to drink, or not the same, or what do you think?" E sought to make the child's response explicit by asking for grounds and justifications ("how do you know?" or "are you sure?" or "can you explain?"). He also tried to verify whether, if the child could distinguish between discussion about the dimensions of the containers or the height of the liquid from discussion about the contents of the containers, the child's responses fell into the latter class ("If you were very thirsty . . ."). E asked S to anticipate the effect of pouring the contents of C into A′ ("and if I pour this juice (C) into here (A′) what will we have? Will there be the same to drink in A and in A′, or not?"). E then poured the contents of C into A', allows the child to see the equality, then poured (or asked S to pour) A into C. Next E repeated the immediately preceding questions.

When the child had given clear responses, E made a counter-suggestion, i.e. proposed a response opposed to that already made by the child, either to verify the conviction of the child's response, or to give an opportunity for a change of mind to be expressed. If the child had given a correct response, the counter-proposal aimed to attract the subject's attention to the different levels of liquid in the two glasses. If a non-conserving response had been made, E reminded the child of the initial equal quantities, or drew attention to the dimension that the child was ignoring. An example of a counter-suggestion would be: "there was one little boy who told me that there is more here (or less, or the same) because the glass is wider. What do you think, is he right or is he wrong? What would you say to him?" or "you say there is more juice in this one because the glass is taller; but you could say there is less here because the glass is thinner. What do you think—is there more in one than the other, or is there the same in each?"

At the end of the experiment, E gave S a straw, and invited the child to choose which glass to drink from. In some cases S asked the child's reasons for the choice.

The subjects were divided into three groups according to their operational level on this pre-test: "conservers", "intermediates" and "non-conservers". The criteria used are those described by Piaget and Szeminska (1941) and used also by Sinclair (1967) and Inhelder et al. (1974).

Pre-test Criteria

First stage: no conservation (NC). At this stage, the child sees the same quantity of liquid in identical glasses, and has no difficulty in recognizing the equality. But if the liquid is transferred to containers of a different form, the child believes that the quantity of liquid increases or diminishes as a function of the dimensions taken on by the liquid in these different containers.

When faced with the counter-suggestions of the E, the child either maintains the original judgment, or formulates other judgments, but these will be equally non-conserving. Being reminded of the initial equal quantities does nothing to modify the child's judgment.

Second stage: intermediate response (I). These subjects oscillate between conservation and non-conservation. From time to time they affirm the conservation of quantity, but their justifications are generally inexplicit and incomplete. They do not seem to see a physical or logical necessity in conservation. They oscillate between a coordination of relations (height and width) and centration on a single dimension.

Third stage: necessary conservation (C). From the outset, these children affirm the conservation of quantities of liquids, independent of the number and the nature of transformations which may be carried out. One or more of the following arguments for conservation will be given: indentity, compensation, reversibility (of which we will give some examples later). The child resists the experimenter's counter-suggestions.

Collective Session

This phase of the experiment took place two to three weeks after the pre-test. Three children were gathered together in the room where the pre-test had taken place. Two of the children (S2, S3) were conservers (C) on the pre-test, and the third child (S1) was either a non-conserver (NC) or an intermediate (I).

Sex was made an independent variable by dividing the trios of children into two types: — in the *homogeneous condition*, all three children were of the same sex; in the *heterogeneous condition*, the non-conserving child was not of the same sex as the conservers. There were 19 trios in the homogeneous condition, and 18 in the heterogeneous condition.

The experimental task, identical in these two conditions, was based on another item of Piaget's liquids test in the choice of materials, but was completely different in presentation.

S3 was seated at the head of the table, with S1 and S2 at the sides, facing each other. E told them that they were going to play a game with some juice, which would be a little different from the game they had played the other time. Glass A was assigned to S1, glass D to S2, and S3 was given the opaque bottle containing fruit juice. S3 was asked to pour juice into the glasses of the other two, so that "they would both have the same to drink, and both would be equally happy". E added that, after having poured out the drinks, S3 should check with S1 and S2 for their approval, and it would not be until all three were agreed on the sharing out of the juice that S3 would be able to have a share (in A″), and all three would be able to drink. E placed glass A′ in front of S3, telling the child that this glass could be used if it would be of any help.

This interaction situation lasted about 10 minutes. In most cases, S1 immediately poured juice from the bottle into A and D (no child began by pouring from the bottle into A and A′, then transferring to D). Some children tried to equalize the levels in A and D, others did not. After this, S1 and S2 gave their views, either spontaneously, on being questioned by S3, or by E. When conversation did not immediately take place between the children, but there was a tendency to address remarks instead to the E, then E would direct the childrens' attention to the diversity of views among them, and encourage them to explain their reasons for disagreement. E's role was therefore to maintain the conversation between the children, and occasionally reformulate their remarks, especially when one of the children was timid, or an NC child was not listened to by the others. Overall, E's task was to encourage the group to reach agreement, while remaining unobtrusive and uninvolved with the course of the interaction. If, as happened in some cases, agreement was impossible, E simply asked S1 how much juice should be poured into A″, and then all three children were allowed to drink.

Post-test 1

One week after the collective session, subject S1 was placed again in the pre-test conditions, with the only difference that glass D was used in addition to glasses A, A′ and C. This allowed E to question the child about novel transfers of liquid (e.g. comparison of A poured into C with A′ poured into D). The child's attainment was evaluated according to the same criteria, and using the same methods, as in the pre-test.

Post-test 2

A second post-test, identical to the first, took place about a month after the first.

CONTROL CONDITION

Pre-test. This was identical to the pre-test for the experimental conditions.

Post-test 1. Control group subjects did not take part in a collective session, but underwent a post-test 1 identical to that in the experimental conditions, and with the same interval of time between the two sessions.

DATA COLLECTION

During each session, the experimenter was assisted by one or two people whose role as observers consisted in noting down the procedure, the interventions of E, and all the actions and words of the subject in relation to the configuration of the containers and the quantities of liquid. In half the sessions we used a tape-recorder to verify the protocols, and this showed that, with practice, the observers' records were sufficiently complete.

Results

QUALITATIVE ANALYSIS OF OBSERVED BEHAVIOURS

Pre-test

The behaviours observed during the pre-test were exactly those described by Piaget and Szeminska (1941), permitting us to distinguish between conservers, intermediates and non-conservers.

Among the 100 children tested, 44 were conservers, leaving 56 children available as experimental subjects. For reasons beyond our control (school timetabling, absences, holidays) 7 among these were not finally available.

Following the pre-test, then, our population was defined as 11 intermediate subjects, and 38 non-conservers—a total of 49 subjects roughly equally divided between girls (23) and boys (26).

Collective Session

According to the nature of particular groups, this session involved a small or greater number of interventions by the experimenter, but in all cases the children had verbal exchange with each other, whether giving instructions, demonstration, advice or explanation.

First example (extract from protocol of a collective session).

(...)
Ama (S1) pours juice up to the same level in A and D
Pat (S2) "There isn't the same to drink."
Bru (S3) "No, Pat will have less."
Pat "You should pour it like this" (pours D into A').
Ama (pours A' into D) "There is more in here." (D)
Pat "They are the same."
Bru "They are the same."
Ama "No." (takes some juice out of D, pouring it back into the bottle) (silence)
Exp "The game is that they both have the same to drink, but Pat drinks out of this glass (D) and Bru drinks out of this one (A)."
Ama puts some more juice in D to equalize the levels in D and A
Pat "That's not right."
Bru "She's doing it all wrong. You should take A'."
Ama "follows Bru's instruction, and equalizes the levels in A and A'
Bru "Now pour." (A' into D)
Pat "There, now they are both the same!"
Exp "Is there the same everywhere?"
Bru "Yes."
Pat "Yes."
Ama "No, this one (D) has less," ... "yes, the same."

Second example.

(...)
Isa (S1) pours juice to equal levels in A and D
Exp "Do Ma and Na have the same to drink?"
Isa "Yes."
Ma (S2) "No."
Na (S3) "No."
Isa "That one (D) has a little bit less in, because it's thin."
Ma "Yes, I think you have to put some in a bit higher, I think."
Isa pours a little juice from the bottle into D
Ma "Oh yes."
Isa (to Exp) "Some more?"
Exp "I don't know, you have to ask them."
Isa (to Ma and Na) "Some more?"
Ma and Na "No."
Exp (to Ma and Na) "Well, have you been given the same to drink?"
Ma "I think so."
Isa "That one (D) is so thin, I must put some more in."
Na "Put a little bit more in."
Ma "I know what you should do, put that in there (D in A')."
Isa not understanding Ma's instruction, pours some from the bottle into A'

Ma "No."

Exp "Why do you say no?"

Ma "Because I thought she should pour that (D) into here (A') to see if it's the same."

Na "Put this glass (A') near to this one (A″)," (puts them together) "they are the same."

Exp (empties D into the bottle) "I want Ma to drink from this glass (D) and Na from this one (A)."

(silence)

Exp (to Isa) "Ask Ma if she has an idea."

Ma "You take what you have poured into here (A') and put it in this glass (D)."

Isa pours A' into D

Ma "They are the same."

Isa and Na "They are the same."

Exp (to all three) "Now, is there the same to drink . . .?"

Isa, Ma and Na "Yes."

Isa "The glass isn't magic!"

In the two examples above, the conserving children have essentially watched over events to make sure that equality was achieved, but they made relatively few attempts to explain their remarks to the non-conserver, who merely followed their instructions. This is not the case in the following examples, where we see the conservers giving justifications for their statements, and the non-conservers either accepting or opposing these.

Third example.

Ala (S1) pours equal levels of juice into A and D

Mo (S3) "Ge is going to have more."

Ge (S2) pours D into A', points out the inequality between A and A', asks Ala to equalize the levels, then pours A' into D

Exp (to all three) "Are they the same?"

Ge "Yes."

Exp "Why?"

Ge "We looked."

Exp "Do you all agree?"

Ala and Mo "Yes."

Ge "It was put into the big glass, and after it was put in the little one it was the same."

Mo "This one (D) is taller. The other one (A) is a bit shorter, but fatter."

(. . .)

Ge "No the glass isn't magic. There is just as much. It's taller."

Mo "Taller but not so round."

(. . .)

Fourth example.

(Pat has glass A, Ale glass D)
Fa (S1) pours juice into A and D; the level in D is higher
Ale (S2) "No, Pat has more (A)."
Pat (S3) "No, there's more in this one (D)."
Ale "No, this is thinner (D), that one's thicker (A). Perhaps they're the same, perhaps there's more, perhaps there's less. I can't see."
Exp "I would like Ale and Pat to have the same to drink."
Pat "They're not the same."
Ale "No."
Fa "No, because the glass is thicker."
Fa pours D into A'
Ale "You saw; I've got even less."
Fa "Shall I put some more in?"
Ale "Of course!"
Fa equalizes the levels in A and A'
Ale "Right!" (pours A into D) "I bet you're going to say there's more!"
Exp "If you drink what's in this glass (A') and you what's in this glass (D) will you have the same to drink?"
Fa "No."
Pat "No."
Ale "Yes."
Exp "Explain what you all mean."
Ale "This (D) was poured into here (A). It was the same. The glass isn't magic."
Exp "But here (D) it's higher . . ."
Ale "Yes, I know but it's thinner. If you pour this (D) into here (A) they will be the same."
Exp "Fa, what do you think?"
Fa "Yes."
Ale (pours D into A) "Look!"
Pat points out a very small difference in the levels of A and A'
Fa equalizes A and A'
Ale "Oh! you're not going to count the drops!"
(. . .)

While in most cases, both conserving subjects took part in the verbal exchange and made use of their operational reasoning, in the example above, one of them, Ale, led the conversation and the other one, Pat, seemed to waver between positions.* The reverse case has sometimes

* It was not part of the study, as specified in the Introduction, to look at the conditions which can retard intellectual development, or bring about a regression. However, having observed some subjects who were conservers on the pre-test who later, in the collective session, behaved more like non-conservers, we selected six conservers at random and gave them a post-test. In all six cases, the subjects remained conservers, and gave operational arguments in support of their statements.

happened (though rarely), that a subject who was non-conserving on the pre-test behaved from the start like a conserver when in the collective situation, in which case the role of the two conservers was more restrained. Thus:

Fifth example.

(. . .)

Exp "I'm going to give Ger (S2) this glass (D), Mor (S3) this glass (A), and Fra will give you some juice so that you both have the same amount to drink."

Fra (S1) pours juice into A and D, leaving the level lower in A

Exp "Are they the same?"

Mor "Ger has got more."

Fra "Yes."

Ger "No."

Exp "Agree amongst yourselves."

Fra "I'm going to pour that (D) into here (A') and I'm going to measure." (carries this out)

Ger "I had even less!"

Fra equalizes the levels in A and A'.

Ger "They're not equal."

Fra equalizes again, taking three attempts.

Ger "They are the same."

Fra "Yes."

Exp "I would like Ger to drink out of D."

Fra pours A into D

Exp "Is there the same to drink?"

Fra "Yes."

Exp "Why?"

Fra "There (D), it's taller and thinner."

Exp "Do all three of you agree?"

Fra, Ger and Mor "Yes."

(they drink their juice)

Post-test 1

The subjects individually underwent a post-test, in the conditions described. Once again, their behaviour was similar to that described by Piaget and Szeminska (1941), divisible into three categories: non-conserving, intermediate and conserving. There were a few different cases:

(a) Subjects who were non-conserving on the pre-test, and still non-conserving on post-test 1; thus the behaviour of Fa hardly changed at all.

Pre-test.

(...)

Exp "You're going to put some juice in this glass (A) and this glass A') so that we'll have the same to drink."

Fa pours equal levels in A and A'

Exp "Are they the same, or . . . ?"

Fa "Yes."

Exp "Watch me pour my juice (A) into here (C). If I drink this and you drink that (A) will we have the same to drink, or will one have more?"

Fa "No."

Exp "What is the difference?"

Fa "There's more in A."

Exp "Why?"

Fa "That one (C) is smaller, that one (A) is bigger."

Exp "And if I pour that (C) into here (A) will there be the same in here (A) and here (A'), or more, or less?"

Fa "Yes, the same."

Exp pours C into A) "Are they the same?"

Fa "Yes."

Exp "And if I pour this (A) into here (C), will they be the same?"

Fa "There will be less in this one (C)."

Exp pours A into C, and makes a counter-suggestion about the width of C

Fa "There is more here (A)."

Exp "Which one do you want to drink?"

Fa "This one (A)."

Post-test 1.

Fa equalizes the levels in A and A'

Exp (pours A into C) "Now what?"

Fa "They're not the same because this glass is wider (C)."

Exp "So there is more, or less?"

Fa "Less in this one (C)."

Exp "What do you think about it?"

Fa "Before, in A, it was the same, but now it's wider."

Exp "So?"

Fa "Here (C) it's smaller, there (A) it's bigger."

Exp "Is there the same amount, or more in one glass?"

Fa "Before there was the same. Now there is less in this one (C)."

(...)

Exp "Now I'm pouring this (A) into here (D). Now, is there more, or less, or the same to drink, or what do you think?"

Fa "There's more in this one (D)."

Exp "Why?"

Fa "Because this (D) is thinner and bigger."

Exp "Which one do you want to drink?"

Fa "This one (D)."

(b) Subjects who were non-conserving on the pre-test, but intermediate on post-test 1.

Pre-test.

> *Isa* Has established equality A and A' E has poured A into C.
> *Isa* "There isn't the same."
> *Exp* "Who has got more?"
> *Isa* "Me."
> *Exp* "How is that?"
> *Isa* "This glass (C), it's fatter and smaller."
> *Exp* "Where is it fatter?"
> *Isa* points out the width
> *Exp* "And how much is there to drink? Is there more in it, or less, or the same?"
> *Isa* "There's less in it."
> *Exp* "If I put it back in this glass (A), how much will there be to drink then?"
> *Isa* "It will be the same."
> *Exp* "And if I put it back in this one (C)?"
> *Isa* "It's less."
> *Exp* "So you think there's less in it, but I might think there is more to drink in this one (C), because this glass (A) is thin, so there might be more in it (C)—is that right, or not?"
> *Isa* "That's right."
> (. . .)
> *Exp* "Do you want some to drink?"
> *Isa* "Yes."
> *Exp* "Which glass do you want to drink?"
> *Isa* "That one (A)."
> *Exp* "Why?"
> *Isa* "Because there's more in it."

Post-test 1.

> Isa has equalized the quantities of juice in A and A^1
> *Exp* "I'm going to give you your juice; I'm going to pour it in this glass (C). There. Now if I drink all the juice in this glass (A), and you drink all the juice in this glass (C), will we both have the same amount to drink, or . . . ?
> *Isa* "Yes."
> *Exp* "So if I gave it you in this glass (C), it would be the same?"
> *Isa* "Yes, it's (C) wider."
> *Exp* "But here (A) it's taller."
> *Isa* "Because it's (C) fatter."

Exp "If it's fatter, is there more, or is there the same?"
Isa "No, it's the same. There's more in this one (C) because it's wider."
Exp "What if I pour this (C) into here (A')?"
Isa "There will be the same."
(Exp transfers the contents of C into A'. Afterwards, Exp pours A' back into C)
Isa "It's the same as before, but here (C) it's fatter, so there's more."
Exp "But this one is taller (A)."
Isa "No, this one (C) has more."
Exp "How much is there to drink?"
Isa "There's more in this one (C)."
(. . .) (A is poured into D)
Isa "There's more in this one (D), but it's thinner."
Exp "How much is there to drink, is there more, less, or the same?"
Isa "Here (D) it's taller, and it's lower there (C), but (D) it's thinner and that's (C) fatter."
Exp "But what about the juice? If someone was very thirsty, which one would you give them to drink?"
Isa "This one (D)."

(c) Subjects who were intermediate on both pre-test and post-test 1.

Pre-test.

(equal quantities were poured into A and A', then the contents of A' poured into C)
(. . .)
Exp "If you drink this one (C) and I drink this one (A), will we both have the same amount to drink, will we both be happy, or will one of us be happier than the other?"
Ica indicates that Exp, with the glass (A) will be more satisfied
Exp "Why?"
Ica "There's more."
Exp "There's more. How do you know?"
Ica "I don't know."
Exp (. . .) "Now have I got less, or the same as you?"
Ica "No, there isn't more. The same."
Exp "Are you sure? how can you tell?"
Ica "I don't know."
(. . .)
(A is once more poured into C, after demonstration of the equality between A and A')
Ica "They're the same."
Exp "Why?"
(silence)

Exp "Do you like fruit juice?"
Ica "Yes."
Exp "You can drink some, from this glass (C) or the other one (A). Which do you want?"
Ica "That one (A)."
Exp "Why?"
Ica "I don't know!!"

Post-test 1.

(Ica has equalized the levels in A and A' several times, and then affirmed the equality)
Exp "Now I'm going to pour my juice in here (pours A into C) . . . is there the same amount of juice, or . . . ?"
Ica "Yes."
Exp "Yes? do you know? why?"
Ica "No, I don't know, but I think it's right."
(. . .)
(after several manipulations, A' is poured into C)
Ica "No, they aren't the same." (. . .) "They're the same."
Exp "A little boy who came here told me that there isn't the same amount here (A) and here (C). What would you say to him?"
(silence)
Exp "Could you explain to him that there is the same amount, or not the same?"
Ica "No."
(. . .)
Exp "Which glass would you rather drink?"
Ica "They're the same."

(d) Subjects who were non-conserving on the pre-test, and conserving on post-test 1.

Pre-test.

Ama has equalized the levels in A and A', and confirmed the equality)
Exp pours A into C (. . .)
Exp "Now, do you think there's the same to drink in each, or not?"
Ama "There's less (in C)."
Exp "Why? they're not the same?"
Ama shakes head
Exp "Why? can you make me understand why?"
Ama "There's less here (C) than here (A)."
(. . .)
Exp "A little boy told me there's the same to drink, because A is taller, and C is wider. Do *you* think they're the same?"

Ama "No!"

(. . .)

Post-test 1.

(Ama pours the same amount of juice into A and A′)

Exp "I would like to drink out of here (D) the same amount of juice that there is in here (A′)."

Ama pours A′ into D

Ama "It's the same, because in here (A′) it was the same. Now I'm adding it (meaning 'pouring it') here (C)."

Exp "How is that?"

Ama "The same, because it was the same in this glass (D)."

Exp "But it went higher, then?"

Ama "Yes, but there's the same as there was in here (A′)."

Exp "How do you know it's the same as in there (A)?"

Ama (pouring D into A′) "Because when I put it in here (D) it was the same thing as in there (A′)."

Exp "Why did it go higher when it was poured in this glass (D)?"

Ama "Because it's taller and thinner."

Exp "But it was taller and thinner, does that mean there's more juice, or not?"

Ama "No!"

Further Example.

Pre-test.

(. . .)

(A = A′, Exp pours A into C)

Fra "There's more here (A) than here (C)."

Exp "Why?"

Fra "Because it's (C) smaller."

Exp "But it's wider."

(silence)

Exp "Do you think there's the same to drink, or not the same?"

Fra "Not the same, because this one (A), it's bigger than this glass (C)."

(. . .)

Exp "Which one do you want to drink?"

Fra indicates C

Exp "Why do you want this one (C)?"

Fra "Because there's less."

Post-test 1.

(. . .)

(A = A′, Exp pours A into C)

Exp "What now?"

Fra "They're the same."

Exp "Why?"

Fra "This one's (C) wider. There isn't more because this glass (C) is wider, and this glass (A) is taller."

(. . .)

(A = A'). Exp pours A into D.

Fra "They are the same because this glass (D) is taller and this glass (A) is wider."

(Exp then pours A' into C)

Exp "Now, is there the same to drink, or more, or less, or what do you think?"

Fra "They're the same."

(e) Subjects who were intermediate on the pre-test, and conserving on post-test 1.

Pre-test.

Exp "You pour juice into here (A) and here (A') so that they both have in the same to drink."

Cla carries this out

Exp "Is that right?"

Cla "It's right."

Exp pours A' into C

Exp "If I drink the juice in this glass (C) and you this glass (A), how much will we have?"

Cla "I've got more, because this glass (C) is smaller, and that one's bigger (A')."

Exp "Yes, the glasses are different. But what about the amount of juice to drink?"

Cla "It's the same."

(. . .)

(A = A', Exp pours A into C)

Exp "How much is there to drink?"

Cla "There's more there (A) than here (C)."

Exp "But before you said they were the same."

(. . .)

Post-test 1.

(A = A', A has been poured into C)

Exp . . . "Have we got the same amount of juice to drink?"

Cla "No. They are the same, but now they're not the same, this glass (C) is smaller."

Exp "How's that?"

Cla "Now they're still the same, but there's more height there (A)."

Exp "They're the same? but how can it be that it's higher?"

Cla "Because before they were the same. But this glass (A) isn't so wide."

(Exp pours A' into D)

Cla "It's still the same."
Exp "But a little boy who's just been here thought that there was less in this glass (D) because it's very thin. What do you think?"
Cla "It's the same."
Exp "How would you explain it to him?"
Cla "If we had another glass like this one (D) we could pour that (C) in it, and it would be the same as here (D)."

Post-test 2

Subjects' behaviour on post-test 2 was similar to that on post-test 1, as indicated in the examples, and varied from non-conservation to conservation with operational arguments.

DEVELOPMENT OF RESPONSES IN CONTROL AND EXPERIMENTAL
CONDITIONS

We were able to determine the level of each subject's responses at three points in the experiment (pre-test, post test 1 and post-test 2). Did the level of response change more frequently in the experimental conditions than in the control conditions, which would indicate a subsequent effect of the collective situation in which children interacted? Did the two experimental conditions have a comparable effect?

Comparisons of Subjects' Levels on Pre-test and Post-test 1

Table 1 allows comparison of subjects' levels on the pre-test and on post-test 1, in control and experimental conditions.

TABLE 1

Development between pre-test and post-test 1: NC and I subjects, experiment 1

Level on post-test 1	Experimental conditions		Control condition	
	NC on pre-test	I on pre-test	NC on pre-test	I on pre-test
NC	11		9	
I	9	2	1	1
C	8	7	0	1
Total	28	9	10	2

In the experimental conditions, 24 out of 37 children progressed along the scale of levels NC-I-C, while in the control condition this is the case for only 2 out of 12 subjects. Comparison of the progress made by children who have experienced the collective session with that made by children in the control condition who have experienced only the pre-test and post-test 1 shows beyond doubt that maturation cannot be responsible for the marked progress shown by the experimental children. (For all subjects, i.e. NC and I: chi-squared with correction = 5·70; d.f. = 1; $p < 0·01$, unidirectional hypothesis. For NC subjects only, the exact probability is $p = 0·0068$ (Finney et al., 1963).

The two experimental conditions had similar effects, in that comparable levels of progress were made whether interaction was with same sex partners (11 out of 19 subjects progressing) or with other-sex partners (13 out of 18 subjects progressing).

Previous work on identification and imitation (see Kagan, 1971, pp. 62–66) would have led to the prediction that in the same-sex condition the perception of similarity with the models would have facilitated imitation of the models. This did not occur in this experiment perhaps because, as we shall show later, what occurred was not a matter of simple imitation.

The results show, then, that in both experimental conditions there was an effect subsequent to social interaction, and that sex was not a relevant variable.

The question remaining concerns the durability of the progress indicated by post-test 1.

Comparison of Subjects' Levels on Post-test 1 and Post-test 2

Table 2 allows comparison of subjects' levels on post-test 1 and post-test 2.

TABLE 2

Development between post-test 1 and post-test 2: Experiment 1

		Level on post-test 1			Total
		NC	I	C	
	NC	9	2	0	11
Level on	I	0	3	2	5
post-test 2	C	2	6	13	21
	Total	11	11	15	37

The table shows that:

15 subjects maintained the progress they had made between the pre-test and post-test 1.

8 subjects made further progress between the two post-tests.

4 subjects had regressed to the pre-test level by the time of the second post-test.

The progress indicated by post-test 1 therefore seems to be durable. Why had some subjects progressed further between the two post-tests? It could be hypothesized that the collective session in the course of which the children had had to interact "triggered off" in them the same process of structuration, but slower. This possibility is supported by the fact that Inhelder *et al.* (1974) have also noted a phenomenon of staggered development: "it happens in somes cases that, at some time between the end of the teaching procedures and post-test 1, but particularly between post-tests 1 and 2, certain subjects pass from a fluctuating result to a completely operational solution, or mark a clear progress from one sub-level or category of hierarchical response to another. During the course of the interval between the two post-tests (from 2 to 6 weeks), the acquisitions initiated by the teaching procedures gradually bring about a set of integrations whose precise nature of course eludes us, but the results of which clearly indicate that they are internal reorganisations of the same order as those which occurred (in other subjects) at the time of the teaching situation" (Inhelder *et al.*, 1974 pp. 296–297).

Analysis of Subjects' Arguments in the Post-tests

In order to clarify this process of structuration, we did a qualitative analysis of subjects' responses in the post-test, and in particular we compared these responses with the explanations or justifications given by their partners in the collective sessions. If the arguments produced by the children who have progressed are different from those of their partners, this will show that they are not simply a reflection of the discussions heard during the collective session.

For the 23 children who had conservation responses, (21 conservers on post-test 2, to whom we add the 2 conservers who regressed to the intermediate level on post-test 2), Table 3 shows the operational arguments used by their partners in the collective session (A), and those

TABLE 3

(A) Arguments given by conserving subjects in the collective session (numbers correspond to individual subjects)

	1	2	3	4	5	6	7	8	9	10	11	12	13	14	15	16	17	18	19	20	21	22	23
IDa	+		+		+	+		+	+	+	+	+	+		+	+	+		+	+	+	+	
IDb	+												+			+				+			
CO	+	+		+		+	+	+	+		+	+	+	+	+	+	+		+			+	+
Rinv		+			+	+						+											
Rrec								+															

See text for explanation of abbreviations.

(B) Arguments given by subjects on post-test 1

	1	2	3	4	5	6	7	8	9	10	11	12	13	14	15	16	17	18	19	20	21	22	23
IDa			+		+	+	⊕	+	+				+				+			+		+	+
IDb							⊕																
CO	+	+	⊕		⊕	+					⊕	+	+	+				+	+	⊕	+	⊕	+
Rinv							⊕					+	⊕							⊕			
Rrec				⊕																			

"Novel" arguments are encircled. These are arguments which had not previously been heard by the subject in the collective session.

(C) Arguments given by subjects on post-test 2

	1	2	3	4	5	6	7	8	9	10	11	12	13	14	15	16	17	18	19	20	21	22	23
IDa	⊕	+			+	⊕	+	+	+	+	+					+	+						+
IDb																							
CO	+		⊕	+	⊕	+	+	+	+	⊕	⊕	+	+	+	⊕	+	+	⊕	+	⊕			+
Rinv					+	+						+	⊕	⊕							⊕	⊕	
Rrec													⊕										

introduced by themselves at the time of the post-tests (B and C). These operational arguments have been classified into the three types identified by Piaget (identity, compensation and reversibility) which correspond to the operations constituting the concept of conservation. However, since the aim here was not simply to discern the operations taking place, but also to determine the originality of the child's reasoning, it was necessary to set up two sub-types for identity and reversibility. Although these two sub-types denote the same operations as their corresponding main types, they remain two very different modalities of formulation. Below we give some examples of arguments given by subjects to justify conservation, classified according to type and sub-type:

Identity
IDa: "Because before it was the same."
IDb: Because nothing's been added, and nothing taken away, it's just what there was in the glass."
(We have not included explanations such as "because it's the same juice" or "it isn't the same glass but it's the same thing" which could have been taken for arguments from identity. In very many cases, it is difficult to decide on the status of such utterances: are they simple statements of conservation, or genuine arguments *for* conservation? We have taken the precaution of acting against the direction of our hypothesis, and excluding from the analysis all utterances which were not clearly arguments.)

Compensation
CO: "It's the same amount of juice because this glass is thinner, but taller as well."

Reversibility
Rinv: (reversibility by inversion) "Because if you put this juice (which has been poured from A into C or D) into another glass like this one (A') you'll see that it's the same."
Rrec: (reversibility by reciprocity) (the contents of A have been poured into C) "Because if you pour this juice (in A') into another glass like this (C) you'll see that it's the same."

In view of the criteria used to distinguish levels, the 23 subjects represented in Table 3 were able by definition to produce arguments for conservation. But the analysis of these results shows that 13 of these subjects used one or more arguments which had not been used by their partners in the collective session. Among these novel arguments are 3 from identity, 7 from reversibility and 7 from compensation. It will be noticed that since the argument from identity was frequently given by conserving children during the collective session, it has a very low probability of appearing as a novel argument in the post-tests.

These novel arguments can in no way be accounted for as imitations of partners' behaviour. They are therefore the sign of novel elaboration in the subject, at the level of operational structures.

Discussion of results

The results indicate advance in a large number of subjects. Could this advance be due to the lapse of time between sessions, permitting a certain degree of maturation, or to other events occurring concurrently with the advance? Are we witnessing a test-retest effect, in which the subject being tested for the second time is merely familiarized with the task and the experimenter? These hypotheses must be rejected following comparison of the experimental groups' results with those of the control group.

One question, however, remains open: the effect of the subject's own activity during the collective session, independently of the social interaction. The control group subjects did not experience the same activity. Could this factor be responsible for such a large difference in development? The following experiments will attempt to resolve this problem by varying the types of social interaction and comparing their effects.

First, however, we need to attempt an explanation of the findings so far. Is there any way in which theories of social learning and simple imitation could account for them?

The first difficulty for such an account would be in explaining why non-conserving children should imitate conserving children. In the collective session, the conservers were not presented to the non-conservers as models, but as partners in a joint task. On the other hand, it is possible, although this was not intended, and the situation was not a didactic one, that the subject perceived the conserving children as being more confident, and that this caused the subject to identify with them and imitate them. This is a plausible hypothesis. At the moment, all we have is evidence which annuls the hypothesis that identification occurred as a function of the sex of the conserving partners.

Yet, supposing it were possible to show that the subjects had a tendency to imitate their partners, how then could we explain their new ability to produce arguments other than those they had heard at the time of the interaction? This new ability cannot derive from the assimilation of others' behaviour, which would in any case be impossible in the absence of the necessary structures, but must derive from nothing less than the *creation* of new operational structures.

Consider now the results of the post-tests. The experimental subjects had advanced by the time of post-test 1, and significantly more so than the control subjects. Furthermore, they had made extra advance between post-test 1 and post-test 2. Responses which had been acquired through imitation would have been vulnerable to forgetting during the weeks separating the two post-tests, and in any case it would be difficult to explain how they could have improved with time.

Even those authors in the social learning tradition who have managed to find durability in behaviour change have not been able to explain it within the framework of "modelling". Thus, in work on the imitation of models for moral judgment,* Cowan *et al.* (1969) have shown that a behaviour change brought about by such techniques is more likely to persist if it is in the direction of cognitive development for the child, than if it is in the opposite direction. In order to explain this differential durability, these and other authors have had to appeal, beyond a "modelling effect", to "a cognitive reorganization already going on within the child" (Sternlieb and Youniss, 1975, p. 895)— which is, moreover, a "development from within the child" (ibid., p. 897).

However, as we have already emphasized, the effect which appears in our experiment is not only durable, but improves with time. An explanation by imitation will not serve here. These phenomena are only comprehensible if the collective session is seen as having triggered off a process of restructuring.

Our results show, then, that the progress made by the children in this experiment is most probably of an *operational* nature.

Conclusion

What are the implications of this research? The experiment was designed to show that certain social interactions can modify the cognitive structure of a child, and has in fact shown that, in many cases, a child of around 6 years who is non-conserving or intermediate on pre-test in relation to a precise concept such as the conservation of a quantity of liquid; who then interacts for about 10 minutes with two conserving peers in a collective task making use of this concept, undergoes as a result of this a process of development at the operational level which leads to mastery of the concept. The specific contribution of this

* The research cited on the durability of effects is concerned only with moral judgment; unfortunately we know of none concerning more strictly operational notions.

experiment is the demonstration that this behaviour change is not a learning of individual behaviours, but consists in a development of the subject's cognitive structures. The experiment also shows that this is a type of development which cannot be explained—at least not entirely explained—by the imitation of another's behaviour.

Certain fundamental problems are raised, however, which suggest several further studies. The first problem is that of the modification of cognitive behaviours. There are a number of features, including the fact that the subjects gave arguments in the post-tests which were novel in relation to their own reasoning on the pre-test, but also novel in relation to those given by their partners in the interaction, which indicate that the changes observed were deeper than surface behaviours, and that they involved operational structures. But the method of investigation used, which was limited to a single test and a small number of items, although rendering this interpretation highly plausible, offered no means of observing the *amplitude* of such an effect on the level of operational structures. In particular, we would like to know the extent of generality of such a change. This deficiency in the experiment calls for a second, more clinical investigation of these structural changes. This could be done at the level of the test, even. The addition of items would permit us to observe the child's behaviour more closely, and would also avoid errors due to freak responses. This type of exploration could be supported by the use of other tests which would evaluate the extent to which an observed change was limited to the concept in play at the time of the interaction, or whether the change was more general and affected other concepts. From the evidence of other studies on conceptual generalization, however, which have shown very limited effects, we could not expect to find strong effects.

A second problem has been pointed out by Rose (1973), who has shown that young subjects tend always to reply affirmatively to questions put to them by an adult experimenter. Our first experiment, although including the precaution of open-ended questions and counter-suggestions, is not immune from this problem. Since the correct solution was always the conservation of an equality of quantities ("there is the same amount") it is possible that an error of interpretation was made on the basis of the affirmative responses of those subjects who did not also provide arguments. Could these responses have represented simple acquiescence, or were they true affirmations? A more systematic way of discerning the underlying thinking would be to ask questions to which the correct answer is sometimes the affirmation of an equality of contents, and sometimes the negation of equality. The inclusion of an item on the conservation of inequalities would meet this requirement.

The use of inequalities would also serve to make sure that there were no misunderstandings between the child and the experimenter at the level of instructions. Our instruction in the collective session in effect required the children to bring about a fair sharing-out of the fruit juice. In their conversations, this requirement was often translated into a kind of watch-word: "they must be the same!" It is possible to ask whether some subjects did not aim exclusively at this objective—being able to say that there was the same amount—and that they gave this response on the post-test purely because, since the experimenter himself was transferring the liquid between containers, the result must be correct, and the amounts had therefore been made "the same"! A control for this is evidently not necessary for subjects who gave operational arguments in support of their affirmations, but it would be valuable in the case of subjects who merely affirm conservation, and whose responses therefore have a doubtful status.

A further experiment would also provide the opportunity to concentrate on non-conserving subjects, leaving out intermediate subjects who are more likely to progress in any case. An effect with non-conservers would be more valid than with children who are already closer to operational behaviours.

A number of questions arise concerning the types of interaction and the changes in intellectual structure observed in experiment I. In attempting to maximize the chances of bringing about such changes, we included many factors which seemed likely to have an effect. Thus, we wanted to confront non-conserving (NC) children with views clearly different from their own, and we placed them in a situation with conserving partners. To make sure that the NC subject participated in the activity, we had this child perform the sharing-out. But this accumulation of possible causes now makes it impossible to evaluate the relative contribution of each.

It is possible that it was not the clarity of the opposing viewpoint which brought about a restructuring in the subject, but the pressure exerted by an opposing majority. According to Piaget's analysis (1958), it seems most unlikely that knowledge—as opposed to opinion—could be transmitted in a coercive relationship, and so it is difficult to impute a role to majority pressure. Even so, the question remains whether the fact that the two conservers were at the same developmental level had an effect in itself, or whether this was merely one way of ensuring that the NC was confronted with effective behaviours. And what are effective behaviours? Following work done by Moscovici and Faucheux (1972) in the area of perception, some studies of opinion (Paicheler, 1974; Mugny, 1975) have demonstrated the influence which can be exerted by "consistent" behaviour. Does the same apply in the field of logical knowledge? Supposing it does, would "interindividual consistency" between the two conserving partners be required, or would consistency over time in the case of one of the partners only be sufficient? In other words, what would happen if the conserving subject was in a minority?

More importantly, we need to know whether the specific character of the interactions in experiment I was the cause of the progress observed, or whether the cause was simply being placed in a social situation with other children, irrespective of their number, their roles, their points of view, or their developmental levels, which brought about decentration and subsequent cognitive reorganization in the subject.

3

The Conservation of Quantities of Liquids: The Effect of Social Interaction on Individual Cognitive Structure

The first experiment has demonstrated statistically an effect of interaction on individual cognitive structure. This work needs to be followed up with a clinical investigation which will look at two aspects in greater depth: the nature and role of interactions, and structural transformation in subjects. This approach calls for a double extension of the experimental paradigm, to permit observation of different types of interaction, and to allow the use of different operational tests of the obtained changes.

These, then, are the aims of the second experiment: to extend the means of observation of children in interactions, and to undertake a more thorough clinical study. Though the results may be regarded as confirming those of the preceding experiment, they will not have been arrived at in a comparable fashion. The method of investigation used here is a contrasting one of clinical analysis of a small number of subjects observed in a wide variety of situations, which will explore the plausibility of a whole range of hypotheses concerning the mechanisms operating.

There are, however, two major hypotheses underlying this clinical study. The first is that progress attained at the operational level will be apparent on several different items of the conservation of liquids test; that this attainment will be more specifically present in relation to conservation because it will have been directly brought into play by the task in the social interaction situation, though the subject's progress on other operational tests will be linked to this progress. Progress in the liquids test, therefore, will be accompanied by progress in other concepts and, conversely, a poor performance on several tests may indicate that there is little progress possible in the acquisition of the conservation of liquids.

In testing this hypothesis, we will make use of three other tests of concrete operations, and more specifically of different types of conservation which appear to be acquired almost simultaneously by the child; conservations of number, of the quantity of matter, and of length. It is possible, however, for number to be slightly advanced and for length to be retarded relative to matter and liquids, and for this reason the tests relevant to these different types of conservation are given a different role in the study.

The second major hypothesis concerns the effect of the composition of the subject's two partners. Each partner's level of understanding of the task is likely to entail a different interaction, a more or less developed coordination of actions, and therefore a greater or lesser effect on the subject subsequently.

From these two major hypotheses, together with the analyses previously described, we have derived a number of secondary hypotheses about the individual tests, the effect of different types of interaction, and the mechanisms operating (including the majority effect) which will be presented in the course of reporting the research, for greater clarity.

Technically, we aimed at a collection of data which was the most complete possible, and therefore we intended to make an audiovisual recording of all the sessions. In fact, however, for various reasons (timetabling, availability of rooms and materials, breakdowns of equipment, etc.) we were forced to limit this ambition, and we finally obtained video-recordings of about half the subjects, the remainder being described by detailed notes.

Experiment II

Using an experimental paradigm similar to that of the first experiment, this second experiment was conducted between January and June, 1974 in a different school, this time situated in a suburb of Geneva. The experimental room was an unused staff room which was placed at our disposal.

SUBJECTS

Pilot investigations showed that subjects in the first year of the primary school (6–7 years) were more often conserving than those in the school where we had carried out the first experiment. We therefore had to include subjects from the second year of infant school (aged 5–6 years), amongst whom there were some conservers. A total of 91 children took the pre-test. Of these, we retained only those who were clearly conserving or non-conserving. We had two reasons for excluding intermediate subjects; firstly, intermediates are inherently more likely to advance operationally, hence evidence of advance in non-conservers is more interesting and a severer test of our thesis; secondly, this exclusion enabled us to limit the number of experimental variables. (In fact, an error in classifying the protocols led to the inclusion of a trio with an intermediate subject, thus creating an unforeseen fourth experimental group. We have included this trio in the results, but only in analyses which are independent of the type of experimental group.) The attempt to compose experimental groups containing equal representation of school years, and trios of children from the same school year also caused us to lose a large number of subjects, because of the high frequency of conservers in the first year of primary school and the inverse frequency in the second year of infant school. The experimental "mortality" was further increased by external factors such as the availability of rooms and children, sickness, absences, school outings, and so on, even given the great cooperativeness of the staff.

The different experimental groups, composed in conjuction with the pre-tests, were set up in parallel with each other so that observations could be made at the same point in the school year for each group. The composition of the groups was therefore a function of performance on the conservation of liquids pre-test, and of the "reserve" of pre-tested (and available!) partners. The sum of all these constraints did not finally allow a perfectly equivalent representation of the school years in the different experimental groups. While pointing this out, we do not believe that this omission poses serious problems, since our criteria of analysis are developmental levels, rather than school years. Our final research population consisted of 54 children. The experimental groups were made up of 38 children, including 12 from the first year of primary school, and 26 from the second year of infant school, distributed as follows (a more detailed description will be given later):

Experimental group I (2 C + 1 NC)
15 children including 5 NC subjects, making up:
    3 trios from the first year of primary school. Mean age = 6·10 years.

2 trios from the second year of infant school. Mean age = 5·11 years.

Experimental group II (1 C + 2 NC)
18 children including 12 NC subjects, making up:
  2 trios from the first year of primary school. Mean age = 6·5 years.
  4 trios from the second year of infant school. Mean age = 6·1 years.

Experimental group III (3 NC)
9 children including 9 NC subjects, making up:
  3 trios from the second year of infant school. Mean age = 5·10 years.

Experimental group IV (created inadvertently)
3 children including 2 NC subjects and 1 I subject, making up:
  1 trio from the first year of primary school.

Control group (not experiencing a collective situation)
9 NC subjects:
  2 from the first year of primary school. Mean age = 6·6 years.
  7 from the second year of infant school. Mean age = 6·0 years.

MATERIALS

For the conservation of liquids test, the materials used were the same as those in the first experiment (3 identical glasses, A, A' and A", a glass C which was wider and lower than the A vessels, a glass D which was taller and narrower than the A vessels, an opaque bottle containing fruit juice, and some straws). To these were added a series of four identical glasses which were very much smaller than A (about one-fifth of the capacity).

For the conservation of number test we used two series of coloured counters.

Two balls of plasticine were used for the conservation of matter test.

The conservation of length test used two metal "sticks" of equal length (16 cm) and four smaller metal "sticks" which were a quarter of the size of the larger ones (4 cm).

METHOD

Each experimental group was seen four times. The pre-test was followed by a collective session after an interval of one to two weeks. One week later, the first post-test took place, and then, after a month, the second post-test. The control group took the pre- and post-tests at the same temporal intervals, but did not experience a collective session.

All subjects were questioned in the same manner, this being modified similarly for all groups in the light of subjects' performance on the conservation of liquids test. Since the different tests, which were complementary, were used for different purposes, not all subjects took all the tests. The conservation of number test, which a child may succeed in earlier than the others, was designed to provide a comparison within the non-conservers of liquid—were some of them more advanced operationally than others? The conservation of length test answered to the same purpose in the case of liquid *conservers*, permitting us to distinguish between "original" conservers and those who became conservers during the course of the experiment. All subjects took the conservation of matter test, which permitted a comparison between subjects' development in terms of conservation of matter, and their development in terms of conservation of liquid, or, more generally, related progress in the conservation of liquid, such as was attained in the first experiment, to overall operational progress.

In all the conservation of quantity tests, one item was reserved exclusively until the post-test.

Pre-test

Each subject was tested individually for the conservation of liquid (the procedure will be discribed below). Subjects who were found to be conservers went on to an item testing the conservation of inequalities of liquid. For intermediates, the procedure was suspended at this point.

The pre-test for the conservers was then completed with two items on the conservation of matter and one item on the conservation of length.

The non-conservers' (of liquid) pre-test was completed with tests of the conservation of matter and the conservation of number.

Collective Sessions

For all experimental groups, the instructions and materials used in this session were identical to those in the first experiment.

Post-test 1

As in the pre-test, all subjects were run individually in post-test 1, which consisted of a test of conservation of equality of liquid with a supplementary item (transfer of the liquid into the four small glasses), a test of the conservation of inequality of liquid, and finally tests of the conservation of length and the conservation of matter (3 items).

Post-test 2

This test was also run individually, and consisted of the totality of items on the *conservation of the equality and inequality of liquid*.

EXPERIMENTAL GROUPS

Three experimental groups were formed, taking into account subjects' performance on the conservation of liquids pre-test:
  Group I (I NC with 2 C) (trios with a majority of conservers)
  This consisted of subjects who were NC on the pre-test, and who were placed together in the collective session with two subjects who were C on the pre-test.
  Group II (2 NC with 1C) (trios with a majority of non-conservers)
  NC subjects were placed together with another NC subject and a C subject in the collective session.
  Group III (3 NC) (homogeneous trios)
  NC subjects were placed together with two other NCs.
  Group IV (2 NC + 1 I)
  This trio was obtained by chance, and consisted of two NC subjects with one intermediate subject.

CONTROL GROUP

This comprised NC subjects who did not take part in the collective session.

INSTRUCTIONS AND QUESTIONING PROCEDURES

The approach was similar to that in the first experiment, but the questions envisaged a larger number of situations concerning the notion of the conservation of liquid, and concerned other tests of conservation.

THE CONSERVATION OF LIQUID TEST

Procedure

All children took the conservation of liquids test and were questioned according to the procedure described in detail in the report of the pre-test in experiment I. To the items used in this previous pre-test we added two from the previous post-test, which used glasses C and D simultaneously. After the child had confirmed equal quantities of liquid in the two identical glasses A and A', they were then questioned about the conservation of quantity when A was poured into C, then back into A, then into D and again back into A, and finally when A and A' were simultaneously poured into C and D respectively.

Subjects who were found to be conservers on this test then went on to two items on the conservation of the *inequality* of initial quantities: (1) A contained a larger quantity than A', and the contents of A were poured into C; (2) the contents of A and D were unequal, but the heights of liquid in the two glasses were the same; then D was poured either into A' or into C.

All subjects did all the tests of equality and inequality, in the post-tests, with the additional item of fractionating a quantity of liquid contained in A (equal to the quantity in A') into four small glasses.

Criteria

The criteria were the same as those in experiment 1, but were more refined in view of the more complete questioning adopted in this experiment.

Non-conservers. The absence of conservation was the characterizing feature of these subjects' behaviour. We distinguished several levels within this stage, following the classification of E. Ferreiro (1971):

(1a) Subjects who are incapable of "reversibility", so that if the initial situation consists of equal quantities in A and A', and one of these, say A', is poured into C and later returned to A', these subjects do not see that the initial situation of equality between A and A' is thereby reinstated. They are obliged to carry out the pouring operations themselves in order to see the reinstatement.

(1b) Subjects who oscillate between reversibility and its absence.

(1c) The presence of reversibility: these subjects are able to foresee the reinstatement of equal levels of liquid in A and A', and also the reinstatement of equal quantities, but they do not conserve in the course of the pouring operations themselves.

(1d) These subjects are the same as those in (1c), but in addition they spontaneously suggest the return pouring operations in order to attain the initial equal quantities in A and A', even though they do not always conserve during the pouring operations.

Intermediates. The behaviour of these subjects is characterized by oscillation between denial and affirmation of conservation. Two levels can be distinguished:

I These subjects occasionally affirm conservation, but do not support this with arguments, and are not resistant to counter-suggestions. Initially, they do relate the dimensions.

I⁺ Subjects similar to those in 1, but who occasionally offer arguments in support of conservation.

Conservers. These subjects affirm conservation independently of the number and the nature of transfers of liquid.

C⁻ Conserve on all items concerning the conservation of equality, and provide operational arguments. Nevertheless, they are only at an intermediate level when inequality is in question. (Note that we decided to classify these subjects as conservers, using their success on equality items as the criterion, so as to maintain consistency of criteria in the two experiments.)

C Complete construction of the notion of conservation. Subjects affirm conservation on all items, and justify it using arguments of the type described in experiment 1.

THE CONSERVATION OF NUMBER TEST

This technique was based on that used by Piaget and Szeminska (1941), and again by Inhelder *et al.* (1974).

Procedure

The procedure was similar to one which was used in research we will present later (experiment III), and which will be described in detail then. In this case, however, we used a much smaller number of situations. Briefly, the procedure was as follows.

The experimenter took between 6 and 8 green counters, and placed them on the table in a straight line. The Exp. then asked the child to do the same with yellow counters: "take some yellow counters and put them in the same way; use the same number as me, so that both our lines are the same, with one having neither more nor less in it than the other" (or with a similar instruction). Once this equality had been achieved by the child, E then changed the arrangement of one of the lines by spacing out the counters more widely. Next, these counters were replaced in their original configuration. Finally, the other line of counters was shortened by closing the gaps between the counters. During the course of these changes, E questioned S about the equivalence of the sets of counters: "Is there the same number of greens and yellows, or are there more greens, or more yellows, or what do you think? . . . How do you know?" According to the subject's responses, E proposed counter-arguments in order to verify whether the subject had understood the instructions, to test the solidity of the responses, and in particular to see whether conserving responses were resistant to systematic observations concerning the length of the lines. If the child was unable to establish equality at the outset, E set up two lines of counters by placing successive pairs of counters in such a way that a counter of one colour always had a counter of the other colour in a corresponding position below it.

Finally the test was repeated with 12 counters.

Criteria

Non-conservers. These subjects attempted to establish equality either haphazardly, or by setting up a global correspondence. They may have established equality by constructing the lines counter by counter, or by enumerating the counters. However, even if they managed to establish equality, and possibly also conserved this equality for the smaller sets of counters, they were unable to do so for the sets of 12.

Intermediates. Equality was set up correctly, counter against counter; but responses oscillated between conservation and non-conservation, both between and within items. Their conserving responses were not supported with explicit and complete arguments, unless they resorted to counting.

Conservers. These subjects gave stable conservation responses on all items, including those involving the larger set of counters. Their affirmations were justified either by counting* or by arguments which were characteristically operational (identity, reversibility, compensation).

THE CONSERVATION OF MATTER TEST

This test was the same as that used by Piaget and Inhelder (1941) and Inhelder *et al.* (1974).

Procedure

The experimenter gave the child two balls of plasticine, each about 5 cm in diam. and asked that the two balls be made equal, so that both contained the same amount of plasticine. By questioning, E made sure that the child established the equality of quantity. "Here I've got two balls of plasticine. I would like to have the same amount of plasticine in each ball . . . Let's pretend this is dough to make a cake with, and you're going to eat this ball of dough, and I'm going to eat this one. Will we have the same amount to eat, or will you have more, will I have more, or what do you think?" After this presentation, the E took one of the two balls and flattened it into a "biscuit" of about 8 cm in diam. "Now, is there the same amount of dough in the ball and the biscuit (More to eat . . . Why? Can you tell me how you know? etc. . . . " According to the subject's responses, E formulated counter-arguments concerning the initial quantities (in cases of non-conservation) or the perceptual dimensions (in cases of conservation). Thus, for example: "look here (the biscuit)—it's very flat, and very thin; don't you think there'd be more to eat there (ball)?" Before re-forming the initial ball, E

* Counting is not an operational argument. It appears at a previous level, (intermediate) when the problem of quality is correctly resolved. However, we included as "conservers" those subjects who used counting to affirm the *evidence* of conservation.

asked the child: "If I make another ball with this biscuit, will we both have the same to eat?" E then re-formed the biscuit into a ball, and asked the child to confirm the equality. If necessary, the balls were made more and more nearly equal until the child judged the quantities equal.

The third transformation was to make 8–10 "crumbs" out of one of the balls. The procedure was as in the previous cases, with emphasis on comparing the set of crumbs with the ball.

Criteria

These were, up to a point, analogous with those used in the acquisition of the conservation of liquids.

Non-conservers. These subjects considered that the equality of quantities had disappeared when one of the balls was transformed. Thus, for example, "there is more in the ball because the sausage is very thin" or "there is more in the sausage because it's longer". There was limitation of attention to only one dimension, with occasional switching from one dimension to another but without the ability to coordinate them. Reminder of the initial quantities did not modify these subjects' judgment. Some of them anticipated the return of the matter into equal balls, but others did not.

Intermediates. These subjects oscillated between affirmation and denial of conservation when the transformations were made. In particular, they were swayed by the counter-suggestions of the E. On the other hand, they correctly anticipated the return to the initial equal quantities.

Conservers. The conservation of quantities was seen as evident throughout all the transformations. Their judgments were accompanied by one or more arguments, which were defended against counter-arguments: "they are the same because nothing has been added, and nothing taken away" (identity), or "it's the same here and there because if you remade a ball it would be the same" (reversibility), or "the sausage is long, but it's thin, so they're the same" (compensation).

THE CONSERVATION OF LENGTH TEST

This test was based on the original test of Piaget *et al.* (1948). It will be discussed further, together with other items, in experiment V.

Procedure

After making sure that the child understood the designation of "stick", E placed on the table before the child a stick of 16 cm, and a second stick parallel to the first and coterminous with it:

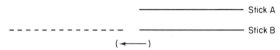

E then asked the child to confirm the equality of length, and displaced stick B, still parallel with A, to the left. The subject was asked: "Are these two sticks the same length, or is one of them longer than the other?" In order to make sure that the child understood the question, illustrations were used, such as: "if we say that this stick (A) is a road, and this stick is another road, (B) is there further to walk on this road (A), or is there the same to walk as on this one (B)?" or "if a little ant walked all along this road (A) (walking the length with two fingers), and another little ant walked all along this road (B), did one of them walk more than the other, or did they both walk the same?" If the subject's responses were conserving, E drew the child's attention to the lack of alignment between the extremities (right-hand, for example) of the sticks. If the responses were non-conserving, E asked the child to recall how the sticks were arranged initially: "What was it like before? Were the two roads the same length then, or what do you think?" After having replaced the sticks in their original position, E began the same type of questioning, but after displacing the other stick (A), in the opposite direction. E asked the child to fully explain the response.

The next item was to place before the child one of the 16 cm sticks (A), and, parallel to this, 4 small sticks placed end to end. The equality of lengths was established using questions analogous to those above. The 4 small sticks were then made into a zig-zag "road" which was coterminous with A at one extremity:

"Now, is there as far to walk on this road (A) as on this one (C)? Do the little ants who walk on these roads go the same distance, or not, what do you think? How do you know? etc. .... " The four small sticks, were then replaced in their initial positions, after which they were re-formed into a different "road":

and the procedure was continued as in the preceding items.

Criteria

Non-conservers. Length was not conserved if one of the identical sticks was displaced. The child attended only to the "extension" to the left or to the right. Similarly, the total length of the 4 small sticks, which was the same as that of A, was not conserved when the configuration of the "road" was changed. Furthermore, the child's judgment was not swayed at all when the lengths in the initial configuration were recalled.

Intermediates. These subjects either gave conserving responses on some items and not others, or on the same item they oscillated between conserving and non-conserving responses. The justifications of conserving responses were not sufficiently explicit.

Conservers. Length was conserved in every situation, and judgments were supported with operational arguments such as "the two sticks are the same. You have only moved one" (identity); or "if you put the little sticks back to make a straight road like before, you'll see that they're both the same, so they're the same length" (reversibility); or, pointing successively to A and the identical but displaced B: "Here (A) it goes further (to the right), but here (B) it also goes further (to the left)" (compensation).

Results

The results and their analysis will be presented in three sections. First, they will be discussed in relation to the results of experiment I; are the findings of the first experiment confirmed, and does the second experiment dispose of the problems outstanding from the inadequate first control condition? Secondly, we will consider in more depth the operational nature of the effects of interaction. Thirdly, we will be concerned with the types of interaction in relation to the amplitude of cognitive effects, in framing hypotheses to account for these effects.

DEVELOPMENT OF BEHAVIOUR IN EXPERIMENTAL AND CONTROL
CONDITIONS: COMPARISON WITH EXPERIMENT I

The subjects' responses were completely analogous to those described by Piaget and his co-workers, and to those obtained in experiment I. We can therefore proceed to the same qualitative analysis, using the criteria set up to determine the subjects' levels on the pre-test, post-test 1 and post-test 2. In fact, the criteria used in experiment II, which were more detailed than those used in experiment I, allow a more detailed evaluation of the intermediate and conserving subjects' responses, although they do not help us to differentiate among the non-conservers. For this, the questioning would need to be more subtle on the items concerning "reversibility", in order to be sure that the counter-suggestions made to the subjects do not lead them to anticipate a return to equal levels in the two initial glasses. The protocols of the sessions show that we did not always leave the subjects the *possibility of an initiative* in expressing reversibility, and that we cannot therefore distinguish between those at level (1d), who suggested pouring back to retrieve the initial equal quantities, from those at level (1c) who understood this possibility without suggesting it, or from those at level (1b) who partially understood it. Since none of our subjects were incapable of reversibility (1a), the sub-levels within non-conservation lose their interest for us. For this reason, we do not discuss them in the presentation of results.

There is also a problem arising from an item involving the transfer of liquid into 4 small glasses in the post-tests: some subjects affirmed conservation for this transformation, but do not for the others. In order to be able to compare the results of the pre- and post-tests, we have left out responses to this item in assigning subjects to levels. We do, however, consider the arguments that the subjects used in justifying these responses.

Table 4 shows the development of subjects taking part in this second experiment, by permitting comparison of their performance on the pre-test and on post-test 1. Recall that all the subjects in this experiment were non-conserving on the pre-test.

TABLE 4

Experiment II: Subjects' development between pre-test and post-test 1 as a function of experimental condition

		Condition I (1 NC + 2 C)	Condition II (2 NC + 1 C)	Condition III (3 NC)	Condition IV (2 NC + 1 I)	Control condition
	NC	1	7	9	1	7
	I	2	0	0	0	1
Post-test 1	I^+	1	0	0	1	0
level	C^-	1	1	0	0	0
	C	0	4	0	1	1
	Total	5	12	9	3	9

In experiment I, non-conserving subjects experienced a collective session with two conserving partners, and by the time of post-test 1 the relatively high proportion of 17 out of 28 of them had advanced in their performance. This result is in fact of the same order* as that obtained in the analogous experimental situation in experiment II (condition I). A similar result was found in condition II, which is a similar condition in so far as non-conservers were in the presence of operational behaviours.

Is the advance made by subjects as a result of these experimental experiences a durable one? Do some subjects progress further in the interval between the two post-tests? If this is the case, we shall see how far the analysis of results in the different experimental and control conditions permit this progress to be attributed to a process of restructuring "triggered off" by the collective session.

Table 5 gives a detailed picture of the changes in behaviour between post-test 1 and post-test 2 in the different experimental conditions of experiment II. Table 6 gives the same information for children who were non-conservers (on pre-test) in experiment I. In condition I in the second experiment, Table 5 shows that the subjects' progress was durable, and moreover that two of the subjects progressed further to attain conservation. These results are exactly in the direction predicted

---

* The clinical nature of experiment II did not permit the collection of data for a large number of subjects, which prevents any quantitative statistical comparison.

TABLE 5

Experiment II: Subjects' development on operational tests in experimental and control conditions

The table is constructed with initial reference to subjects' levels of attainment on the conservation of liquids test. Their levels on the other tests are shown alongside their names. The following abbreviations are used: N = conservation of number test; M = conservation of matter test; L = conservation of length test; + = conserving on the test under consideration; i = intermediate; − = non-conserving; × = subject did not take the test.

Condition I (1 NC + 2 C)

Level on "Liquids" test	Pre-test			Post-test 1			Post-test 2
C⁺					M	L	Gio / NatD
C				Mag	+	+	Mag
I				Gio	−	−	
				NatD	i	−	
				Jos	−	−	Jos
NC		M	N				
	Mag	i	+				
	Gio	−	+				
	NatD	−	i				
	Jos	−	−		M	L	
	Pat	−	−	Pat	−	−	Pat

Condition II (2 NC + 1 C)

Level on "Liquids" test	Pre-test			Post-test 1			Post-test 2
					M	L	
C				Eti	+	+	Eti
				Jeap	−	−	Jeap
				Mar	i	+	Mar
				Ver	+	−	
C⁻				Med	i	i	
I⁺							Med / Mau
I							
NC		M	N				
	Eti	−	+				
	Jeap	i	i				
	Mar	−	+				
	Ver	−	−				Ver
	Med	−	−		M	L	
	Mau	−	−	Mau	−	−	
	Mam	−	+	Mam	−	−	Mam
	Cel	−	−	Cel	−	−	Cel
	Vep	−	−	Vep	−	−	Vep
	Eli	−	−	Eli	−	−	Eli
	Mac	−	−	Mac	−	−	Mac
	Gah	−	−	Gah	−	−	Gah

Condition III (3 NC)

Level on "Liquids" test	Pre-test			Post-test 1			Post-test 2
C							Sop Yvo Deh
C⁻							
I⁺							Yva Vef
I							Cor Jer

		M	N		M	L	
NC	Sop	−	− ⟶	Sop	i	X	
	Yvo	−	− ⟶	Yvo	−	−	
	Deh	−	− ⟶	Deh	−	−	
	Yva	i	i ⟶	Yva	i	−	
	Vef	−	− ⟶	Vef	−	−	
	Cor	+	+ ⟶	Cor	+	i	
	Jer	−	− ⟶	Jer	−	−	
	Tam	−	i ⟶	Tam	−	− ⟶	Tam
	Ced	−	− ⟶	Ced	−	− ⟶	Ced

Condition IV (2 NC + 1 I)

					M	L	
C				Nata	i	i ⟶	Nata
I⁺				Cla	i	− ⟶	Cla
		M	N				
I	Nata	i	−				
NC	Cla	X	−				
	Abe	−	− ⟶	Abe	−	− ⟶	Abe

Control condition

					M	L	
C				Ane	+	+ ⟶	Ane
I				Fab	+	+	
							Dan
		M	N				
NC	Ane	i	+				
	Fab	+	+				Fab
					M	L	
	Dan	−	− ⟶	Dan	−	−	
	Fre	i	− ⟶	Fre	i	− ⟶	Fre
	Mar	−	+ ⟶	Mar	−	− ⟶	Mar
	Eri	−	− ⟶	Eri	−	− ⟶	Eri
	Ste	−	− ⟶	Ste	−	− ⟶	Ste
	Gin	−	− ⟶	Gin	−	− →?	
	Syl	−	− ⟶	Syl	−	− ⟶	Syl

TABLE 6

Experiment I: Development between post-test 1 and post-test 2 in subjects who were non-conserving on pre-test

| | | Level on post-test 1 | | | |
		NC	I	C	Total
	NC	9	2	0	11
Level on					
post-test 2	I	0	2	1	3
	C	2	5	7	14
	Total	11	9	8	28

in experiment I, which placed non-conservers in homologous conditions, and whose progress was in general maintained (17 out of 28) or carried further (7 out of 28). The first experiment also found regression in 3 subjects. This did not occur in condition I of the second experiment, but it did in condition II for 2 subjects; of the other 10 subjects, 9 retained their post-test 1 levels, and 1 had improved further by post-test 2.

How does development compare in the different experimental conditions and the control condition? In conditions I and II, which confronted subjects with one or two conserving partners, progress is apparent on the first post-test. In several cases, these subjects make further progress between the two post-tests. In condition III, by contrast, subjects who were with others of the same level (non-conserving) showed no progress by post-test 1, but a high proportion of them had attained a higher level by the time of post-test 2 (7 out of 9). Should the superior performance on post-test 2 for all these conditions (and for the subjects of experiment I) be attributed to maturation, to personal experiences of the child, or to familiarization with the questioning procedure—that is to say, to factors independent of the experimental manipulation, which was controlled social interaction?

The answer to this question is provided in the analysis of our control subjects' development. These subjects experienced the same questioning procedure (and so were equally familiarized with it), and at the same intervals of time (thus they had the same opportunities for maturation or for personal experience). Only 1 out of 8* of these control

* One subject was absent at the time of post-test 2.

subjects progressed between the two post-tests, while one of the 2 subjects who showed progress on post-test 1 later regressed. The results of this control condition are therefore clearly different from those of condition III: in the one condition, subjects progressed very little, in the other very much more. These results favour the hypothesis of a re-structuring process initiated by the interactive session in condition III.

On the basis of a comparison between the control condition and condition III alone, it is not possible to exclude the possibility that it was merely acting upon the material, permitted by the collective session task, which brought about the process of re-structuring. But such a hypothesis would not explain why progress should have been more rapid in conditions I and II than in condition III.

THE EFFECT OF INTERACTION ON INDIVIDUAL COGNITIVE STRUCTURES: ITS SIGNIFICANCE FOR THE DEVELOPMENT OF OPERATIONS

We used two techniques to approach a deeper clinical analysis of individual operational changes. The first was to extend the conservation of liquids test itself. The second was a parallel administration of other tests diagnostic of cognitive structures. The results of these tests are now analysed in turn.

THE CONSERVATION OF LIQUID TEST (EXTENDED VERSION)

(1) The addition of new items concerning the conservation of the equality of quantities meant that we had more time in which to question each child, and also that there was more opportunity for the child either to reinforce the coherence of their responses, or to reveal difficulties of coordination in oscillating between one level of response and another. This approach therefore increased the validity of our diagnosis of a subject's developmental level, by giving the subject more opportunities to give explicit expression to their thinking.

The following extract from a protocol illustrates the growing coherence of response which can occur:

Exp pours some juice in A, and the child Ver pours some in A' to establish initial equality

Exp (then pours A into D) "Is there the same amount of juice, or not the same amount, or what do you think?"

Ver "No, you've got more, because you put it in a bigger one (glass)."
Exp "But another little boy told me these were the same. Is he right?"
Ver "No."
Exp "What would we have to do to get the same amount of juice?"
Ver "Empty some in here (A)."
(D is then returned to A: A = A')
Exp "And now have we got the same or not?"
Ver "Yes."
Exp (pours A into C) "Is there the same amount now, or what?"
Ver "Yes."
Exp "Why?"
Ver "It's fatter and shorter here (C), but you can still drink the same amount."
Exp confronts Ver with a counter-suggestion, attributed to "another little boy"
Ver "He wasn't right."
Exp "So we've got the same to drink?"
Ver "Yes."
Exp returns to the preceding situation, pouring C into D and asking the child to compare A' and D; Ver then affirms conservation
Exp "But before you said that when the juice is in here (D) it's not the same amount, do you remember?"
Ver (pointing to A and A') "Before I saw that it's the same as here."
(. . .)
(A = A': Exp pours some of A' into the bottle: A A', after confirmation of the inequality, Exp pours A' into D)
Exp "Now, do we have the same amount of juice, or not?"
Ver "No. I saw before that you had more in there (A)."
(A is poured into C. Exp asks the child to compare C and D)
Ver "They aren't the same, because you poured a bit into the bottle."
(C is returned to A)
(A and D have the same levels)
Ver "No, (they're not the same) because you put more in (A)."

Another child, Mau, was intermediate on post-test 2, her responses alternating from the start. The second item provides the opportunity for reasoning indicating conservation, but the third item once more reveals non-conservation:

(A = A')
Exp "Is there the same amount to drink in these two glasses?"
Mau "Yes."
(A is poured into C) "Is there the same amount to drink . . .?"
Mau "No, it's thicker and rounder (C)."
Exp "What would we have to do if we wanted each to have the same to drink?"

Mau "To get the same, you would have to put that (C) into here (A)."
(. . .)
  Mau "There's more in C. No, the same amount of juice, but the glasses are different. If you put this (C) back into here (A) you will have the same thing."
Exp "And if we leave this here (C)?"
Mau "It isn't the same."
(C is poured back into A)
Mau "The same."
Exp "And if I pour (A) here (D)?"
Mau "You drink more here (D) because it's taller."
Exp gives Mau a counter-suggestion
Mau "It's (D) thin. You can't drink the same amount. There's more here (D)."
Exp "If you drink this (A') and I drink that (D) will one of us drink more than the other, or will we both drink the same?"
Mau "The same amount of juice, but it's taller there."
Exp "How can that be?"
Mau It's the same amount of juice, even if it's in this glass (D)."
Exp "It's both taller and the same thing?"
Mau "Not the same glass, but the same amount of juice, because I knew that that (D) was in there (A)."
(Exp pours D into C)
Mau "No, it's not the same."
(. . .)
(A = A': A is poured into the four small glasses)
Mau "Hey! you've got more!"
Exp "But the glasses are half empty."
Mau "That one has got more, good, it's the same, not a little bit less."
Exp "How do you mean?"
Mau "Not the same. There's more there (4 glasses)."
Exp "More juice?"
Mau "Yes."

Most protocols, however, show the subject maintaining the same level of response throughout, and the different items only provide the opportunity for them to repeat their first explanation. There were very few subjects who changed their centration or point of view, in spite of the experimenter's counter-suggestions. Even for the intermediate subjects, who one would expect to oscillate between different types of response, it seemed that questions relating to the first item would set the style of responses.

Cor was non-conserving at the time of post-test 1, and invoked the same reasons in all situations:

$(A = A')$

$(A'$ is poured into C)

$(\ldots)$

Cor "I've got more (A). Mine is taller. That one (C) is wider and that one (A) is smaller, so it's me who drinks the most."

Exp "If we both wanted to drink the same, what would we have to do?"

Cor "I'd have to pour this (C) back into here (A')." (this action is carried out, and $A = A'$)

(then A is poured into D)

Cor "There's more here (D)."

(after Exp's counter-suggestion affirming equality, Cor's response is decisive)

Cor "No-o! There it's smaller (D) so you must put it back in A. Then that will make it the same."

$(\ldots)$

$(A = A'$: A is poured into the four small glasses)

Exp "Now will one of us have more to drink, or is it the same?"

Cor "It's less there, it isn't the same. Not the same size."

Exp "Do you think one of us is going to have more to drink?"

Cor "Me, I'll drink more."

Exp "If someone was very thirsty, which one should they drink?"

Cor "The little glasses. It's the same."

Exp "The same?"

Cor "Yes."

Exp "And if I pour the 4 glasses back into here (D), will it be the same thing, or more, or what?"

Cor "That makes more, there (D)."

Exp "What should we do to make them the same?"

Cor "Pour back into there (A)."

At the beginning, one might have thought that since Cor talked about the two dimensions of the glasses, the additional situations would have given her an opportunity to coordinate them and so modify her responses. In fact this did not happen, and apart from a moment of hesitation when the juice was poured into the 4 small glasses, she continued to affirm non-conservation by drawing attention to the differences between the containers.

On post-test 2, Vef gave both operational and pre-operational responses. From the outset, she refers to identity ("you didn't put it back in the bottle"), but at the same time centres herself on the differences in dimensions, which she sees as the cause of inequality. Vef oscillates in this way throughout:

$(A = A'$: A is poured into C)

Vef "That makes less in here (C) because it isn't the same glass any more."

Exp "Is it the same juice?"

Vef "Yes."

Exp "Is there less juice to drink, or the same?"

Vef "Less!"

Exp "There was a little boy, before you, who told me it was the same juice, so it was the same amount to drink. Was he right or was he wrong?"

Vef "He was right because it's still the same juice inside."

Exp "How do you know it's the same juice?"

Vef "Because you didn't put it back in the bottle."

Exp "Don't you think there's more in here (C)?"

Vef "No."

Exp "If you were very thirsty, which one would you drink?"

Vef "This one (A)."

Exp "Why?"

Vef "There's more!"

Exp "But before you said they were the same. Which is right?"

Vef "Both!"

Exp "Explain it again so that I understand properly."

Vef "You didn't put any juice in the bottle, so that makes them the same, only this one (C) is fatter, so that makes less."

(...)

(A = A': A' is poured into D)

Vef "It's the same because D is thinner, so that makes more."

(...)

(A = A': A' is poured into D, and A into C)

Vef "In this glass (D) it's thinner and in this one (C) it's fatter, so there's more here (D) and less in this one (C)."

Exp "If someone were very thirsty, which one should they drink?"

Vef "They should drink this one (D)."

Exp "Is there more in it?"

Vef "Yes."

(...)

(A = A': A is poured into D)

Vef "That makes it thinner here (D) and fatter here (A), but they are the same."

Exp "How do you know?"

Vef "You didn't put any back in the bottle."

(...)

Sop is conserving on post-test 2, and also uses an explanation based on the same argument (compensation) throughout:

(A = A': Sop pours A' into C)

Exp "Is there the same amount of juice, or not?"

Sop "Yes, because the glass (C) is wider, because like that it makes more space for the juice."

(A is poured into D)

(. . .)

Sop "Yes, because it's thinner, it's the same but only because the glass is taller and smaller."

Exp "But there are some children who say that there's more here (D)."

Sop "That's not right."

(D is poured into the 4 small glasses)

Sop "It's the same because the glasses are smaller and thinner, and there's more."

Exp "How do you know there's the same amount of juice?"

Sop "They're thinner, so the juice goes higher up."

(. . .)

Jeap also conserved from the first item on post-test 1, further items merely providing the opportunity for better formulated arguments.

(A = A': A is poured into C)

Jeap "It's the same because it's fatter here, so it's bound to be like that."

Exp makes a counter-suggestion, drawing the subject's attention to the height of the glasses

Jeap "It's fatter (C). It's the same because before the same amount was in this glass (A)."

(A = A': A' is poured into D)

Jeap (ponders, then says) "It's the same, before it was the same in these two (A and A'), and then in these two (A and D). It's taller and smaller (D) and there it's fatter, so there's less. There isn't any juice added."

(D is then poured into the four small glasses)

Jeap "There's more in the small glasses. No, the same because before in there (A and A') it was the same."

The fact that most subjects gave responses of the same kind throughout the test validates the shorter questioning procedure used in experiment I as a means of determining children's developmental levels. It also allows us to observe comparable development in the two experiments, since although the number of test items is different, the number of arguments produced individually by children is about the same in the two cases.

Following the same procedure as in the first experiment, we have laid out the arguments which each child heard from partners in the collective session, and those produced by the child itself on the post-tests, for children progressing to levels I$^+$ or C in each experimental group. The same comparison for the first experiment showed that most of the subjects who had progressed by the time of the post-tests gave novel arguments, i.e. arguments different from those used by their partners, and which they had therefore had to formulate themselves. For the second experiment, this is true for the totality of subjects attaining conservation (C) or a level very close to it (I^+).

These facts confirm our basic hypothesis, which is that the progress shown by these children is of a truly operational nature, and cannot be attributed to simple memorization or imitation.

There is, however, one surprising finding to emerge from this analysis of arguments. While the aggregate of individual behaviours is very similar in the two experiments, in the first experiment there were many more arguments from identity in the collective session. What is the reason for this unexpected difference? Why did the subjects in the second experiment confine themselves to different arguments? It is clearly the case that the argument from identity of type IDa ("before it was the same, so now it must be the same, it has only been poured") is a special one, since it underlies, for conservers, most "demonstrations through action" (the conserver pours D back into A' to affirm equality—"look!"), but why is it only the subjects in the first experiment who formulate this clearly? The two populations did differ partly in school class composition (one being made up entirely of children from the first year of primary school, the other being made up of some first-year, but more second-year kindergarten children) but why should this difference in the rate of acquisition of the concept be reflected in the choice of argument? Why should this be a characteristic of "pre-test conservers" in the collective session, whereas individually they formulated this type of argument well? Arguments from identity are therefore a special problem. Nevertheless, as far as other arguments are concerned the two experiments give similar results, and, apart from arguments from identity, subjects produce arguments which are novel in relation to those of the collective session.

(2) The extension of the conservation of liquids test, in the second experiment, also included an item on inequality. We have already previously pointed out, in justifying their use only with conservers of equality, that these items seem to be more difficult.

What is the specific nature of this difficulty? Undoubtedly the contrast between reality and perceptual appearance is stronger in cases of inequality than in equality. Thus a glass D, which is taller and thinner than A, may not only contain an equal quantity of liquid while having a higher level of liquid, but it may even contain *less* liquid, while having a higher level.

It also appears from a reading of the protocols that one of the causes of difficulty with the inequality items is that they follow immediately after equality items. The child then tries to bring the two situations into some relation with each other (before it was a question of two glasses A and A' containing the same amount of liquid, now, in contrast, the starting-point is two *un*equal quantities), sometimes mentioning the transition from one to the other ("because you've put some juice back in the bottle"), all of which renders more complex the setting in which the conservation questions are put. It is then more difficult for the child to make judgments explicit and to produce arguments for them.

This seemed to be the case for Mag, who, on post-test 1, ended by confusing points of departure which were presented in sequence:

Exp (A=A') "Is there the same amount to drink in these two glasses or not?"
Mag "Yes."
Exp (pours A into C) "And now is there the same amount to drink, or not?"
Mag "No."
Exp "How do you know?"
Mag "It's the same because A' is thinner and C is wider!"
(. . .)
Exp (A>A')
Mag "There's more juice here (A)."
Exp (pours A into C) "And now is there the same amount of juice . . .?"
Mag "Yes."
Exp "How do you know?"
Mag "Because before there was the same amount in this one (A)."
Exp transfers C into A, etc.

Jeap, in contrast, is conserving on all the items in post-test 1. But he bases his arguments for the conservation of inequalities on references to preceding manipulations. If the inequality situation had been presented to him in the first place, he would not have been able to explain the conservation of differences in the same way:

(A=A' is poured into D)
Jeap (thinks for a while, then says) "It's the same. Before it was the same in those two glasses (A and A'), and then in these two (A and D) (it's the same). Here (D) it's higher and smaller, and there (A) it's fatter, so it's less (full). There hasn't been any added."

Exp (pours the contents of D into the four small glasses) "And now?"
Jeap "There's more in the small glasses. No, it's the same because before
   they were the same (in A and A')."
(. . .)
Exp pours the juice from the four small glasses into A'
(then A = A')
Exp pours part of A' into the bottle: A > A'; the inequality is confirmed,
   and A' is poured into D
Jeap "I've got more because some was taken away."

The subjects have difficulty in explaining their arguments on these inequality items. What is revealed, then, by the addition of these inequality items to the procedure?

While, on occasion, they provided further verification of the operational level of subjects, or set limits to it (as in the case of Med, who on post-test 1 only had conserving responses in cases of equality, not of inequality, thus indicating the weak structure of the concept, and partly explaining her "intermediate" level on post-test 2) the main interest of these inequality items is a theoretical one. They have the advantage of being unlike the task in the collective session, which was concerned with equality. Therefore, success on these inequality items requires more than a simple replication of the coordinations developed in the company of other children, and denotes a real mastery of the concept in question. Is this confirmed in our data? In this second experiment, we had 18 conserving subjects, only 4 of whom failed to solve the inequality items. Their level of conservation, therefore, is one which includes behaviours requisite for the complete construction of the concept of the conservation of quantities of liquid.

Subjects' Development on the Different Operational Tests

We are reminded by Inhelder *et al* (1974, p. 298) that the research done by Piaget and Inhelder (1941), Piaget and Szeminska (1941), and Piaget *et al* (1948) has shown that the concept of the conservation of quantity is acquired in a fixed chronological order, which is the following: conservation of discrete quantities, of continuous physical quantities (liquid, matter), and finally of lengths. These notions are underpinned by the same operational systems. The problem of the staggered nature of the acquisition of these concepts raises the question of the causal relations among them, and it is this question which is at the heart of the Inhelder *et al.* (1974) study (see particularly their conclusion on p. 298ff.). Several of the points made in this study will enable us to clarify the nature of the relationships among performances on the different tests we have used, and thence to analyse how the learning triggered by our collective session fits in with the overall pattern of what is already known about cognitive development.

Following these authors, we may expect to find the order of acquisitions which they describe. More specifically, in several of their teaching procedures concerned with the conservation of quantities of liquid or matter, Inhelder *et al.* (1974, chapters I and III and p. 304) found that subjects who broadly progressed already possessed numerical conservation. However "there does not seem to be a direct causal link . . . what we see is a development out of a general lack of differentiation, rather than a direct progress from numerical estimation to estimation of the quantity of matter. In fact, what our procedure has shown above all is that the processes of differentiation begin at different moments, and that they are necessary for operational quantification" (p. 125).

Comparing subjects' performance on tests of conservation of liquid and of matter, these authors confirm (particularly in chapter III) that the first is generally successful slightly earlier than the second, although the difference is not very great.

On the concept of the conservation of length. Inhelder *et al.* (1974, p. 306) write that "it is not a simple generalisation of knowledge previously acquired to a new context, but a genuine reconstruction on a new level. This reconstruction is analogous to that characterizing the establishment of conservations of numerical equivalences, and it takes place in parallel with the development from conservation of discrete entities to conservation of matter, although beginning and ending slightly later".

According to this analysis, then, it seems that in the absence of direct causal links between these concepts, subjects are not likely to directly transfer the totality of their behaviours from one domain to the other, but rather to reconstruct them each time. On the other hand, we can expect to find a parallel development on different tests, the elaboration of one of the concepts facilitating the emergence of another without necessarily entailing it.

Thus an advanced performance on the conservation of number test may indicate a relatively great possibility of progress on the conservation of liquids test, which will, in turn, be linked with the probability of development on the conservation of matter test. Conversely, subjects who are weak on the conservation of liquids are not likely to show advanced performance on the conservation of length.

If the apparent progress of our subjects arises from a genuine operational restructuring, as we are hypothesizing, then we would expect to find that their behaviour following the session of social interaction is compatible with the overall sequence of development as described by Inhelder *et al.* (1974), particularly in relation to their performance on individual tests of conservation.

Table 5, already discussed, show the development of each subject on the conservation of liquids test from the pre-test up to post-test 2, together with their levels on the other operational tests. First of all we will examine the results for each test, then put them in relation with the progress made on the conservation of liquids test, and finally examine the overall development of our experimental and control groups.

THE CONSERVATION OF NUMBER TEST

At the time of the pre-test, among all subjects from both experimental and control groups we had 37 subjects who were non-conserving on the conservation of liquids test. All of these subjects then took the conservation of number test. Nine of them were conserving on this test, 4 were intermediate, and 24 were non-conserving.

These results confirm that success on the conservation of number test may precede success on the conservation of liquids test.

Is it the case that subjects who are at an operational level on this number test are the ones who have progressed most by the time of post-test 1 on the liquid test? In fact, not all of the subjects who have progressed by post-test 1 have necessarily succeeded on the conservation of number in the pre-test: this is the case for only 6 out of 12 subjects. However, it can clearly be seen from Table 7 that, with a very high level of significance,* subjects who were intermediate or conserving on the conservation of number test are more likely to progress in one or other of the experimental groups, or the control group (8 progressing out of 13 subjects), than non-conserving subjects (4 progressing out of 24).

---

* Where the statistical test used is not specified in the text, the test was always the exact probability test (Finney *et al.*, 1963).

TABLE 7

Progress on the conservation of liquids test by the time of post-test 1 as a function of initial level on the conservation of number test: All experimental conditions

| | | Liquids: post-test 1 | | |
		Progress	No progress	Total
Number pre-test	NC	4	20	24
	I or C	8	5	13
	Total	12	25	37

This pattern holds also if we consider only subjects in experimental conditions I and II, for whom the collective session rendered progress likely by post-test1. Once again, a certain number of subjects (4 out of 11) progress in the absence of numerical conservation on pre-test; and there is also a higher proportion of subjects progressing (5 out of 6) amongst those who had already attained a certain level of elaboration of the idea of numerical conservation.

If now we consider, not progress between pre-test and post-test 1, but between pre-test and post-test 2, the same relation appears, in the same direction. Table 8 shows that 9 out of 24 subjects having a better performance on post-test 2 than they had on pre-test were simply non-conserving with respect to number. Yet it was the subjects who were intermediate and conserving with respect to number who made most progress (9 out of 13). In the case of experimental conditions I, II and III, which produced a clear development between pre-test and post-test 2, progress was made by 7 out of 16 non-conservers of number, and by 8 out of 10 conservers and intermediates.

TABLE 8

Progress on the conservation of liquids test by the time of post-test 2, as a function of initial level on the conservation of number test

| | | Liquids: post-test 2 | | |
		Progress	No progress	Total
Number pre-test	NC	9	15	24
	I + C	9	4	13
	Total	18	19	37

These results clearly indicate, then, that a subjects's performance on the conservation of number at the time of pre-test cannot be used to directly predict their development in terms of the conservation of liquids: some subjects may progress in this, while having poor performance on number, while others may not progress even though they showed superior performance on number. Even so, there is a strong tendency, as in the results reported by Inhelder *et al*. (1974) for a certain level of operational elaboration of the concept of numerical conservation to increase the probability of progress with the concept of conservation of liquid, and this is true of both experimental and control groups.

THE TEST OF CONSERVATION OF MATTER

Of the 37 subjects who were non-conservers of liquid on pre-test,*, all took the conservation of matter test on pre-test and on post-test 1. We have seen previously that success on this test is likely to be a little delayed in relation to success on the first. Is it the case that those of our subjects who were advanced on this test were most likely to progress on the conservation of liquids?

A comparison of subjects' levels on the conservation of matter at pre-test with their levels on the conservation of liquid at post-test 1 shows that, contrary to what we had expected, the two subjects who were conservers of matter had a poor performance on the conservation of liquids test at post-test 1. Among the 5 who were intermediate conservers of matter on pre-test, 2 had a poor performance, and 3 had better performances on the liquids test. 22 subjects were non-conserving on both tests, and 7 who were non-conservers of matter on pre-test showed better performance on the liquids test at post-test 1.

TABLE 9

Progress on the conservation of liquids test as a function of initial level on the conservation of matter test

| | | Liquids: post-test 1 | | |
		Progress	No progress	Total
Matter	NC	7	22	29
pre-test	I + C	4	3	7
	Total	11	25	36

* Unfortunately we lack the pre-test data on conservation of matter for one of the condition IV subjects, consequently the relevant tables present data for 36 subjects only.

It does happen, then, that the concept of the conservation of matter is acquired before that of the conservation of liquid, and that mastery of this concept does not entail progress on the other. This is hardly surprising given that the authors reported cited only a slight advance, which does not entail direct transfer from the one concept to the other. Even so, in agreement with the hypothesis that operational structuring which is already advanced in one sphere will render advance probable in another sphere, it emerges from Table 9 (though just missing statistical significance) that subjects who are advanced on the conservation of matter are more likely to progress on the liquids test (4 out of 7) than those who are non-conservers (7 out of 29).

The results are very similar when we come to consider the progress made by the subjects in experimental conditions I and II. The two subjects who were advanced on the conservation of matter at pre-test both made progress by post-test 1 on the conservation of liquid. Their pattern of development conforms perfectly with the theoretical pattern, which predicts that a level of operational structuring of the concept of conservation of matter renders more likely the same concept with respect to liquids.

If the asynchrony between success on these two tests really is slight, then it is of interest, over and above the prediction of progress in performance on one test from performance at pre-test on the other, to observe whether a subject develops in a parallel manner in these two spheres. If such development were found, when only one of the two domains were the object of the procedure bringing about learning, then this would be further evidence in favour of our hypothesis that the progress made in our experiments is truly operational.

Is progress on the conservation of liquids test accompanied by progress on the conservation of matter test? Tables 10 and 11 give this information. In fact the results are highly significant. With the exception of one subject in condition III, it is only those subjects who progress on the first test who progress on the second to an equal level. This is the case for 6 out of 11 subjects (6 out of 9 if we only consider the subjects in experimental conditions I and II), a relatively high proportion given that 4 of these 11 subjects already had on the pre-test a better performance on the matter test than on the liquid test.

Are these parallel acquisitions in more than half the subjects in terms of similar performance on the two tests, or is there a slight advance on the liquids test? Comparison of subjects' levels on the two tests at

TABLE 10

Progress attained by post-test 1 on tests of conservation of matter and liquid

		Liquids		
		Progress	No progress	Total[a]
Matter	Progress	6	1	7
	No progress	5	24	29
	Total	11	25	36

[a] $p = 0.0014$.

TABLE 11

Progress attained by post-test 1 on tests of conservation of matter and liquid: experimental conditions I and II

		Liquids		
		Progress	No progress	Total[a]
Matter	Progress	6	0	1
	No progress	3	8	11
	Total	9	8	17

[a] $p = 0.01$ (Fisher's exact probability test).

post-test 1 shows that, for most of the population, as well as for experimental conditions I and II, more than two-thirds of the subjects (26 out of 36, i.e. 72·2%, and 12 out of 17, i.e. 70·58%) attained a similar level on both tests. The difference in attainment on the two tests in the other subjects appears, as expected, as an advance in the conservation of liquids test for subjects in experimental groups I and II, while the relationship is reversed in the other subjects.

It is a matter for speculation as to why we do not find the expected relationship between the two tests in all conditions. It appears, in particular, that in those subjects who made progress as a result of our experimental procedure attainment on the two tests tends to be parallel. It is the case, however, that the majority of subjects show a slight advance in the concept of the conservation of liquid over the concept of conservation of matter, as previous studies would lead us to expect.

The results from the conservation of matter test confirm once more, then, that the progress stimulated by the social interaction sessions is analogous to that observed in other developmental studies.

THE CONSERVATION OF LENGTH TEST

This test was given, on pre-test, to subjects who were conservers of liquids, and on post-test 1 to all experimental and control subjects*

We have seen previously that success on this test is generally acquired later than on the other tests considered here. We might therefore expect that only those subjects attaining a relatively high level on the other tests would show conservation on this test. Table 12 shows that, of the 12 subjects who had progressed on the conservation of liquid by post-test 1, 6 were intermediate or conserving on length (this result is highly significant). This result becomes 4 out of 9 if we consider only subjects in experimental conditions I and II.

TABLE 12

Subjects' levels on the conservation of length and conservation of liquid tests at post-test 1

| | | Liquids | | | |
		NC	I	C	Total[a]
	NC	23	4	2	29
Length	I	1	0	1	2
	C	0	1	4	5
	Total[a]	24	5	7	36

[a] $p = 0.0028$ by the exact probability test, combining scores within each quadrant.

All subjects who are intermediate or conserving on the conservation of length test are conservers of matter (see Table 5). These results seem to confirm, both for experimental groups I and II and for the total population, the relative delay in acquistion of the conservation of length, but at the same time the link between this concept and the development of the concepts of conservation of liquid and of matter.

Table 13 shows the levels on the other two tests, at pre-test, of subjects possessing the concept of the conservation of liquid. Data are missing for some subjects, because it was not until this experiment was underway that we realized the interest of comparing, by means of these tests, those subjects who were conserving on pre-test with those who *became* conservers during the course of the experimental conditions. Do all these subjects present the same pattern of levels? Table 13 also gives the levels on the other tests of those subjects in the four experimental conditions who had become conservers of liquid by post-test 1.

* With the exception of one subject who, through an oversight, was not tested.

TABLE 13

Performance of liquid conservers on the tests of conservation of
length and conservation of matter

Liquid	Subjects	Matter	Length
	San	C	NC
	Mic	C	I
	Nie	C	C
	Ari	C	C
	Phi	C	I
Conservers	Ale	C	C
on pre-test	Deu	C	C
	Pat	C	C
	Val	C	I
	Ant	C	NC
	Sad	NC	NC
	Mai	C	C
	Mag	C	C
Experimental	Eti	C	C
subjects	Jeap	NC	NC
conserving on	Mar	I	C
post-test 1	Ver	C	NC
	Med	I	I
	Nata	I	I

With the exception of one subject in condition II, the two groups of children have levels which are either equal, or superior in the case of matter. These results correspond to the usual sequence of development. The subjects in the two groups also have similar levels on the conservation of length test. However, those subjects who have already acquired the conservation of liquid by the time of the pre-test are more often conservers of matter (11 out of 12) than the others (3 out of 7). If the patterns of acquisition are comparable in the two groups, it is possible that the slight inferiority on the conservation of matter test is due to the recency of operational structuring in the experimental subjects.

CONCLUSIONS

From this analysis of results concerning the development of subjects' performance on the different operational tests used in experiment II, there emerge two important points.

The first is the confirmation that, in a large number of cases (more than 70%) the operational structuring following social interactions in the collective session extends beyond the concept of the conservation of liquid to encompass the conservation of matter. This is clear evidence that the progress made by our subjects is more fundamental than the mere adoption of behaviours relevant to a single task.

The second point is that the progress made by our subjects following the collective session conforms to what is known of the pattern of normal cognitive development; this shows that our experimental procedure stimulates more than specific learning, and induces genuine cognitive development.

Inhelder *et al*. (1974, pp. 295–297) identify three categories of phenomena which must be taken account of in any interpretation of the relationship between learning and the general mechanisms of development. Do these three categories of phenomena show themselves in our results?

The first is the demonstration of the possibility of facilitating, and therefore accelerating, cognitive development. This possibility allows Inhelder *et al*. to reject the maturationist interpretation of development, and to stress the role of the environment. On the basis of our results, we can also reject a simple maturationist interpretation, since a comparison of development in the experimental and control groups clearly indicates the role of social interaction.

The second type of phenomenon has already been pointed out in Chapter 2: progress made by post-test 1 is not only durable enough to be evident also on post-test 2, but may have made further gains. Inhelder *et al*. attribute this extension of acquisitions triggered off by the experimental procedure to a process of internal reorganization.

Finally, Inhelder *et al*. point out that the nature and extent of progress is always, and strikingly, *a function of the initial level of development* of the subject, or in other words of the subject's potential for assimilation. In most cases, the hierarchical pattern of attainments found in the pre-tests is maintained in the two post-tests. This fundamental phenomenon may be described as the non-crossing of most lines of cognitive change. Furthermore, and this is a finding which seems to us particularly revealing of the laws of development, the differences between subjects' levels of development are greater at the end of the experiment than they were at the beginning. These differences therefore tend to increase during the course of learning, which would seem to indicate that the experimental situations, the exchanges with the experimenter, are experienced differently according to the cognitive level of each subject, even when the differences between them are minimal" (p. 295) (their italics). The effect of the environment is therefore subject to the internal potential of the subject to "appropriate and transform external data according to the laws of organisation" (p. 296).

These three types of phenomena are evident in our experiments: the non-crossing of the majority of lines of development (see Table 5), the maintenance of the rank order of subjects in regard to their attainments, and the widening of the differences between subjects within this rank order. When this second experiment was planned, we intended a systematic study of the effect of the subject's initial level of development using two other methods: through an analysis of subjects' performance on different operational tests at the time of the pre-test, and through a rank ordering of their performance within the stage of non-conservation of liquid. The first method showed that a certain level of operational development in other domains rendered more likely a degree of progress in the domain chosen for experimental intervention. As we have indicated earlier, the second method we intended to use could not in fact be carried out in the event, because of difficulties we encountered in pursuing a clinical questioning procedure in depth according to the criteria we had judged necessary. Since the problem of the subject's initial level of development is an important one for a constructivist approach to development, this second planned method will be taken up again in the next experiment in Chapter 4.

OBSERVATION OF TYPES OF SOCIAL INTERACTION IN THE COLLECTIVE SESSIONS, IN RELATION TO THE SIZE OF THEIR EFFECTS

As we have seen in Chapter 2, since the main aim of the first experiment was to demonstrate that certain social interactions can bring about development at the level of cognitive structures, a whole series of questions was left open concerning the effective mechanism of these interactions.

Role of the Partners' Level of Cognitive Development

The first of these questions concerns the composition, from the point of view of cognitive development, of the pairs of partners in the collective sessions. Is it necessary, for the interaction to be effective in bringing about cognitive change in the experimental subject, that both partners are conservers of liquid, or would one conserver, or even none, be sufficent?

It was in order to provide an answer to this question that the second experiment placed subjects in different interactive conditions. These conditions were defined in terms of the cognitive levels of the partners (as evaluated on the pre-test). Table 14 recalls these conditions, together with the data from Table 4, so that the proportions of subjects progressing in each case may be seen.

TABLE 14

Number of experimental and control subjects progressing by post-test 1 on the conservation of liquids test

	Progress	No progress	Total
Experimental conditions			
I	4	1	5
(1 NC + 2 C)			
II	5	7	12
(2 NC + 1 C)			
III	0	9	9
(3 NC)			
IV	1	1	2
(1 I + 2 NC)			
Control condition			
(no collective session)	2	7	9
Total	12	25	37

It appears that the situation in which a non-conserving subject interacts with two conservers is more favourable to development than one in which there is only one conserving partner. The number of subjects in condition I is unfortunately too small for us to test this hypothesis statistically, but a comparison between condition II and the experimental condition of experiment I will permit an analogous inference. This comparison shows, however, a clear difference between experimental conditions I and II, considered together, and either condition III or the control condition.

What is the reason for these differences? Does it lie in the different types of interaction which may be occurring in these different conditions?

We can speculate that the role allowed to the subject in the work of the group might lead to a more or less active participation, and thence to a greater or less intellectual activity. If this were the case, then we would expect that non-conserving subjects who were in charge of sharing out the juice among the trio in the collective session would be more likely to progress than those who were merely receivers of the sharing-out. This would explain the difference between the experimental conditions, since in conditon I all subjects were required to do some sharing-out, while only half of the subjects in condition II, and a third of the subjects in condition III, were responsible for sharing-out.

Table 15 gives a comparison of subjects' development after experiencing condition II or III, according to their function in the sharing-out. The comparison appears to show that there is no reason to suppose that the act of sharing-out favours any subject's development. The data from post-test 2 confirm this finding.

TABLE 15

Progress of subjects in experimental conditions II and III by post-test 1 as a function of their role in the share-out

		Progress	No progress	Total
Condition II (2 NC + 1 C)	NC performing the share-out	3	3	6
	NC "receiving"	2	4	6
Condition III (3 NC)	NC performing the share-out	0	3	3
	NC "receiving"	0	6	6
Total		5	16	21

Analysis of the protocols (and video-recordings, when we had them) of the collective sessions showed that none of the children were indifferent to the sharing-out procedure, and that the great majority of them participated actively in it. Only five subjects were relatively less involved, as indicated by long silences, distractibility, failure to take intiative, etc. Even so, this more or less great involvement in the communal activity does not seem to be linked with, or predictive of, progress as measured on the post-tests.

If we then reject the hypothesis which would explain the differences between experimental conditions in terms of the role or degree of active participation allowed to the experimental subject, can we put forward the alternative hypothesis that experimental conditions I and II are more favourable to cognitive development because they place their subjects in the presence of at least one partner with a mastery of the concept of conservation, which is necessary to a just sharing-out?

The answer to this question cannot be given by simply taking account of the levels of the partners on pre-test. We noticed during the course of experimentation that the behaviour of children in the collective session was not always similar to the behaviour they had shown on pre-test. This led us to make systematic observations (supported by video-recordings whenever possible) of childrens' behaviour in the collective session.

From these observations, it emerged that the conserving subjects did not always demonstrate their mastery of conservation in their behaviour with partners. Some of them vacillated between affirmations of conservation and non-conserving points of view, rather like intermediate subjects. Others centred themselves on the height of the juice in the glasses, even if the glasses were of different widths, in other words behaving like non-conservers. On the other hand, some subjects who were non-conserving on pre-test were able to foresee the conservation of quantities of liquid that they poured from one glass to another during the collective session, and they occasionally affirmed conservation, or repeated the affirmations of their partners, thus behaving like intermediate subjects. This is the reason why certain collective sessions in conditions I and II, for example, are very much like the sessions in condition III, if we look at the exchanges which took place between the children.

On the basis of these observations, it is possible to carry out an internal analysis of the data in order to determine which behaviours in the partners favoured the development of non-conserving subjects.*

---

* As we have already pointed out in chapter 1, we did not aim to study the conditions which could lead subjects to regress cognitively. Nevertheless, from the first experiment we wanted to be sure—and this is in fact the case—that interaction with a subject at a lower operational level would not cause a conserving child to regress. Condition II of this second experiment is therefore of particular interest, because the conserver is placed together with two non-conserving partners in the collective session. Accordingly, we gave a post-test to the conservers in condition II. The results show that, not only did the subjects not regress, but those among them who had room for improvement on the tests actually showed improvement. This was the case also for those amongst them who showed intermediate behaviour in the collective session. In terms of improvement, the C^- subject became C; the subject who was non-conserving on the matter test acquired this concept and progressed on the conservation of length; and one subject who was intermediate on this latter test acquired conservation. Similarly, an intermediate subject in condition IV who was placed with two subjects at a lower level had progressed by the time of the post-test to the conservation of matter.

We therefore distinguished five different "constellations" of partners in the collective sessions of experiment II:

Constellation A The two partners show a mastery of the concept of conservation of liquid throughout the collective session.

Constellation B Only one of the partners shows conservation behaviour, the other partner centring on the heights of liquid, and believing that the quantities of liquid change during transfer between vessels.

Constellation C Both partners show non-conserving behaviour.

Constellation D Both partners show intermediate behaviour, alternating between conserving and non-conserving behaviour.

Constellation E One of the partners shows intermediate behaviour, the other non-conserving behaviour.

These "constellations" of behaviour appeared in the following experimental conditions:

Condition I   4 subjects in constellation A
(1 NC + 2 C) 1 subject in constellation C
Condition II   6 subjects in constellation B
(2 NC + 1C)   1 subject in constellation D
              5 subjects in constellation E
Condition III 7 subjects in constellation C
(3 NC)   2 subjects in constellation E
Condition IV   1 subject in constellation D
(2 NC + 1I)   1 subject in constellation E

TABLE 16

Number of subjects progressing on the conservation of liquids test by post-test 1, as a function of the "constellation" of partners in the collective session

		Progress	No progress	Total
"Constellations"	A	3	1	4
in the collective	B	2	4	6
session	C	1	7	8
	D	0	2	2
	E	4	4	8
	Total	10	18	28

Table 16 shows the number of subjects who had progressed by the time of post-test 1 on the test of conservation of liquid for each "constellation" in the collective session. We can answer the question behind this internal analysis by comparing the frequencies of progress attained by subjects according to whether their "constellation" in the collective session comprised at least: a subject having mastery of the concept of conservation of liquid ("constellations" A and B); or a subject showing an intermediate level of conservation behaviour ("constellations" D and E); or no subject showing operational behaviour relevant to this concept ("constellation" C). This comparison shows that progress was more frequent in subjects who had experienced social interaction with partners showing operational behaviours than in subject whose partners showed non-conserving behaviour. It is interesting to note, also, that the sum of "constellations" A and B and D and E stimulate progress in a similar proportion of subjects. It would seem, therefore, that for a non-conserving subject interacting with another child showing an intermediate level of conservation is no less favourable than interacting with a child showing full mastery of the concept. The source of the differences in progress by post-test 1 between experimental conditions I and II and condition III is therefore not to be found in the fact that the first two conditions place the subject together with a partner in full possession of the concept in question, but rather in the reduced probability, in condition III, that subject will meet a view point different from their own. What remains to be clarified is whether this viewpoint needs to be one which produces an adequate response to the problem at hand, or whether it is sufficient for it to be merely different, without being more advanced. The data from this experiment do not permit evaluation of these two possibilities, since the non-conserving subjects all tended to defend the same points of view (centred on the heights of the liquid in the glasses). Experiments to be reported later will, however, return to this question.

Majority Pressure Hypothesis

In the analysis of experiment I, we envisaged the possibility that progress in non-conserving subjects who had experienced the collective session was due to pressure exerted by the majority opinion of the two conservers.

In the data we have discussed so far, we have already found evidence telling against this possibility of explaining cognitive development by a process acting at the level of opinions only, since we have been able to demonstrate that the progress made was the sign of real advance in operational structuring.

Furthermore, if this was a matter of social influence, we would expect the influence process to be linked with the consistency of behaviour of partners having a viewpoint different from that of the subject, as we pointed out in Chapter 2. With regard to intra-individual consistency, it was the conservers in constellations A and B who, either singly or in pairs, really defended a different viewpoint with coherence and persistence throughout the interaction. The results in Table 16 show that this intra-individual consistency was no more favourable to experimental subjects' development than the inconsistent and vacillating behaviour of the intermediate partners in constellations D and E. If we now consider inter-individual consistency, this is found only in constellation A, since in constellation D the two intermediate subjects did not defend a coherent viewpoint. Unfortunately the numbers are too small to properly establish the superiority of this A constellation. If this efficacity of inter-individual consistency needs to be explained in the absence of an effect of intra-individual consistency, then it seems more appropriate to explain it, not as a process of social influence, but in terms of the fact that inter-individual consistency gives a different point of view greater salience in the eyes of the subject.

Influence processes were certainly at work during the collective session, since we observed (and this was the reason for looking at the constellations) that some subjects who were conserving on pre-test and post-test did not show conservation behaviour during the interaction. This was particularly true of condition II, when they were with *two* non-conservers. But none of the results we have indicate that such influence processes are the cause of the cognitive development is our subjects. Although the absence of any indication favouring an influence process does not prove that such a process did not occur, we are bound to look for alternative explanations.

One last observation, on the agreement reached by subjects at the end of the collective session, argues against the role of influence.

The Role of Agreement between Subjects in the Collective Session

The instructions given to the children at the beginning of the collective session stressed that they should reach agreement on a just sharing-out of the juice: this condition had to be met before each child could drink their glass of juice. This instruction was followed in all the sessions, with the exception of one in which agreement could not be reached.

We looked at whether these agreements were based on acceptance of the notion of conservation (conserving agreement), or on acceptance of the idea that different heights of juice in different glasses indicated different quantities (non-conserving agreement).

TABLE 17

Type of agreement reached during the collective session, and subjects' development by post-test 1 on the conservation of liquids test

	Progress	No progress	Total
Condition I (1 NC + 2 C)			
Conserving agreement	3	1	4
Non-conserving agreement	1	0	1
Condition II (2 NC + 1 C)			
Conserving agreement	2	4	6
Non-conserving agreement	2	2	4
No agreement	0	2	2
Condition III (3 NC)			
Conserving agreement	0	0	0
Non-conserving agreement	0	9	9

Table 17 shows, for each experimental condition, whether or not progress took place in subjects as a function of the type of agreement they had entered into. The hypothesis that social pressure from the group brought about cognitive development would predict that the direction of this pressure would be revealed by the type of agreement, and that subjects who had entered into a conserving agreement would be more likely to progress than subjects who had entered into a non-conserving agreement. Results similar to this have in fact been found by Silverman and Stone (1972) and Silverman and Geiringer (1973) who, using a different theoretical framework but a similar experimental paradigm to ours, showed that non-conservers who had shown progress on post-test had submitted to the viewpoint of a conserving partner during the course of interaction. These authors report that, in the great majority of cases, the viewpoint of the conserver prevailed over that of the non-conserver.

In our results, only conditions I and II, which placed non-conservers together with a conserving partner, led subjects to conserving agreements. But these conserving agreements are no more linked than non-conserving agreements to the subsequent development of the subjects. In the first case, 5 out of 10 subjects showed progress on post-test; in the second case, 3 out of 5.

Although the numbers are small, it seems that it is not the fact of agreeing with the viewpoint of a conserver (or conservers) which is in itself the source of cognitive advance in the subject, since some subjects who did this did not advance, while others who did not accede to pressure from the partner nevertheless showed subsequent advance. The presence of a conserver allowed agreement at this level to occur, but the agreement did not cause the development.

These results suggest, therefore, a re-interpretation of the findings of Silverman and his co-workers. Silverman and Stone (1972) and Silverman and Geiringer (1973) claim there is a link between the conserving agreement of a pair at the time of the interaction, and the development of the non-conserving partner by the time of being post-tested. It is possible that, in their experiments, it was only those pairs in which the conserving partner behaved truly like a conserver (in the sense we consider in our analysis of "constellations") which reached agreement at this level, and that in the other pairs the non-conserving subject was in fact never confronted with a point of view different from their own, this being the reason for the non-conserver's failure to develop. This possibility is strongly supported by instances from our experiment: the subject in condition I who experienced a non-conserving agreement with two conservers, who nevertheless behaved liked non-conservers during the interaction; and the four subjects in condition 2, whose partners were conservers behaving like intermediate conservers.

In a recent study, Miller and Brownell (1975) took up the problem raised by Silverman et al. and tried to find out why, in most cases, it is conserving subjects who dominate interactions in which agreements are to be reached. They asked whether this is a general characteristic of their behaviour, regardless of the task, or whether it is a phenomenon specific to the purpose of the interaction, namely, conservation. The experiment they designed to answer these questions found the same result as Silverman et al., in so far as the non-conservers most often conformed to the view of the conserver in problems of conservation. However, they found that this was not the case in tasks which were independent of the cognitive levels of the subjects. In our experiment, we also found a tendency for the opinions of conservers to prevail during the interaction (10 out of 15 agreements reached were conserving agreements), and from observation of subjects' behaviour on video-tape, it can be confirmed that conservers took the initiative more often than non-conservers, asserted their point of view more often, and in general assumed leadership in the situation. What is striking, however, is that these behaviours appear only in those conservers who did not "regress" to non-conserving behaviours during the interaction. The fact that Miller and Brownell (1975, p. 995) found that subjects who "submitted" were different from those who dominated in the same way that non-conservers were different from conservers leads us to think, therefore, that those among their conservers who submitted to non-conservers did not behave like conservers at the time of the interaction; in particular, that they did not assert a conserving viewpoint.

Our interpretation is that the development in non-conserving subjects is not stimulated by influence, persuasion or dominance on the part of conservers, but rather by being confronted with a different viewpoint. Furthermore, this viewpoint need not necessarily be defended consistently, since conservers who behave like intermediates are equally capable of stimulating development in non-conservers. Indeed, the reverse may be the case in some circumstances: we observed five instances in which the conserving subject dominated the interaction to such a degree that angry words were used, and the conserver clearly thought that the non-conserver's ideas were aberrant and absurd; in four out of these five cases, the non-conserver made no advance. Could this be because, in such a situation, the cognitive conflict which should have been aroused by the confrontation of two different viewpoints was masked by the emotional nature of the interaction?

Conclusions

This second experiment had two aims: to confirm the results obtained in the first experiment by more precisely evaluating their significance for operational development; and to allow observation of childrens' behaviour in a collective session by varying the conditions of interaction, so that the processes underlying those social interactions which lead to cognitive development could be studied.

The results of experiment I were in fact confirmed, and the clinical analysis of subjects' behaviour shows that the development of subjects following these social interactions is in the form of a genuine structuring of operations consistent with the normal sequence of cognitive development. The subjects who became conservers demonstrated the operational nature of their acquisition by creating a characteristic style of argument with which to defend their affirmations of conservation. Furthermore, progress in the concept of conservation of liquid (the purpose of the collective sessions) was paralleled by progress in related concepts. Progress in the conservation of liquid *facilitated* progress in related domains, since, as we have seen, it made progress in the conservation of matter and of length more likely to occur. This link was seen also in the reverse direction: some of our results indicate that the degree of progress is a function of the subject's initial level of development. In the next experiment, reported in Chapter 4, we will attempt to verify this point, which is a fundamental postulate of a constructivist approach to development.

We have shown that a comparison of the development of operational behaviours in different experimental conditions and the control condition confirms the role of the collective session in stimulating the operational development indicated by the two post-tests. There was a clear difference between the experimental conditions, according to whether they placed together children with the same, or different, viewpoints. In the first case (condition III), progress was not evident until the second post-test; in the second case (conditions I and II), progress was apparent on the first post-test. Can we suppose that the late progress associated with condition III was also the result of restructuring brought about by the social interaction of the experimental situation?

Other investigations, particularly those of Inhelder *et al.* (1974) have also found phenomena of "staggered" progress similar to those we have found (Inhelder *et al.*, 1974, pp. 91, 115, 246, 265, 283, 297).

These findings can also be placed in relation to those of other research* which has found that an experimentally stimulated change in behaviour, if it is consistent with the general trend of development, can bring about superior performance in experimental subjects as con-

---

* Note that the research cited on the durability of effects has been specifically concerned with moral judgment.

trasted with control subjects which lasts at least a fortnight (Cowan *et al.*, 1969) and may even last as long as six months (Glassco *et al.*, 1975) although no longer evident after a year (Sternlieb and Youniss, 1975), no doubt because the intervening period has allowed the control subjects to catch up as a result of experiencing interactions of the same type.

Since it is known, then, that stimulated advance may continue between post-tests, and that the differential effects of experimental conditions may still be evident six months after the intervention, it seems likely that it is the experimental manipulation which was responsible for the difference between condition III and the control condition in the results of post-test 2. Furthermore, if it is the case that the three experimental conditions involving the coordination of individual actions brought about cognitive development, then we must assume that the same has occurred, only more slowly, in condition III. It is possible that finer testing methods would reveal the effects of the restructuring process as early as post-test 1, but in the absence of such methods we are brought back to the question already raised by Inhelder *et al.* (1974, p. 265)—the "problem of the rhythm of integration" of the individual subject which can "either lead to superior results immediately, apparent on post-test 1, or only after a lapse of time permitting slow development between post-tests 1 and 2".

We have rejected the hypothesis of learning by imitation, because it cannot explain either the general operational advance made by our subjects, or their use of novel arguments in the post-tests. This is corroborated by our analysis of subjects' behaviour, which showed that the influence or pressure exerted by the partners and the submission to a group agreement were not related to the cognitive advance observed.

Our interpretation of the results is that the social interactions which obliged subjects to coordinate their actions with those of others brought about a process of decentration leading to a conflict between the subject's own point of view and that of the partners. This conflict led to the cognitive restructuring revealed by the post-tests. We would hypothesize next that the difference in the size of effects following social interactions (in terms of our experiment, the differences between the experimental conditions) are due to the degree to which this cognitive conflict was expressed or acted out as a function of the difference in points of view. This would explain the differences in effectiveness between conditions I and II as contrasted with condition III, or between "constellations" A, B, D and E as contrasted with C. It is equally possible that the superiority of condition I (or constellation A) lies in the salience it gave to the point of view opposed to the subject's, since the two partners both defended the opposed position in an identical fashion.

We will attempt to verify and add substance to this interpretation in the following chapters, by seeking out the specific characteristics of socio-cognitive conflict which lead to cognitive development. In Chapter 4 we will look at the confrontation between a non-conserver and an intermediate conserver, hypothesizing that this will also bring about development detectable on the first post-test. However, we might expect this confrontation to be less fruitful than one between a non-conserver and a conserver, since an intermediate conserver, who shifts positions, gives a less salient picture of an opposed viewpoint. Chapter 5 will follow up this investigation in a number of experiments which attempt to verify the hypothesis that socio-cognitive conflict is a source of development even if the partner's viewpoint is less developed than that of the subject, in so far as their centrations are different.

4

The Conservation of Number: The Differential Effect of the Subject's Initial Level of Competence

The "prerequisites" for cognitive re-structuring: The notion of minimal competence

The notion of minimal competence is relevant to two aspects of the problem with which we are concerned. Firstly, we have to consider the competence for social interaction which is necessary for the subject to be able to communicate and to enter into inter-individual coordination of actions, cooperation or confrontation—in other words, the "prerequisite for social interaction". Secondly, there is the problem of "prerequisites for cognitive re-structuring", or the level of cognitive competence which subjects must already possess before a given social interaction can bring about cognitive development in them. The third experiment, to be reported next, addresses itself to this latter question.

If we consider that many factors contribute to the development of the individual, and that the social factor is only one of these, it must be possible to demonstrate experimentally that the social factor can only have an effect when other conditions have been fulfilled. The interactionist and constructivist approach has shown that development is not a simple copy of a model, but an active construction on the part of the subject, all knowledge being a continuous construction which includes novel elaboration. In order to relate our thesis on the role of social interactions to what is known about cognitive development, it is necessary to show that social interaction can stimulate constructive activity in the subject only in so far as the subject has attained a level of competence sufficient to benefit from the interaction.

In the preceding experiments, we have shown that the development of the concept of the conservation of liquid which followed the interactive session was paralleled by the development of other operational concepts, and, more specifically, we showed that if the subject was already advanced with respect to the conservation of number or of matter, this made it more probable that there would be an advance in the case of the conservation of liquid.

These experiments will now be followed up systematically by looking at the effects of different levels of performance within the stage of non-conservation on development subsequent to the interaction.

Experiments I and II showed that the progress evident already on post-test 1, relatively soon after the collective session, was stimulated by the conflict of points of view. What conditions need to be fulfilled at the individual level before the subject is aware of this conflict? It is clear that subjects must be able to see the difference of position between their partners and themselves, and that they are capable of going on to try to effect a reconciliation. For this reason, we hypothesize that only those non-conserving subjects who have nevertheless already reached a certain level of conceptual elaboration will have the cognitive basis needed to be able to benefit from the confrontation, and therefore to proceed to an intellectual restructuring.

Experiment III set out to demonstrate the existence of such a prerequisite level of development in non-conservers, and to specify its location in the rank order of levels discernible within the stage of non-conservation.

Experiment III

The aim of this third experiment, then, is to look once more at the effects demonstrated in the first two experiments, but with a more detailed analysis of non-conservers' levels of development. This will also provide the opportunity to verify the generality of the previous results, by showing that analogous effects can be brought about in domains other than the conservation of liquid.

The concept of the conservation of number has been the subject of many studies since the first work of Piaget and Szeminska (1941). It is of special interest, being one of the earliest conceptual developments to be fully documented, and the use of this test will allow us to study the effects of social interaction in children who are at the threshold of the stage of concrete operations. Can these effects be found at an age when cooperation (in the Piagetian sense of coordination of operations) is still barely developed?

Gréco's work (1962) on the progressive elaboration of numerical ideas suggested the possibility that non-conservers' performance on perceptual estimation, placing items into one-to-one correspondence, and enumeration, would be sufficiently diversified for us to be able to distinguish several distinct and ordered levels of non-conserving behaviour on a test of the conservation of number.

We interpreted the effects of social interactions found in experiment II as being due to factors other than simple majority influence. If this is correct, it should be possible to reproduce the results by placing the subject together with a single partner. This is the reason for using couples instead of trios in the present experiment.

The final aim of this experiment is to study the effects on a non-conserver of social interaction with an intermediate conserver. The preceding chapters have suggested that it is the conflict between different points of view which brings about a process of intensive restructuring relatively soon after the collective session (post-test 1). This leads to the hypothesis that the confrontation between a non-conserver and an intermediate conserver should equally act as a stimulus to this intensive restructuring. In order to verify this hypothesis, we set up three experimental conditions, differing according to the level of the partner—conserving, intermediate or non-conserving. In order to increase the chances of differentiating the effects of these three conditions, we have brought forward the time of post-testing to three days, instead of eight, after the collective session.

METHOD AND SUBJECTS

The subjects were children attending the first or second class of two infant schools in a suburb of Geneva. (Experiment II on the conservation of liquid was also conducted in one of these schools.) The children were tested between February and May, 1975, in a classroom at the school, by two adults, one of whom ran the experiment while the other took detailed notes on all that was said and done.

Of the 140 subjects who were pre-tested, there were 65 boys and 75 girls. 68 were in the first class, and 72 in the second. Their ages on the day of the pre-test, ranged from 4·0 years to 7·0 years, the mean age being 5·6 years. The two school classes correspond to two age groups.

For the pre- and post-tests we used two sets of green and yellow plastic counters, 1·5 cm in diameter.

In the interaction situation, these counters were replaced by "Smarties" which had the same diameter but offered a range of 7 colours. The interactive session also used a series of strips of cardboard 3 cm wide and of varying lengths according to the number of circles (1·5 cm) which were drawn on them. Thus they were either 9 cm or 17 cm long, with 5, 6 or 7 circles on them (see pp. 126–127).

These strips were referred to as "plates" during the experiment, the children being asked, and agreeing readily, to make believe that they were plates (from which "Smarties" were to be eaten).

The children taking part in this experiment were younger than those in the preceding experiments, and many precautions had to be taken to make sure that there was rapport with the adults, and that the children understood the situation and the tasks.

Pre-test Procedures

The experimenter (E) collected each child from their class-room, and explained the procedure either in the experimental room itself, or in a neighbouring room. After a brief period in which to establish rapport with the second adult present, and to familiarize the child with the room and the tape-recorder, E sat down at a table, invited the child to sit down beside him, and showed the child the counters. Then questions were put to the child which followed very closely the clinical procedure described by Piaget and Szeminska (1941) in their study of spontaneous correspondence and the determination of the cardinal set of value (continued by Inhelder *et al.*, 1974).

We give here the standardized questioning procedure, but obviously this had to be adapted for individual children, and in particular taking account of their use of the terms of quantification. The same items were presented to all subjects in the same order, except that individual changes had to be introduced as a function of responses, for example returning to previous items, supplementary questions, counter-suggestions, etc.

After reaching agreement with the child on the names to be used for the counters ("counters", "tiddlywinks", etc.) E invited the child to choose a colour. If, for example, the child chose green, the E would then take for himself 5 yellow counters and place these in a line on the table. He then asked the subject to make a numerically equivalent set with the green counters: "Do the same with your counters . . . the same number . . . as many green ones as I have yellow ones . . . no more, no less . . . so that we both have the same". When the child seemed satisfied that the instruction had been carried out, and had thus affirmed the equality of the collections, E then proceeded to change his line by spacing the counters more widely or closely together. "Now", he then asked the child, "if you play with these green counters, and I play with these yellow ones, do we have the same number of counters each, or does one of us have more than the other, or what do you think?" "How is that?", "How do you know?" This item was generally repeated by modifying the configuration of the line a second time. In cases where the child correctly affirmed equality, we sought to find out how this had been achieved: did the child use counting, or global correspondence which would not necessarily lead to numerical equivalence? E's observation was supplemented by questions to elucidate the child's approach: "How did you do it?" or "How do you know?" If, on the other hand, the child claimed to have established two equivalent series when this was not the case, E tried to verify whether this was a result of the child's misunderstanding of the instruction, or an incidental error which would not recur if the item were repeated.

For the next items, E put the counters in a pile, then took 5 counters and placed them in the following configuration:

the child was then instructed: "You see what I've done; do the same thing with your counters . . . the same number so that you and I have the same, neither more nor less". E observed the child's behaviour, then asked for an explanation of what had been done. When the child judged that equivalence had been established, E proceeded to change his configuration by spacing it more widely or closely. The E then formed a line out of his 5 counters. After each of these changes of configuration, E questioned the subject about the equivalence of the collections. He also allowed the subject to manipulate the counters; in fact most of the subjects who considered that equivalence was destroyed by changing the configuration wished to do this.

Throughout this first part of the procedure, the E was careful not to induce a recourse to counting or one-to-one correspondence of items, so as to observe whether the child used these strategies spontaneously. This also served to avoid inducing what might be called "conservation of the *names* of numbers", which appears in statements of the type: "there are six here and six here: they are the same!" indicating in fact that the child has interpreted the situation as requiring the same "label" for each series, while remaining convinced that "there is more" in the longer (or denser) line. If precautions are not taken right at the start of questioning, such pseudo-conserving responses are difficult to distinguish from genuine conservation.

In the second part of the pre-test, in contrast, the E attempted to find out, through suggestion, whether the child was capable of understanding and using one-to-one correspondence, and was able to count. The E also questioned subjects' statements in order to understand their logic and the structure of their reasoning.

E placed 6 yellow counters and 6 green counters in corresponding lines, and made sure that the child correctly judged the equivalence of the collections. E then hid one of the two lines, and asked the child if they could say how many counters were in the hidden line, and, if so, how they knew. If the subject was unable to respond to this, E then revealed the hidden line, asked the questions again, and observed whether the child used correspondence or counting in arriving at an answer. After this, E changed the arrangement of the counters and questioned the child about equivalences in the way described above. (Eventually, E added or removed several counters from the line, and thus demonstrated inequalities to the child.) If the child's responses were conserving, E drew attention to the configuration: "Look how long this line is; aren't there more counters in it?" If the responses were non-conserving, E reminded the child of the initial equivalence by remarks such as: "But don't you remember what we did before? We put the same number of counters down. There was the same number of yellow counters and green counters. Has that changed now? What do you think?" E also reminded the child of the previous one-to-one correspondence: "Do you remember what we did before? We put a yellow counter above every green counter; some children have told me that when you do that, put a yellow counter above each green counter, then you have the same number of yellow and green counters. What do *you* think?"

Once the numerical equivalence between two lines of counters was admitted by the child, E hid his line with his hand, and asked the child: "How many counters are there in this line?" adding, if necessary: "Can you count them?" If the child succeeded in stating the number of counters, E ended the pre-test by asking: "And how many counters do you think there are under my hand? Can you guess? How do you know?"

Pre-test Criteria

According to subjects' operational level as indicated by this pre-test, they were placed in three categories: conservers, intermediates and non-conservers. The criteria used were those described by Piaget and Szeminska (1941) and also used by Inhelder *et al.* (1974). We also distinguished four levels within the stage of non-conservation.

First stage: absence of conservation (NC). The child gives non-conserving judgements in different situations. Either the configurations are evaluated perceptually in terms of qualitative similarity alone, or intuitive comparisons are made but still equivalence is considered to be destroyed when the configurations are changed. Four levels are distinguished within this stage.
First level: non-conserving, using global perceptual evaluation (NCg).
The child stops at global evaluations of collections, does not establish one-to-one correspondence, and is concerned solely with qualitative resemblance. Evaluations are based on the space occupied, or the density of elements. The child cannot count a collection of six elements.
Second level: non-conserving, using one-to-one correspondence, but not knowing how to count (NCo).
The child uses one-to-one correspondence, but judges that equivalence has been destroyed if the configuration is changed with resulting loss of visual and spatial correspondence. The elements are placed closer together or wider apart in order to re-establish equality previously perceived, but the child does not know how to count.
Third level: non-conserving, knowing how to count (NCc).
The child knows how to count, or sometimes uses counting, but does not use one-to-one correspondence. Counting alternates with global

perceptual evaluation. If the configurations are changed, the child judges it necessary to re-count the elements, and is in general not satisfied to find the same number (or "number name") applicable to rows of different dimensions. If two rows are in one-to-one correspondence, and the number of counters in one row is known, the child does not necessarily infer the number in the second row. (Note that these subjects therefore know how to count in the sense of establishing a one-to-one correspondence between words—one, two, three, four, etc. and the counters in a line. It is very likely that they would be able to establish a one-to-one correspondence between the counters of two rows as well, if the instructions explicitly requested this, which was not the case in our procedure. What interests us here is the fact that the subjects at this level did not, of their own accord, make use of one-to-one correspondence between rows of counters in responding to the experimenter's questions. Their counting behaviour which is not yet a genuine numeration, does not enable them to establish the equivalence of collections in all cases.)

Fourth level: non-conservers using one-to-one correspondence, and knowing how to count (NC4).

The child uses one-to-one correspondence, and counts in order to verify or explain the equivalence of collections. Conversely, the child may count from the beginning, and only clearly establishes a one-to-one correspondence in order to show the E that there is the same number of counters in the two configurations. However, if the changes in configuration are very great, the child may consider it necessary to count afresh, or may cease to affirm equivalence, even if it is admitted that the original configuration may be re-formed with the same counters.

Second stage: intermediate conservation (I). There is alternation between the behaviours of the first stage (NC4) and of the third stage. Collections are set up using correct one-to-one correspondence. The child's judgment is either conserving for some situations and not for others, or the child hesitates and alternates in the same situation. There is a pseudo-conservation of the "name" of the number of counters, which is distinct from conservation of the quantity of counters. In other words, the child knows that the result of counting will always be the same, regardless of changes of configuration, but thinks that the quantity of counters does change.

Third stage: conservation (C). The child carries out one-to-one correspondence without seeking perceptual information. The number of
counters is considered to be unaffected by changes of configuration (the
child stating, for instance: "they are the same, they haven't changed! I
counted them. There are still 6 there and 6 there"). Stable, conserving
judgments are given in all situations. These are justified by one or more
of the following arguments:

argument from *"identity"* "There is the same number of green and
yellow counters, because before they were the same and none have
been added or taken away, they are just closer together."
argument from *"reversibility"* "You can put them back like they were
before, and see that there's the same amount" or "if you spread the
counters out in this line, it will be the same as this one. They have the
same."
argument from *"compensation"* "It's longer here (the line) but the counters aren't so close together, so they have the same."

Collective Session

This phase of the experiment took place between one and four days
after the pre-test. Two children were taken together to the same room
where the pre-test took place, and were seated at a small table, facing
each other. After a short period to establish rapport, E presented the
experimental material, "Smarties", and told the children that they
would be able to eat them after the game, but only if they managed to
divide the "Smarties" equally between them. E then took up the strips
of cardboard and asked the children to pretend that these were plates:
"We're going to pretend that these are plates", or "look at these strips
of cardboard that I've cut out; can we pretend that they are plates?"
(When this precaution was taken in introducing the material, the
children readily accepted the convention of "pretending", whereas if it
was omitted the question of what function the cardboard strips had in
the game seemed to disorientate them.)

The E then placed about 15 "Smarties" in the middle of the table,
gave plate A (9 cm long, 5 circles) to one child (S1) and plate B (17 cm
long, 5 circles) to the other (S2). E explained that the circles drawn on
the plates were "places to put the 'Smarties'", but that they didn't have
to use these places if they didn't want to. E then said: "You can take the

"Smarties" and put them on your plates, but only if you both take the same amount. You mustn't have more, or less, than your friend. You must both have the same amount, both be satisfied, otherwise it won't be fair. How are you going to do it?" In some cases, one of the two children carried out the distribution, and in other cases each child took their own "Smarties". When the distribution was completed, E asked the two subjects whether in fact they had divided the "Smarties" equally between them, if so how this had been achieved, or should have been achieved, and pressed them to find some way of agreeing on the fairness of the division. Once agreement was reached, E exchanged the plates between the two partners in order to test the consistency of the agreement. The procedure was then repeated, using different plates. "Now that you've understood the game, we'll try again with different plates. Then we'll eat the 'Smarties'." The pairs of plates then used consecutively were: B and C (both 17cm long, but with 5 and 7 circles) and A and D (both 9 cm long, with 5 and 6 circles). At the end of the last sharing-out, E allowed the children to eat the "Smarties", and asked them if they were both satisfied with the division.

Post-test

The post-test took place for each child individually two to four days after the collective session. The conditions, procedure and scoring were exactly the same as for the pre-test.

EXPERIMENTAL CONDITIONS

There were three experimental conditions, according to the conservation level (as determined in the pre-test) of the partners in the collective situation:

Condition (a) One of the children was conserving on the pre-test, the other non-conserving.
Condition (b) One of the children was intermediate on pre-test, the other was non-conserving.
Condition (c) Both children were non-conserving on pre-test.

In conditions (a) and (b), the non-conserving subject was placed together with a partner whose level was superior to their own. In condition (c), the interaction was between two children of the same level.

COLLECTION OF DATA

In each session, the experimenter was assisted by a colleague who took notes on the sequence of events and the actions and utterances of the subject(s). At the same time, systematic cassette recordings were made which permitted checks to be made on the completeness of the protocols.

Results

QUALITATIVE ANALYSIS OF BEHAVIOUR AND ITS DEVELOPMENT

Pre-test

Qualitative analysis of the 140 pre-test protocols showed that the subjects' behaviour was entirely similar to that described by Piaget and Szeminska (1941). The sub-stages defined for the non-conservers discriminated among them sufficiently to set up four distinct levels, as had been anticipated.

TABLE 18

Level on the conservation of number pre-test as a function of school class

| School class | Level on pre-test | | | | | | |
	NCg	NCo	NCc	NC4	I	C	Total
First class	16	2	10	26	7	7	68
Second class	0	0	4	6	11	51	72
Total	16	2	14	32	18	58	140

Table 18 shows subjects' levels in the two school classes. These data indicate that, although there is no clear transition, children attaining the highest level on this test of conservation are in the older class. Such a result confirms the link between development and the construction of the concept of conservation, already indicated by Piaget and Szeminska (1941). This link will be seen again in relation to the stages defined by these authors, and also to the levels of non-conservation which we have set up ourselves.

Collective Situation

On the pre-test, 64 children were classified as non-conservers. Of these, 40 were distributed across the three experimental conditions, the remaining 24 having served as pilot subjects for pre-testing, experimental procedures, or determining the levels of non-conservation; or having had to be discarded because of timetable clashes or absences which interfered with the required temporal intervals between sessions.

In the three experimental conditions, most of the non-conserving subjects came from the younger class. Their mean age was between 5 years and 5 years 4 months.

In the collective sessions, in all the experimental conditions there were interactions between the children: questions, comments, demonstrations, commands, advice and explanations. In order to standardize the procedure, the experimenter (according to the levels of the partners) was obliged to intervene in his attempts to make sure that the children talked among themselves, rather than addressing him or carrying out actions which did not stem from mutual agreement. It appeared here, as in experiments I and II, that it was situations (a) and (b), which placed together children of different levels, which gave rise to most exchanges and conflicts between partners, and in which there were fewest interventions by the experimenter.

Post-test

The same range of behaviours was apparent on the post-test as had been observed in the pre-test, making it possible to use the same criteria of evaluation to determine each subject's level on the conservation of number test.

DEVELOPMENT OF BEHAVIOUR BETWEEN PRE-TEST AND POST-TEST

Many of the children progressed between the pre-test and the post-test. There were two degree of progress:

(1) *"sub-stage progress"* *(pp)* The subject progressed from one sub-stage to another within the stage of non-conservation, e.g. from NCg to NCo.

(2) *"stage progress"* *(P)* The subject progressed to a higher stage of conservation, a non-conserver becoming an intermediate conserver or a conserver.

There was only one child who performed less well on the post-test than on the pre-test. This was a subject who had been classified as NC4 on pre-test, but who performed at NCg level on post-test. The following protocols illustrate the two degrees of progress.

"Sub-stage Progress" (pp)

The subject here is Phi, whose level was NCc on pre-test, and NC4 on post-test.

Pre-test.

> *Exp* (places 5 green counters in a row, and says to *Phi*) "Take some of the yellow counters, and take as many as I have, so that there will be the same number of green and yellow counters."
>
> *Phi* sets out 9 yellow counters
>
> *Exp* "Are there more yellow counters, more green ones, or are there as many of each?"
>
> *Phi* "Not the same."
>
> *Exp* "Make it so that there are the same number of green and yellow ones."
>
> *Phi* "Must take those away." (leaves 6 yellow counters)
>
> *Exp* "Is there one row with more in, or are they the same?"
>
> *Phi* "One of them has more." (takes away one more yellow counter, leaving 5)
>
> *Exp* "Now, do they have the same, or does one have more?"
>
> *Phi* "Not more."
>
> *Exp* (spaces out the green counters to form a longer row) "Do we have the same amount of green and yellow counters to play with, or does one row have more?"
>
> *Phi* (spaces out his yellow counters, and adds more to his line which then contains 8)
>
> *Exp* "Are there more yellow counters, more green ones or do they both have the same?"
>
> *Phi* "The same."
>
> *Exp* (spaces out further the 5 green counters in his row) "Now, have we got more yellow counters to play with, more green ones, or the same, what do you think?"
>
> *Phi* "Not the same."
>
> *Exp* "One of us has more?"
>
> *Phi* "Yes; you."
>
> *Exp* "What should we do so that we both have the same?"
>
> *Phi* "I'll put that one down there, and that one, and that one (. . .)"(—changing the arrangement of the 5 green and the 8 yellow counters)
>
> (. . .)

Exp (places 6 green counters in a row) "Now you do it so that you have the same as me; you must have as many yellow counters as I have green ones."

Phi makes a row of 7 yellow counters

Exp "Can you count them?"

Phi "1, 2, 3, 4, 5, 6" (green)
"1, 2, 3, 4, 5, 6, 7" (yellow)

Phi "They're not the same."

Exp "Are there more yellow ones, more green ones, or the same amount of each?"

Phi "Take that one away." (Leaving 6 yellow counters.)

Exp "What now?"

Phi "They're the same."

Exp spaces out the green counters

Phi "There are more green ones," (and counts) "1,2,3,4,5,6" (green)

Exp "What about the yellow ones?" "1,2,3,4,5,6" (yellow) (and adds two yellow counters to his line to produce a length comparable to the green line containing 6 counters)

Post-test.

Exp (takes 5 green counters and places them in a row) "Take as many counters as I have."

Phi (places 4 yellow counters in a row) "There are more green ones."

Exp "Well, take some more so that we've got the same."

Phi adds one yellow counter

(...)

(Phi picks up some counters, hesitating; he tries both adding and removing yellow counters, but fails to produce a satisfying solution. He seems to be looking at the length of the lines and the spaces between the counters)

Exp "Well now, what have we got to play with?"

Phi (arranges the counters in one-to-one correspondence) (there are 4 yellow and 5 green) "They're not the same, there's one missing." (adds a yellow counter) "There!"

Exp pushes the green counters more closely together

Phi "There are more green ones."

Exp "What do we have to do to get the same amount of counters each ?"

Phi (is silent, then says) "You have to put one below, one above, one below (etc.)." (he pushes the yellow counters closer together, and places them in one-to-one correspondence with the green counters)

(...)

Exp (places 6 yellow and 6 green counters in one-to-one correspondence; the child assents to the equivalence) "If I hide the green counters, can you tell me how many of them there are?"

Phi silence

Exp "How many yellow ones are there?"

Phi "1,2,3,4,5,6"

Exp (discloses the green counters) "How many green ones?"

Phi "1,2,3,4,5,6"

Exp spaces out the green counters

Phi "The same."

Exp "I'm going to play with the green counters, and you with the yellow ones. Have we got the same amount of counters, each of us, to play with?"

Phi "No, there are more green ones."

Exp invites Phi to recount the two rows; he finds 6 yellow and 6 green

Exp "Do we have the same or not?"

Phi "No, there are more green ones."

"Stage progress" (P)

(a) First example: Dor, whose level on pre-test was non-conserving (NC4), and whose post-test level was intermediate (I).

Pre-test

Exp has taken 5 green counters and arranged them in a row; the child takes 5 yellow ones

Exp "Have you taken as many as me?"

Dor "Yes, that's enough."

Exp (spaces out the green counters) "If you play with the yellow counters, and I play with the green ones, do we both have the same number of counters to play with, or does one have more, or what do you think?"

Dor "There are more green ones."

Exp "What if I do this?" (pushes the green counters closer together, so that the green line is shorter than the yellow one) "Are there more green ones, more yellow ones, or are they the same number?"

Dor "There are very few green ones and a lot of yellow ones."

Exp "And if I play with all the green ones, and you play with all the yellow ones, do we both have the same amount to play with . . .?"

Dor "I've got more and you've got less."

Exp "What would we have to do to both have the same?"

Dor "You have to push them all together" (she pushes the counters together, and adds some) "so that the two lines are the same."

Exp "What now?"

Dor "They're the same."

(the counters are all put in a heap; Exp takes out 5 green counters and arranges them as the four corners of a square, with one in the centre; Dor copies the figure with 5 yellow counters)

Exp "Now, are there more green ones, more yellow ones, or the same number of each?"
Dor "The same."
Exp pushes the green counters closer together
Dor "You've got very few, I've got a lot."
Exp "Of what?"
Dor "Counters."
(the counters are once more put in a heap; Exp places 5 green counters in a line; Dor places 5 yellow counters in one-to-one correspondence with the green ones)
Exp (hiding the green line with his hand) "If I hide my counters, can you say how many I've got?"
Dor (probably counting mentally, but making an error) "6!"
Exp "How do you know?"
(silence)
Exp "And how many have you got?"
Dor "6!"
Exp "And if I put two more green counters in my line?" (does this) "how many have I got?"
Dor "8!"
Exp "How do you know?"
Dor "Because you put two more."
(. . .)

Post-test.

(Exp has put 5 counters in a line; Dor 5 yellow counters)
Exp "Have we both got the same number of counters, or has one of us got more than the other?"
Dor "I've got more." Removes a yellow counter, leaving 4.
Exp "Are you sure?"
Dor "Yes."
Exp "How do you know?"
Dor "Because I counted them!"
Exp "Oh, yes! go on then!"
Dor "1,2,3,4 and . . ." (adds a yellow counter) there, 5! Not two, because that makes 6!"
(so now there are two equal lines of five counters; Exp spaces out the green counters)
Dor "You've got more!"
Exp "How many have I got?"
Dor "You've got 6 and me 5!" (whereas there are in fact 5 green and 5 yellow)
(. . .)

(Dor has affirmed the equivalence of two lines of 5 counters; Exp closes up the line of green counters)

Dor "There are more yellow ones."

Exp "This is a long line" (pointing to the yellow counters)" and this is a short line; but are there more yellow *counters*, or more green ones, or are there the same number of each?"

Dor "More yellow ones."

Exp "What shall we do to have the same number each to play with?"

Dor "I've only got to put them closer together"

(the counters are put together in a heap; Exp makes the square figure with one counter in the centre, using green counters; Dor copies the figure with yellow counters)

Exp "Did you use the same number of counters as me?"

Dor "Yes."

Exp spaces out his green counters to make a larger figure

Dor "There are more green ones!"

Exp "How do you know?"

Dor "Because yours is bigger than mine, and if I make mine bigger it's the same."

(. . .)

Exp reforms his counters into a line

Dor "It's the same." (miming the action of putting the yellow counters also in a line)

Exp "And what if you leave yours like that, in a "flower"?"

Dor "It's the same, because we both took the same. We both had five."

Exp spaces out his counters, thus lengthening his line

Dor "You've got more because it's more spaced out."

Exp "Yes, but if I play with all these green counters and you with all these yellow ones . . ."

Dor "You've got a lot more."

(. . .)

(Dor considers that two lines comprising respectively 7 yellow counters and 7 green counters are equivalent; Exp pushes the green counters closer together)

Dor "I've got more and you've got very few."

Exp "How many have I got?"

Dor "I've got seven as well."

Exp "Have we both got the same number to play with?"

Dor "I've got more because they're more spaced out."

Exp "I've got a little line and you, you've got a big line, but have I got more *counters* than you, or less, or the same amount?"

Dor "The same."

Exp "But why?"

Dor "Because I counted them."

Exp "But before you said they weren't the same"

Dor "They're the same!"

These protocols show that, on the pre-test, Dor was centring on the configuration formed by the counters. In the course of questioning, it became clear that Dor would use one-to-one correspondence to establish equivalence. She knows how to count the series of counters, and is even able to guess the number of counters in the line (previously constructed by one-to-one correspondence) hidden by the experimenter's hand. However, at no time did she envisage that a change of configuration could fail to change the quantity of counters. On the post-test, in contrast, Dor sometimes affirms conservation, particularly in the case of the "flower" figure, when she uses an argument from identity ("it's the same because we took the same number of counters"). But non-conserving responses follow, which are based on the length of the lines. Dor also oscillates in her counting responses. Even though she can use counting to establish the numerical equivalence of the lines, or to justify her conserving judgments, the idea does not seem to be solidly established. She will claim that a change in the spacing of the counters does not leave their number invariant, or she will consider that the number remains the same but the quantity changes.

"Stage Progress" (P)

(b) Second example: Oli, whose level on pre-test is non-conserving (NCc) and on post-test conserving (C).

Pre-test.

> (Exp places 5 green counters in a line and says to Oli) "Take the same number of counters as me!" (Oli constructs a line with 7 counters, starting from the end of the experimenter's line and forming an angle of about 60° with it; with no attempt at a one-to-one correspondence)
>
> *Oli* "There! we've both got the same."
> *Exp* spaces out the 5 green counters making up his line
> *Oli* "There are more green ones if you put them like that."
> *Exp* "But if I play with the green ones and you with the yellow ones, shall we both have the same, or will one of us have more? Is there the same number of counters, or are there more green ones or more yellow ones? What do you think?"
> *Oli* "There are more green ones."
> *Exp* (pushing the 5 green counters closer together) "If I put my counters like that, and you do too." (the 7 yellow counters are placed likewise)
> *Oli* "There are more yellow ones."

(. . .)

Exp (takes 5 green counters and places them in a square with one in the middle) "Take the same number!" (Oli does the same with 5 yellow counters; He makes a smaller figure)

Exp "Are there more green ones or yellow ones?"

Oli "There same."

Exp "How do you know?"

Oli "Because they're the same number."

(. . .)

Exp (forms two lines of 5 counters, placing them in one-to-one correspondence)

Oli (comments) "Six!"

Exp "How do you know! Explain it to me."

Oli "Like that!"

Exp "How?"

Oli "I counted. 1,2,3,4,5,6" (in fact there are 5 yellow and 5 green counters)

Exp "Count them again."

Oli "1,2,3,4,5,6"

Exp "And what if it's like this" (spaces out the green counters) "are there the same number of yellow counters and green counters, or does one of us have more than the other?"

Oli "There are more green ones."

Exp "How many are there?"

Oli "Still 6"

(. . .)

The protocol shows that Oli does not use one-to-one correspondence, although he knows how to attribute the same number ("six", whereas in fact there were 5 counters) to the two rows constructed by the experimenter. He uses counting, but does not have full mastery of it: he makes systematic errors. This often unskilled use of counting nevertheless allows him to succeed with the flower figure (unless he knows the game of dominoes, in which the 5 piece bears the same figure, and this helps him to see that the same configuration in different sizes is the same?) but does not serve him, whatever formulation may be suggested to him by the experimenter, in seeing the equivalence between the two lines of unequal length but the same number of counters.

Post-test.

Exp (takes 5 green counters and places them in a row) "Take the same number; take as many as I have." (Oli constructs a second line using one-to-one correspondence with 5 yellow counters; he appears to count mentally)

Oli "There!"

Exp "How do you know there are the same number?"

Oli "Because I counted them."

Exp (spaces out the green counters and says) "If I play with all these green counters, and you play with all these yellow ones, do we both have the same number, or is there one of us who has more?"

Oli "We still have the same."

Exp "How do you know?"

Oli "There's still 6." (in fact there are 5 counters)

Exp (pushing the green counters closer together) "You leave yours like that. There. If I play with the green counters and you with the yellow ones, are there more green ones, more yellow ones, or do we both have the same?"

Oli "The same."

Exp "How do you know?"

Oli "There are still 6."

Exp "There was a little girl who came here before you, and she told me that this is a little line, so there are less counters in it. Do you think she was right, or wrong?"

Oli "She was wrong."

Exp "How would you explain to her what is right?"

Oli "Say to her that there are 6."

(. . .)

(Exp places the 5 green counters in the flower figure; Oli imitates this figure with some difficulty, using 5 yellow counters; Exp spaces out the green counters) "Do we have the same number of counters each, or does one of us have more than the other?"

Oli "No-one has more."

Exp "How do you know?"

(Oli counts mentally, then says) "The are 6." (in fact there are 5)

Exp "For both of us?"

Oli "yes."

Exp spaces out the green counters

Oli "We've got the same."

Exp puts them in a line

Oli "Still the same!"

Exp spaces out the counters in his line

Oli "Still the same!"

(. . .)

(Exp places two lines of 7 counters each in one-to-one correspondence; when the equivalence has been affirmed, he then puts the 7 green counters in a heap)

Oli (counts them) "The same, still the same."

Exp "Even though mine are in a heap?"

Oli "Yes."

Exp "How many have I got?"

Oli "Six." (in fact there are 7)

Oli's responses in the post-test differ sharply from his responses in the pre-test, in that he still affirms conservation whatever changes of configuration are presented to him. He never appears to doubt or hesitate between different points of view, which allows us to conclude that he has progressed beyond the intermediate stage. Nevertheless, it is clear that this acquisition is recent, and still in the process of being completed, since Oli has great difficulty in justifying his judgments. He justifies them by counting (even though his counting is inaccurate, in contrast to the notional grasp of it which he appears to have acquired): "They're the same because I counted them!". He also invokes counting to formulate an argument which is close to the idea of identity: "—How do you know we still have the same?" "There are still 6!" he replies, without counting.

THE EFFECT OF INTERACTION AND THE ROLE OF SUBJECT'S AND
PARTNER'S INITIAL LEVEL

As we have just seen, the analysis of pre- and post-test protocols shows greater or lesser degrees of development at the level of cognitive structuring. Is there also evidence of the differential effect of experimental conditions of the kind we previously obtained in the case of conservation of liquid? More specifically, is there evidence that non-conserving subjects are more likely to progress if they are placed together with a partner at a more advanced level, than if they interact with a partner at the same level, with the same point of view as their own? We hypothesized that progress should occur with either a conserving or an intermediate partner (i.e. in either condition (a) or (b)); but we expect that, since the conflict of viewpoints will be greater in the first condition, this will be the more effective.

Table 19 shows the results of the post-test for each of the experimental conditions. The expected order of effectiveness of conditions is confirmed, in so far as non-conservers tend to progress more frequently if they are confronted with conservers (condition (a) 6 progressing out of 14) than if they are placed together with intermediates (condition (b) 2 progressing out of 10). The effect of interaction with a partner at a more advanced level (conditions (a) and (b) 8 progressing out of 24) is greater than with a partner at the same level (condition (c) 2 progressing out of 16). However, these are tendencies which do not reach statistical significance.

TABLE 19

Progress (P) evident on post-test in the three experimental conditions as a function of initial level on pre-test

		NCg		NCo		NCc		NC4		Total	
						Level on pre-test					
	P	No progress	P	No progress	P	No progress	P	No progress	P	No progress	
(a) NC + C	0	1	0	0	1	2	5	5	6	8	
(b) NC + I	0	1	0	0	1	3	1	4	2	8	
(c) NC + NC	1	4	0	1	1	1	0	8	2	14	
Total	1	6	0	1	3	6	6	17	10	30	

Our second aim was to find out what prerequisite conditions need to be fulfilled before a child can be affected by an interaction. We should therefore look at the differences between the experimental conditions again, focussing on those children who did make progress.

Table 20 presents data on the development of all non-conservers between the pre-test and the post-test. It shows that the subjects most likely to progress were those who were most advanced within the stage of non-conservation (NCc and NC4 subjects; 9 out of 32). Of the others within this stage, there were 8 at the sub-stages NCg and NCo, only one of whom progressed, and this subject's progress was of the sub-stage type.

TABLE 20

Development between pre-test and post-test of non-conservers in all experimental conditions

		NCg	NCo	NCc	NC4	I	C	Total
				Level on post-test				
	NCg	6	0	1	0	0	0	7
Level on	NCo	0	1	0	0	0	0	1
pre-test	NCc	0	0	6	1	1	1	9
	NC4	1	0	0	16	5	1	23
	Total	7	1	7	17	7	2	40

Why did the non-conservers at the lower sub-stages fail to benefit from the interaction? Most probably because they did not understand what was going on in their interaction with a partner of a higher level.

We observed that the task in the collective session was almost always dealt with using counting and one-to-one correspondence by the higher-level children. For the NCo subject, who was unable to use counting in the pre-test, the partner's behaviour was unfamiliar in two ways: first, the partner used counting, and second, the partner referred to the results of this counting (the conservers always, the intermediates occasionally) to prove that the quantities of "Smarties" were conserved. It is possible to imagine that, for the NCo subject, it was particularly difficult to grasp *how different* the partner's viewpoint was, both in using counting, and in appealing to the significance of counting. If this is so, then the difficulties must have been even greater for a NCg subject, who faced not only the same difficulties as the NCo subject in understanding what counting was all about, but in addition had the problem of trying to understand one-to-one correspondence. The first acquisitions these subjects have to make, then, are those (superior to perceptual global evaluation) which permit the construction of two collections which are equivalent, even if they only recognize them as such in the case of configurations which do not present perceptual conflict. The interactive task was not centred on these abilities; rather, it required the children to have recourse to them in effecting a fair distribution on the basis of conflicting configurations (represented by the "plates"). In other words, the interactive task was not designed to evoke the strategies which the NCg and NCo subjects were to acquire (hence their relative ineffectiveness), but it pre-supposed them, thus making it impossible for these subjects to properly participate.

In the light of these results and our interpretation of them, then, it would appear that in order to be able to participate in a given social interaction—and therefore to benefit from it— subjects must already have acquired abilities which are called upon during the interaction. Within a constructivist approach, it is necessary to show that these prerequisite abilities also are developed during the course of social interactions.

We have just seen that the point of the collective session was to induce coordinations of behaviours which would lead to the setting-up of numerically equivalent collections from perceptually conflicting configurations, and that these interactions were therefore more likely to lead to development in the idea of conservation of number ("stage progress") than to the acquisition of the elementary strategies of counting and one-to-one correspondence for simple configurations ("sub-stage progress"). For this reason, it is appropriate to compare the three experimental conditions in terms of their success in inducing stage progress. The comparison is made only for those non-conservers shown by the preceding analysis to be cable of progressing as a result of interaction—NCc and NC4 subjects. Table 21 presents this compari-son.

TABLE 21

Stage progress (P) in NCc and NC4 subjects as a function of experimental condition

	NCc		NC4		NCc + NC4		Total
	P	No progress	P	No progress	P	No progress	
(a) NC + C	1	2	5	5	6	7	13
(b) NC + I	1	3	1	4	2	7	9
(c) NC + NC	0	2	0	8	0	10	10
Total	2	7	6	17	8	24	32

Primarily, we find in this experiment on the conservation of number the same phenomenon that we have already seen in experiment II on the conservation of liquid—that non-conservers are more likely to progress if they are confronted with a conserving partner (conditions (a) 6 out of 13) than if the partner is, like them, a non-conserver (condition (c) 0 out of 10). This result is statistically significant (Fisher's threshold of $p=0.025$). Condition (a) in this experiment differs from the homologous condition in the preceding experiment (condition I) in that the non-conserver interacts, not with two, but with only one conserver. This shows clearly that, as we had earlier reasoned, it is not necessary for the non-conserver to be confronted with a conserving majority for the effect of interaction to occur.

Our hypothesis was that the effectiveness of the collective situation in bringing about cognitive development lies in the fact that it confronts non-conservers with viewpoints different from their own. This is the case for conditions (a) and (b), but not for condition (c). In fact conditions (a) and (b) are the only ones in which stage progress (P) is apparent on post-test, making them significantly different from condi-tion (c) (exact probability $=0.034$). Analysis of subjects' development in condition (b) also reveals a trend in line with this hypothesis, but the trend does not reach statistical significances: non-conservers progress following interaction with an intermediate partner, but not with a non-conserving partner; and progress following interaction with an intermediate partner is less frequent than with a conserving partner— probably because the conflict between viewpoints is less salient in this case than with a conserver.

Finally, the protocols of this third experiment give rise to an observation which was not intended to be an experimental one. For ethical reasons, as in the preceding experiments, we took the precaution of verifying, by means of post-tests, that the conserving subjects in condition (a) did not regress significantly following their interaction with less advanced partners. The same precaution led us to look at the development of the 10 intermediate subjects in condition (b).

Table 22 gives the post-test levels of intermediate subjects as a function of their partner's pre-test level. Only one intermediate subject regressed (to non-conserving sub-stage NC4), and half of them (5 out of 10) benefited from the interaction with a less advanced partner, and became conservers. Since the development of subjects interacting with less advanced partners was not one of the planned observations in this study, we did not include the control group which would have permitted evaluation of its relative importance. Failing this, we can however, simply compare this observation with that obtained from experiment I on the conservation of liquid (Table 1), in which 7 out of 9 intermediates who interacted with more advanced partners (conservers) made progress. These observations suggest that interaction with a less advanced partner may be as profitable as with a more advanced partner, and it is a suggestion which we put to experimental test in the next chapter.

TABLE 22

Post-test levels of intermediate subjects in condition (b) as a function of partner's pre-test level

| | | Partner's pre-test level | | | |
		NCg	NCc	NC4	Total
Intermediate	NC4	0	0	1	1
subjects'	I	0	3	1	4
post-test levels	C	1	1	3	5
	Total	1	4	5	10

Conclusions

This experiment on the conservation of number has permitted the generalization to younger children, and to a different domain of conservation, of the effect of social interaction demonstrated in the previous experiments. The experiment also allows specification of the individual and social conditions prerequisite to the effect.

Without necessarily agreeing with contemporary criticism of some Piagetian research on learning (Lefebvre-Pinard, 1976) it is important to point out that we are not subject to this criticism, since the subjects who progressed most in this experiment, like those in experiment II, were well below the operational level—and this in relation to a concept which is one of the first to be constructed when the stage of concrete operations is reached.

In Chapter 3, in a theoretical approach similar to that of Inhelder *et al.* (1974) we attempted to show that the progress induced by social interaction is compatible with what is already known concerning the laws of development. In fact we had already been able to reject a simple maturation hypothesis in favour of an explanation in terms of processes of internal reorganization. It then remained to show that the effect of social interaction is constrained by the subject's internal potential to proceed to the assimilations and accommodations necessary to be able to cooperate; and that the nature and extent of progress made is a function of the subject's initial level of development.

While this experiment, like the two preceding ones, has shown that social interaction induces learning not only in intermediates but also—and this was its major interest—in non-conservers, the aim of the third experiment was more precise. It was to determine whether there is a minimum initial level which non-conservers need to have reached before they can benefit from the type of interactions to which we exposed them. We therefore distinguished between two types of minimum initial competence: the prerequisites for social interaction, and the prerequisites for cognitive re-structuring.

The first conclusion which can be drawn from our results a concerns the second set of prerequisites: only those subjects who already, on pre-test, performed at one of the higher levels of non-conservation, were able to benefit from the social interaction we provided to the extent that their post-test performance showed cognitive re-structuring. Such results are not novel. Cowan *et al* (1969) and J. P. Murray (1974), among others, have shown (though working within a different theoretical tradition) that the susceptibility of children to "modelling" or conditioning depends on their initial developmental level. A point of clarification is important here: our interpretation of these results is not that below a certain level of development the subject is totally impervious to models or conditioning, or unable to participate at all in social interaction, but rather that such results show that there is a minimum developmental level at which *these specific experimental procedures* begin to have an effect. The question arises whether different experimental procedures might not produce effects in younger subjects, though probably these would be ineffective, lengthy or uninteresting for older subjects. A more relevant and precise question, it seems to us, would be to seek the conditions which would induce development in younger children which would take them to the point where they could benefit from the established procedures. From our own research, we have been able to specify the developmental level at which children begin to benefit from social interaction of the type we exposed them to. We have also shown why such joint activity is not able to induce development in children at the lower levels of non-conservation. We hypothesized that there are other interactive situation which could induce development in these subjects—situations in which they would be exposed to behaviour at the level immediately superior to theirs. We have already seen that it is precisely these behaviours (one-to-one correspondence and counting) which are prerequisites for the social interactions brought into play by the sharing task we used in this experiment.

Our results from this third experiment agree with those of Lefebvre and Pinard (1972), Miller (1973) and especially Lefebvre and Pinard (1974). The latter have shown, using very detailed analysis which reveals differences in level of mental development among pre-operational children, that it is not sufficient to create a situation of supposed conflict for the child to experience it as such.

In our experience also, it is not sufficient to place a non-conserving subject together with a partner of a superior level of development for the non-conserver to understand the nature of the conflict between their different viewpoints, and especially to understand on what points there is opposition. It seems that the non-conserver is unable to do this without recourse to one-to-one correspondence or counting together with the partner—that is, unless the non-conserver's level is at least NCc or Nc4.

Lefebvre-Pinard (1976, p. 106) writes on this point: "if we wish the pre-operational child, who is naturally sure in all his assertions and insensitive to contradiction, to benefit from a conflictual method, we must first of all seek to undermine the child's certainties by making him sense the inadequacy of his habitual notional rules before exposing him to properly conflictual situations". Our experiment III brings support to this view by showing that if the child possesses certain behaviours already, social interaction can undermine the child's certainties by means of the very conflict which they create. But this is only possible when certain prerequisite conditions have been met.

These conditions are seen to be of two types. First, they are *social*, since they must include the coordinated action which will induce the behaviours for which the subject is ready (from the point of view of the sequence of developmental acquisitions). Secondly, they are *individual*, since the subject cannot take part in this exchange unless already capable of understanding what the exchange is about.

It therefore appears that these two types of prerequisite are in fact closely intertwined. For a certain type of social interaction to occur, the subject must have minimum cognitive competencies in order to be able to participate in the interaction, and, if this condition is met, the interaction then brings about a process of cognitive re-structuring in the subject. The development which results from this subsequently allows the subject to participate in other interactions which will in their turn be the source of new development. This is a spiral model of developmental progression which is similar to that described by Piaget (1974a, p. 86).

We had hypothesized, within an interactionist and constructivist approach to development, that the progress induced by interaction would occur only if subjects had already reached a level of minimum competence. If the experiment confirms this hypothesis, the detailed examination of the results suggests several more precise interpretations which need experimental investigation.

Finally, this experiment appears to confirm our hypothesis on the role of conflict between the subject's and the partner's points of view. It is certain that confrontation with a partner who has full mastery of the concept in question is the source of cognitive re-structuring, but it seems that confrontation with a partner who is merely intermediate may also be. If this is the case, and that indices such as the progress made by conservers on other tests in experiment II, or the development in intermediates following interaction with less advanced subjects, combine to show that it is sufficient in certain conditions for the viewpoints to be merely different, then the problem of the relative levels of the partners has to be considered in more general terms. The research reported in the next chapter aims to show experimentally that subjects are able to benefit from social interaction with others in so far as the other's centrations are *different* from those of the subject— whether deriving from a higher, or a lower developmental level, or even from within the same level.

If such a demonstration can be made, the question still arises as to the differential effect of the type of confrontation (non-conservers with conservers, intermediates or other non-conservers). In other words, what is the role of the developmental gap between partners, in terms of the salience of cognitive conflict? The results of the third experiment already suggest the hypothesis that too great a gap will prevent the conflict in viewpoints from becoming apparent—at least to the less advanced child—and therefore from being socially experienced by this child.

5

The Effect of Interaction with Less Advanced Partners and the Role of Conflicting Centrations

The experiments reported in the preceding chapters have shown that, in certain conditions, social interaction between children can bring about cognitive development of an operational nature.

However, the first three experiments were exclusively concerned with subjects who were cognitively less advanced than their partner or partners in the interaction. There were two reasons for this constraint. The first lay in the nature of the genesis of the concept under study. The acquisition of both the conservation of liquid and the conservation of number is characterized by three stages which provide the only theoretically valid criteria with which to categorize subjects according to their level of development. It follows that the scale of evaluation used must always be a 3-point scale, even if differentiations are possible within the three stages. It should also be noted that several studies of learning have underlined the special status of intermediate subjects. In investigations like ours, therefore, it would seem prudent to confine attention to effects in subjects at the other two stages: non-conservers and conservers. Here we meet the second reason for the constraint on the preceding experiments: only non-conservers were able to show progress, since the conservers, in the terms of the experiments, had already reached a ceiling in development of the concept under study. The only change they could show would be regression. Is it possible that experiments concerning concepts which could be evaluated on a more extended developmental scale could be devised, which would show whether more advanced subjects might benefit equally from social interaction?

Whereas social learning theories would not make this prediction, but rather the reverse— that subjects would regress when confronted with a model having a less advanced level of behaviour (Rosenthal and

Zimmerman, 1972)—the research we have so far presented does offer several pieces of evidence in favour of such a prediction.

We have already seen that, for the effects on non-conservers of interaction with more advanced children, explanations in terms of the imitation of models are not adequate. Such explanations cannot account for the subjects' creation of novel arguments to justify their conserving responses, or for the further development of responses between the post-tests, which clearly indicates a continuing process of cognitive re-structuring.

Furthermore, the contribution to the effect of interaction of the partner or partners' developmental level, the composition of groups, and the "constellations" of behaviours deployed in the groups leads to the hypothesis that the cause of the cognitive development observed is to be found in the conflict of centrations which the subject experiences during the interaction. The interaction obliges the subject to coordinate their actions with those of others, and this brings about a decentration in the encounter with other points of view which can only be assimilated if cognitive re-structuring takes place.

If these are not imitation processes, but interactive processes, it should be possible to confirm this by showing that it is not necessary for the subject to be confronted with a more advanced partner in order to benefit from the interaction. This hypothesis is already corroborated by some previous observations. In the three experiments we have reported, children who interacted with less advanced children do not regress. (The one exception is an intermediate who became non-conserving (NC4) after interaction with another NC4 in experiment III). More particularly, the second experiment showed that conservers were able to benefit from interactions, in that they made progress in domains related to the one under study. Finally, the third experiment showed important gains in intermediates who interacted with non-conservers.

The aim of this chapter is to demonstrate more specifically the possibilities for progress in the more advanced partner in interactions. The two experiments in which this is done then lead on to a third experiment which focuses on the role of the type of conflict brought about by different centrations.

Progress following interaction with a less advanced partner: copying geometrical shapes

As we have already indicated, this fourth experiment required the categorization of children according to their developmental level on a scale sufficiently extended to obtain two clear categories, "less advanced" and "more advanced", within each of which there was room for further advance. It was therefore necessary for the cognitive domain chosen to be broad enough for continued advance, while being sufficiently well defined to be able to compare levels of performance within it.

For these reasons, we chose a domain which has been the object of some very exact research by Piaget and Inhelder (1948): elementary spatial relations in children's drawing. The choice of this domain also allows us to generalize our findings in the preceding experiments from judgments to representations, and from language-mediated responses to drawing. The age range we chose was the same as that in the experiment on the conservation of number, and therefore roughly corresponds to the beginning of the stage of concrete operations.

In their studies of the child's representation of space, Piaget and Inhelder give detailed descriptions of the development of the child's behaviour in copying different geometrical designs. These descriptions are verified in our research. Basing ourselves on Inhelder and Piaget's work, we selected eight geometrical figures which presented different degrees of difficulty in copying, to children aged between 4 and 5. For each of these figures, we therefore possessed, thanks to the previous work, a description of the development of copying behaviour which could be used to evaluate subjects' performances on pre-test and post-test.

METHOD

We had a test which would allow us to evaluate, not only the graphic quality, but also the spatial properties of the children's copies from these eight geometrical figures. All the subjects were pre-tested individually, then invited, either individually or in pairs, to make a cardboard representation of a certain number of geometrical figures (related to but different from those used in the pre-test). Subjects were then post-tested, using the same test as in the pre-test.

The subjects in this experiment were children aged from 4·0 to 5·6 years, who were in kindergarten classes. Half of the subjects were from a private school in Geneva, the other half were from a large state school in a suburb of Geneva. The children from each school were equally distributed among the different experimental conditions.

Each child was selected at random from their class, taking no account of age, sex or scholastic standing, but it was of course impossible to constrain 4-year-old children to cooperate with an .unknown experimenter: about three children in each class refused.

MATERIALS

Materials for the pre-test and the post-test consisted of:

A series of 8 large white cards, 10·5 cm long and 7·5 cm wide. Each card bore a different geometrical figure in black felt: a cross with its arms in the standard horizontal and vertical positions, a cross with its arms as diagonals, a rectangle, two equal intersecting circles, two equal contiguous circles, a square with a top-left to bottom-right diagonal, an equilateral triangle inside a circle, and a diamond (see Fig. 1);
Sheets of white paper 15 cm long and 10·5 cm wide;
A soft-lead pencil.

Materials used in the experimental session were:
A large sheet of green card (22 cm × 31 cm) which bore the following figures, cut out of red gummed paper: equilateral triangle, square, two equal and contiguous circles, parallelogram, lozenge atop an insoceles triangle (see Fig. 2);
A sheet of white paper 22 cm × 31 cm, a sheet of red gummed paper, a soft-lead pencil and round-ended scissors.

Procedure

The experimenter (E) went to the child in the class-room, and invited him or her to follow him into a neighbouring room. E then took care to establish rapport with the subject, to introduce the other person present, and in general to prepare the child for the novelty of the situation. (This preparatory phase is essential in order to win the confidence and

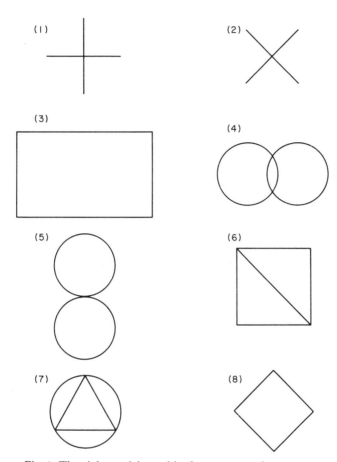

Fig. 1. The eight models used in the pre-test and post-test.

cooperation of children of this age.) The E sat the child down next to him at a small table. When the child was at ease, E repeated what he had already said to the child in the classroom: "I would really like you to do some drawings for me. I'm making a collection of drawings, so I'm asking all the children to do me some, and then I'll put them in my collection. Would you like to do me some? (etc. . . .)" E gave the child a sheet of white paper and the pencil. The first model card (the standard cross) was placed above the child's sheet of paper on the table, and E said: "I'd like you to do me a drawing that is like this one on the card", avoiding any verbal description of the figure. It was sometimes necessary to repeat this instruction several times in different ways, for example: "Do you see this drawing on this card? Can you do me one the

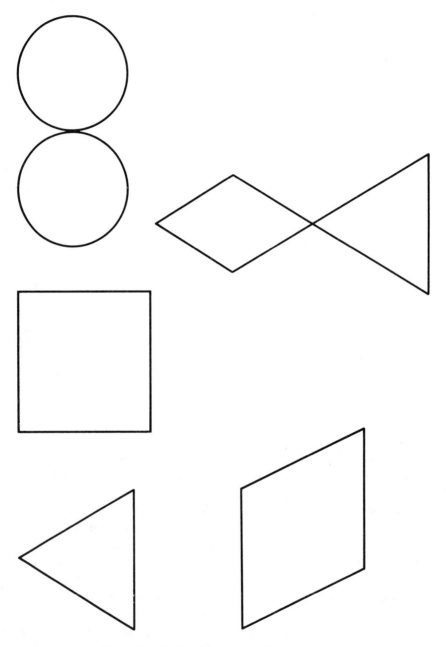

Fig. 2. The models used in the collective session.

same on your piece of paper?" or "draw me the same thing on your sheet of paper." Usually, the child would then do the drawing. If the child hesitated, drew nothing or made an error and then stopped, the E made encouraging remarks such as ("you've already done part of it" or "what are you looking at?" or "how are you doing?") but made no judgmental comments. In some cases, he would suggest that the child begin afresh on another sheet. When the child had finished copying the figure, unless he or she was clearly satisfied with the result, the E asked: "Well; is it O.K. like that?" in order to allow the child to re-begin if an improvement was felt to be possible. The E then took the child's copy and placed it, face downwards, on the pile of drawings making up his "collection". The child was given another sheet of paper and the next model card, and so the procedure continued until all 8 figures had been completed.

Criteria for Evaluating Drawings

The E assigned a score to the best copy (of each figure) produced by each child. The score was determined by the criteria presented below, which represent an ordinal scale of evaluation of the spatial characteristics of subjects' performance. The scales have three, four or five points according to the complexity of the model. These scales permit ready comparison between pre- and post-test performance on each item for each subject, and also reveal progress in the quality of execution. In sum, the greater the subject's mastery of the spatial operations implied in the reproduction of the figure, the greater the number of points awarded.

For each of the 8 figures we give below, in the order of their developmental acquisition, the different drawing performances and the scores assigned to them.

(1) *Cross in standard position*

Formless	0
Indistinct crossing of two lines	$\frac{1}{2}$
Distinct crossing of two lines	1
One line horizontal, the other vertical	2
As above, with equal lines	3

(2) *"Diagonal" cross*

Formless	0
Indistinct crossing of two lines	$\frac{1}{2}$

Distinct crossing of two lines   1
The two lines cross at right angles, forming angles of
    about 45° with the horizontal and the vertical   2
As above, and the lines are equal   3
(3) *Rectangle*
Formless   0
A closed figure   1
As above, with angles   2
A polygon with four sides (even if slightly curved)   3
Rectangle   4
(4) *Two equal intersecting circles*
Formless   0
Two closed figures   1
Two intersecting figures   2
Two intersecting circles, correctly oriented   3
As above, and relatively equal   4
(5) *Two equal contiguous circles*
Formless   0
Two closed figures   1
Two closed figures with:
—either correct orientation
—or in contact   2
Two contiguous circles in correct orientation   3
As above, with relatively equal circles   4
(6) *Square with a diagonal*
Formless   0
A closed figure with a line   1
Rectangle with diagonal (in any direction)   2
Rectangle with diagonal correctly
    oriented and adjusted   3
Square and diagonal correctly
    oriented and adjusted   4
(7) *Equilateral triangle inside a circle*
Formless   0
A closed figure   1
Two closed figures   2
A circle and a triangle   3
Triangle with its three points touching the circle   4
As above, with an equilateral triangle   5

(8) *Diamond*

Formless	0
A closed figure	1
A figure with four angles and four sides	2
As above, with an angle at the base	3
Diamond	4

The subject thus obtained a score for each figure, and a "total score" corresponding to the sum of these 8 scores. It should be noted that these are only ordinal scales. This is taken account of in the analysis of results by counting the number of figures for which a change of score has been recorded. The "total score" is a global index permitting us to classify the subjects into two groups according to their developmental level: less advanced and more advanced.

EXPERIMENTAL SESSION

After the pre-test, all subjects were divided into two experimental groups for the experimental session which took place one week later. There were two experimental conditions: the first was a collective situation in which subjects, with a partner, attempted to reproduce (with drawings and cut-outs) a set of geometric figures. The second condition posed the same task, but subjects attempted it individually.

Subjects were assigned to either one of the two experimental conditions following an alternating principle as they completed the pre-test, subject to the constraints that the two groups were equivalent in respect of pre-test total scores, and that the first group had to contain subject pairs of different developmental levels.

Collective Condition

Two children, one less advanced (L) and one more advanced (M) (according to their pre-test score) were brought together to the experimental room and seated side by side at a small table. After an interval for familiarization and the establishment of rapport, E explained the situation to them as follows: ". . . you've both come here because I want you to do something very special for me. Look at this green card; I've put some shapes on it that I cut out of this red gummed paper. Now I'm going to give you this sheet of white paper (E places this in front of them, turning it widthways like the model, and placing it directly under the model) and this red gummed paper, and I want you to copy this picture to make another one just like it. You can do it together".

E then said to L: "You draw the shapes with this pencil on the gummed paper. Then give your drawing to M, who will cut it out, and then together you can stick it on the white sheet so that it will make the same picture as mine". The E reformulated these instructions to M, gave L the pencil and M the scissors. "Now, be careful to make a picture just the same as mine. If it goes wrong, tell me and you can start again."

The subjects began the task. The E's role was then to see that both children had understood the instructions (occasionally the children checked with each other), that the task was carried out, and to make sure that both children were involved in it, if necessary. The E also intervened to encourage the children to express explicitly what they could only initially indicate by means of mime or gesture. Occasionally, E would make supportive comments, without being evaluative, such as: "There now! what shape is that? What shape are you going to do next? etc.". When the task was completed, E asked the children whether they were satisfied with what they had done, whether or not it was difficult, and allowed them to talk about the task if they seemed to want to.

In this collective session, the E's role proved to be more delicate than in the experiments on conservation. During the sharing-out tasks, we observed that the contradictions between the subjects' points of view led them to make the "cognitive reasons" for their assertions explicit; and that the non-conservers (the less advanced subjects in the situation) usually were not aware that their responses were less adequate than those of the conservers. The conservers, in fact, seemed to be perceived by them as merely "different", not "better". In contrast, in the present task we found that many of the less advanced subjects were spontaneously dissatisfied with their own efforts at drawing; more especially, their more advanced partners were quite ready to make adverse judgments on their efforts, which were felt more for their emotional than for their cognitive content. The experimenter, then, had to try to avert such judgments, and direct the children's attention to the completion of the task itself: "Will this one do, this drawing that your friend has done?", "Why?", "Tell him how it should be changed." The children seemed to understand this approach.

Individual Condition

In this condition the subject, who was either L or M, carried out alone the drawing and cutting-out task just described. The instructions were the same, except that the E made all comments and remarks to the same child, and therefore did not dissociate the roles of drawing and cutting out.

As they carried out both components of the task, these subjects in fact had more opportunity to act on the material than did the subjects in the collective condition. Bearing in mind the role of physical activity in cognitive development, it seems likely that the individual condition would create better conditions for cognitive development than the collective condition. This possibility only affects the experiment's validity in so far as the size of the obtained effects might be reduced, since the possible effect of the individual condition would be in the opposite direction to that of the principal hypothesis of a greater effect of the collective condition, due to the social interaction permitted.

Post-test

The experimental session was followed, after one week, by an individual post-test. The procedure and analysis of results were the same as in the pre-test.

Results

Table 23 gives pre-test and post-test scores for subjects in the collective condition. The difference between the two scores is indicated as progress (+), regression (−) or no change (O). Table 24 gives the same information for subjects in the individual condition.

On the basis of the pre-test scores, the eight pairs of subjects in the collective condition were divided into eight M subjects and eight L subjects, as shown in Table 25.

There were 13 subjects in the individual condition, and their range of initial levels was comparable to that of subjects in the collective condition. It would have been preferable to set up two groups of eight in this condition also, and thus to have avoided the overlap between the two categories (M and L) in the case of subjects whose scores were between

TABLE 23

Copying geometrical shapes: Differences between pre- and post-test scores in the collective condition[a]

		Shape																						
		(1)			(2)			(3)			(4)			(5)			(6)			(7)			(8)		
	Pair	Pre	Post	Diff.	Pre	Post	Diff.	Pre	Post	Diff.	Pre	Post	Diff.	Pre	Post	Diff.	Pre	Post	Diff.	Pre	Post	Diff.	Pre	Post	Diff.
M Partners	I	3	3	O	2	3	+	4	4	O	4	4	O	3	4	+	4	4	O	4	4	O	3	3·5	+
	II	2	3	+	3	3	O	4	4	O	4	4	O	3	4	+	4	4	O	4	4	O	3	3	O
	III	2	2	O	2	2	O	3	3	O	2	1·5	—	2·5	2·5	O	2·5	3	O	4	3	—	1	1	O
	IV	1	2	+	2	2	O	3	3	O	1	3	+	2	2	O	3	3	O	3	4	+	3	3	O
	V	1	2	+	1	2	+	3	3	O	2	3	+	2	3	+	2	3	+	2	3	+	2	2	O
	VI	2	2	O	2	2	O	2	2	O	2	2	O	2	2	O	2	3	+	2	3	+	2	2	O
	VII	2	2	O	2	2	O	3	3	O	1	3	+	2	2	O	2	3	+	2	3	+	2	3	+
	VIII	2	2	O	2	2	O	3	3	O	1	3	+	2	2	O	1	1	O	2·5	3	+	3·5	3	—
L Partners	I	1	2	+	1	1	O	4	4	O	3	3	O	2	4	+	2	3	+	3	3	O	2	2	O
	II	2	1	—	0	0	O	3	3	O	3	3	O	3	3	O	0	3	+	2	3	+	3	3	O
	III	1	1	O	1	2	+	3	3	O	1	3	+	2	3	+	1·5	1	—	2	3	+	2	2	O
	IV	1	1·5	+	0·5	1	+	3	3	O	3	3	O	3	3	O	0	0·5	+	2	2	O	2	1·5	—
	V	2	2	O	1	0	—	3	4	+	3	2	—	3	2	—	1	1	O	2	2	O	1	1	O
	VI	2	2	O	1	2	+	3	4	+	1	1	O	2	2	O	1	1	O	3	3	O	1	1·5	+
	VII	0	1·5	+	0	0	O	2	2·5	+	1	3	+	2	2	O	0·5	0·5	O	2	2	O	1	1	O
	VIII	2	1	—	1	1	O	1	1	O	1	3	+	2	2	O	1	1	O	2	2	O	1	1	O

[a] +, progress; —, regression and O, no change.

TABLE 24

Copying geometrical shapes: differences between pre- and post-test scores in the individual condition[a]

Subject	(1) Pre	Post	Diff.	(2) Pre	Post	Diff.	(3) Pre	Post	Diff.	(4) Pre	Post	Diff.	(5) Pre	Post	Diff.	(6) Pre	Post	Diff.	(7) Pre	Post	Diff.	(8) Pre	Post	Diff.
1	3	3	O	3	3	O	4	4	O	3	3	O	4	4	O	3	4	O	3	3	O	3	4	+
2	2	3	+	2	2	O	4	4	O	3	3	O	3	4	-	3	4	+	3	4	+	3	3	O
3	2	2	O	2	2	O	3	3	O	2	3	+	3	3	+	4·5	3	-	4·5	4·5	O	3	3	O
4	2	2	O	2	2	O	3	3	O	2	3	+	2·5	2	-	3	2	-	3	3	O	2	3	+
5	2	2	O	2	2	O	3	3	O	2	2	O	2	4	+	3	3	+	3	3	O	3	3	-
6	1	1	O	2	2	O	3	3	O	2	2	O	2	3	+	3	3	O	3	3	O	3	3	O
7	2	2	O	1	0	-	3	4	+	2	2	O	2	2	O	3	2	+	3	3	O	1	2	+
8	2	2	O	0·5	0·5	O	3	3	O	1	1	O	3	3	O	2	1	O	2	2	O	2	2	O
9	1	2	+	1	2	+	3	3	O	3	2·5	-	2	2	O	2	2	+	2	1	-	0	1	+
10	0·5	0	-	0	0	O	3	3	O	3	2	-	3	2	O	1	0	O	1	2	+	2	2	O
11	2	2	O	1	1	O	3	3	O	1	1	O	2	2	O	2	3	+	2	2	O	1	2	+
12	1	1·5	+	0	2	+	3	3·5	+	1	2	+	2	2	O	2	1	O	2	2	O	1	2	+
13	1	2	+	1	1	O	3	3	O	1	3	+	1	2	+	1	1·5	+	1	2	+	1	2	+

[a] +, progress; –, regression and O, no change.

14 and 19. This was impossible, however, due to organizational reasons beyond our control—particularly, the frequent absences of the children.

In any case, we had not planned a comparison between the L and M subjects, for several reasons. Firstly, the nature of the scale of evaluation meant that there was a ceiling on the performance of the M subjects, since a child who obtained the maximum score on the pre-test could not "progress" further. Secondly, it was very likely that the rate

TABLE 25

Comparison of progress made in the two experimental conditions for the two levels of subjects, copying geometrical shapes experiment

		Collective condition			Individual condition	
	Pair	Pre-test	ε^a	Subject	Pre-test	ε
M subjects	I	27	3	1	27	1
	II	26	3	2	24	1
	III	19·5	−2	3	22·5	1
	IV	17	4	4	19·5	0
	V	16	5	5	18	1
	VI	16	3	6[b]	19	1
	VII	17	3	7[b]	15	2
	VIII	17	1	8[b]	14·5	0
	Total	155·5	20		159·5	7
	Mann-Whitney U with correction: U=11·5; $p<0.05$ (two-tailed)					
L subjects	I	18	3	6[b]	15	2
	II	16	1	7[b]	14·5	0
	III	13	5	8[b]	19	1
	IV	14·5	2	9	13	2
	V	13	0	10	12·5	−2
	VI	14	3	11	13	2
	VII	8·5	3	12	11	5
	VIII	11	0	13	10	6
	Total	108	17		108	16

[a] The number of shapes on which the subject has progressed by the post-test, minus the number on which the subject has regressed.

[b] Some subjects are included in both groups, since the groups are not being compared.

of acquisition was very different at different points on this ordinal scale. Instead, we have used the same "pool" of subjects in order to compare the effects of the collective and the individual conditions, while separating the subjects into more and less advanced.

Table 25 summarizes the data in the preceding tables, facilitating comparisons between the two experimental conditions for each developmental level. The table shows that the majority of subjects showed more cognitively advanced performance on the post-test. For the L subjects, there is no difference between the collective and the individual conditions: gains apparent on post-test (ε) are comparable for both conditions. In contrast, the M subjects benefited from sharing the task with an L partner (Mann-Whitney U: $U = 11 \cdot 5$ with correction; two-tailed $p < 0 \cdot 05$).

It would appear, then, that this experiment confirms the hypothesis that social interaction can be a source of cognitive development even if the interaction is with a less advanced partner.

But why do we not find the same difference between the experimental conditions for the less advanced children? First of all, it should be pointed out that the social interaction did not have an adverse effect in their case, since their post-test scores are comparable to those of their peers in the individual condition. At least three hypotheses can be suggested: there could be a prerequisite level of development, below which social interaction is not beneficial; there could be an interference between emotional and cognitive aspects of the interaction in relation to the particular experimental task chosen, since, as we have already pointed out, in this experiment, unlike the preceding ones, the less advanced subjects were aware of the more advanced subjects' superior performance, and the latter were quite ready to pass adverse judgments on their partners' performances. It is possible that the affective implications of these judgments inhibited any positive cognitive effects of the interaction. A third hypothesis arises from the fact that the conditions of the interaction were different for subjects of different levels. It was built into the experimental design that the role of the "cutter-out" was always assigned to the M partners, which meant that only these subjects worked on the product of their partner. They therefore had a more truly "collective" experience: they received the partner's product, decided on its acceptability, perhaps returned it for correction, or adjusted it for errors when they cut it out. The L subjects, on the other hand, being responsible only for the drawing, had a task which, at least in its initial phase, was more independent of the partner.

The role of the experimenter in this experiment was difficult to interpret, since there was no way of knowing whether the subjects understood his interventions in the sense intended and because of this difficulty, we are planning further experiments to look at the same type of performance as that involved in drawing, but using tasks which call for minimal involvement by the experimenter.

Work already under way on cognitive conflict has shown that the effects of interaction appear just as reliably when the experimenter's role has been a much less important one.

Cognitive development and conflicting centrations

The preceding experiment produced results which confirmed our prediction that social interaction is beneficial to cognitive development even if the partner in the interaction is cognitively less advanced. The more advanced subjects appeared to derive systematic advantage from activity which was coordinated with less advanced partners.

We account for these facts, and those we have previously demonstrated, by placing them within the general framework of a constructivist approach to development, in which cognitive development is seen as arising from processes of re-structuring linked to the activity of the child. The specific contribution of our experiments has been to show the importance of social interaction in bringing about these processes of re-structuring. The analysis of this phenomenon in different experimental situations leads us to the hypothesis that it is the element of *conflict* in these social interactions which is the source of their impact.

A situation of social interaction provides not only the opportunity to imitate another child, and thereby the possibility of conflict with one's own way of doing things, but also and more often, the opportunity to elaborate actions with another child, and thus to coordinate centrations even though these may initially be different.

This difference may give rise to conflict among children as long as it is perceived without being assimilated into a joint system. If the child possesses the intellectual prerequisites for recognition of the conflict, the contradiction cannot be ignored, since the co-presence of the individuals, especially if there are manifest relevant behaviours, guarantees the co-presence of different centrations. The child is then obliged, here and now, to compare self and other, and to effect a re-structuring which will integrate the diverging positions. In so far as the child does not have mastery of the operations relevant to the task, the contradictions coming from others, whatever their levels of development, serve to bring the cognitive differences between them into sharp focus, and thus lead to a coordination which will reduce the conflict.

The notion of conflict holds a central place in this theoretical perspective on development: cognitive conflict created by social interaction is the locus at which the power driving intellectual development is generated. This thesis opens the way to a whole new series of experiments which would study the effects of different types of interaction on this cognitive conflict. There are two questions which already seem particularly important. First, there is the role of cognitive conflict itself. Is it possible to verify experimentally that the source of progress such as we have observed is immediately present not in the gap between subjects' developmental levels, but in the divergence between the centrations arising from them? Second, we have already pointed out in the preceding experiment that the nature of the task and of the social relation is important in determining the form taken by the cognitive conflict and its effects.

The first question has already been experimentally investigated (Mugny *et al.*, 1976). Using a new paradigm to study the conservation of length, the hypothesis was that the conflict of centrations is a sufficient condition for cognitive development to result from social interaction. More specifically, we sought to find out whether non-conservers would progress after experiencing contradiction from another non-conserver whose centrations were nevertheless opposed. The conservation of length is a particularly appropriate area for this demonstration, since it permits the elicitation of two unambiguously different judgments as the result of similar reasoning. In the experimental session, after the equality of two small rulers placed side by side was established by the subject, one of the rulers was displaced. All the non-conservers overestimated the length of one of the rulers (generally the displaced one) with reference to a scheme of evaluation which caused them to consider that one of the rulers "went further" and was therefore "longer". The subject was then confronted with an adult confederate of the experimenter who overestimated the *other* ruler, using the same argument. The contradiction facing the subject here does not derive from the expression of judgment from a more advanced level of development, and consequently the progress observed in the subjects cannot be explained in terms of imitation of a model (see also Perret-Clermont *et al.*, 1976).

Our experimental design in this experiment included three conditions which subjects underwent individually (mean age: 6·3 years):

A condition of conflict between similar points of view (SC): this corresponds to the example just given, in which the confederate gives a judgment after that of the subject, directly contradicts the subject, and is centred on the opposite observation to that made by the child.

A condition of "major" conflict (MC) in which the confederate proposes a correct judgment (conserving) accompanied by a conserving argument as follows: "It goes further here, but it goes further here as well, so they are both the same".

A control condition: The confederate does not appear.

Immediately before and after the experimental session, the subject was pre- and post-tested respectively. The pre-test consisted of a test of conservation of equal and unequal lengths. The post-test was similar, except that the items were presented in reverse order. A second, identical post-test was given 10 days later by an experimenter who did not know which experimental condition the subject had been assigned to.

TABLE 26

Subjects' levels on the two post-tests of conservation of inequality and equality of length

			Experimental conditions						
			Control condition n = 13			Similar conflict n = 20			Major conflict n = 19		
			Level on conservation of inequality								
			NC	I	C	NC	I	C	NC	I	C
Level on conservation of equality	Post-test 1	NC	12	1	0	5	2	4	1	0	0
		I	0	0	0	0	1	0	0	2	0
		C	0	0	0	2	2	4	9	3	4
	Post-test 2	NC	10	2	0	4	7	0	1	0	1
		I	0	0	1	0	0	2	2	2	0
		C	0	0	0	1	1	5	5	4	4

Table 26 give subjects' post-test levels in three categories (non-conservers, intermediates and conservers). Table 27 shows the number of subjects who had progressed according to the post-tests, whether in respect of equality or inequality, in the different experimental conditions.

As we had predicted, progress (which was relatively stable and often parallel in the equality and inequality tests) took place only in experimental subjects, confirming that not only conflict with a point of view more advanced than one's own, but also conflict with a point of view of the same level as one's own, can be beneficial. The experiment confirms, then, that conflict is an essential element, and that the development brought about by social interaction is not uniquely tied to the gap between partners' developmental levels. Subjects' development was not, however, identical following the two experimental conditions, leaving the possibility that the processes of cognitive re-structuring are different according to whether the partner offers a correct or incorrect model of behaviour.

TABLE 27

Frequencies of progress on post-test 1 (P1) and post-test 2 (P2) in the different experimental conditions: Conservation of length

Tests of conservation	Experimental conditions					
	Control		Similar conflict		Major conflict	
	P1	P2	P1	P2	P1	P2
Equal lengths	0	1	9**	9*	18**	17**
Unequal lengths	1	3	13**	15**	9*	11

* p 0·05; ** p 0·01: Significant differences from the control condition (Fisher's test).

The hypothesis concerning the imitation of models calls for a more detailed exposition of the results. It was, in fact, the case that subjects in the SC condition tended to progress more than the others on the tests of inequality. Was this because they had implicitly understood that they were meant to follow the example of the confederate in affirming the inequality of the rulers? While it is not impossible that this was the case for some children, this interpretation does not explain the fact that some of the children in this condition became conservers, and used operational arguments to support their *conserving* judgments. Further-more, this interpretation leaves quite unexplained the progress recorded by post-test 1 in 13 out of 20 subjects, and by post-test 2 in 15 of the subjects, on the test of conservation of equality. Similarly, one might suppose that the subjects in the MC condition, who tended to progress more on the equality items, had "learned" to imitate the adult in the experimental session by saying "they are both the same". How-ever, in this case, how is it possible to account for the fact that, out of 17 arguments given on the first post-test to justify the conservation of equality, 12 were novel, and that 11 out of 19 arguments given on post-test 2 were also novel? Here again, the imitation explanation cannot account for the progress made on the test of conservation of inequality (9 out of 19 on post-test 1; 11 out of 19 on post-test 2).

The experiment adds further questions to those raised previously. For instance, how far can the particular status of an adult interacting with a child be responsible for the effects obtained? If we compare the present results with our previous ones, this possibility seems unlikely. Yet the possible role of child-adult relationships in these effects should be examined, both for theoretical reasons and because these relationships are so important in the educational context.

Finally, this notion of cognitive conflict which accounts for so many of our results also suggests a re-interpretation of some work done by Doise and Mugny (1975) which we have already had occasion to mention in Chapter 2. They studied the relations between individual and collective performance in a task of motor coordination (the "cooperative game"), and showed that groups of children are capable of a better performance than individuals at a certain level of development, i.e. during the phase of elaboration of the operations necessary for accomplishment of the task. The following interpretation of these results might be offered: In the phase during which the necessary operations are elaborated, the subjects' actions are poorly coordinated, and the social situation of conjoint activity puts individuals' actions in conflict. The necessity to resolve this conflict both brings about the superiority of the group performance, and explains the effect of the interaction on individuals' later performances. This interpretation needs, of course, to be experimentally confirmed, though we already have some findings which can be reported.

TABLE 28

Comparison of pre-test and post-test results of subjects aged 7–8 (level 1): coordinated motor activities experiment

Group	Subject	Pre-test score	Post-test score	Progress
I	1	3	6	3
I	2	0	6	6
I	3	6	9	3
I	4	3	0	-3
II	5	0	12	12
II	6	0	3	3
II	7	0	0	0
II	8	0	0	0

TABLE 28

Comparison of pre-test and post-test results of subjects aged 7–8 (level 1): coordinated motor activities experiment

Group	Subject	Pre-test score	Post-test score	Progress
III	9	0	12	12
III	10	0	0	0
III	11	3	0	−3
III	12	3	3	0
IV	13	0	9	9
IV	14	0	0	0
IV	15	0	0	0
IV	16	0	6	6
V	17	3	6	3
V	18	0	3	3
V	19	0	3	3
V	20	0	3	3
VI	21	0	9	9
VI	22	6	6	0
VI	23	0	0	0
VI	24	3	0	−3
VII	25	6	0	−6
VII	26	9	6	−3
VII	27	0	3	3
VII	28	0	0	0
VIII	29	0	0	0
VIII	30	3	15	12
VIII	31	3	9	6
VIII	32	3	9	6
IX	33	0	15	15
IX	34	0	0	10
IX	35	0	0	0
IX	36	3	9	6
X	37	3	3	0
X	38	0	0	0
X	39	0	3	3
X	40	0	6	6
Total	40	60	174	114

Student's t = 4·32; p <0·01.

We extended the paradigm used by Doise and Mugny, and adapted their material. First, we gave subjects an individual pre-test. They were then formed into groups of four for the experimental session of social interaction, and finally given a post-test identical to the pre-test. The pre- and post-tests consisted of questions bearing on how the subjects represented to themselves the actions required by the task. The analysis of the responses involved giving a score to each child indicating developmental level (maximum score: 24 points). The children at the lowest level (level 1) were aged between 7 and 8, and had very poor mastery of the action representation called for in this "cooperative game". It was also at this level that there was a significant difference between individual and collective performances. If the interpretation we have suggested is correct, we should be able to discover for these level 1 children the existence of a cognitive benefit following the interaction. Table 28 gives the data which permit comparison between pre-test and post-test results for these children. The difference is highly significant (Student's t = 4·32; p <0·01).

6

Results in a Sociological Perspective

Our results have already been discussed in detail as they were reported. The discussion here will be confined to the implications of these results for the problems pointed out in Chapter 1, and the possibilities of pursuing further research within a sociological framework.

General discussion of results

SOCIAL INTERACTIONS AND COGNITIVE DEVELOPMENT

In certain conditions, a situation of social interaction which requires subjects to coordinate either their actions or their points of view can bring about a modification in their individual cognitive structure. The experimental demonstration of this effect, and the collection of data which clearly show the operational nature of this re-structuring and its compatibility with the known sequence of intellectual development, are the major contributions of this research.

Several experiments have been reported, focussing on different concepts such as the conservation of liquid, the conservation of number, "graphic space", the conservation of length, in children ranging from 4 to 7 years in age. These experiments have brought about cognitive change in these children following social interaction, changes which are related to the processes of cognitive structuring recognized as fundamental to mental development (Inhelder *et al.*, 1974).

What are the reasons for the beneficial effect of social interactions on individual thought, and through what mechanisms is this effect brought about?

The work reported here offers some answers to these questions, and thereby enters the debate on the role of the social environment in learning. There are several conflicting conceptions in this debate. In the contemporary research published in English, two main trends can be distinguished as the successors to work on operant conditioning. The first, termed "social learning", tries to explain the child's acquisition of behaviours by processes of imitation, in particular imitation of models ("modelling effect"). The second comprises theories of equilibration ("equilibration model") according to which all cognitive change comes about through a process of re-structuring. This process can be induced experimentally by presenting the child with a model whose behaviours are developmentally more advanced, thereby creating a disequilibration between the model's expected behaviour and the model's actual behaviour (see for example Kuhn, 1972, p. 834). This approach is explicitly inspired by Piaget, but we shall see that the role accorded to the superiority of the model indicates a too narrow interpretation of the interactionist and constructivist conception of development put forward by Piaget.

The behavioural and conceptual acquisitions stimulated by exposure to a developmentally "superior" model have been studied widely. Turiel (1966) and McManis (1974) have worked on moral development; Rosenthal and Zimmerman (1972) and Zimmerman and Rosenthal (1972, 1974) on concept-formation; and others more specifically on conservation: Waghorn and Sullivan (1970), Zimmerman and Lanaro (1974), J. P. Murray (1974), Botvin and Murray (1975), and Cook and Murray (1975). While the modelling effect can be corroborated by several facts reported in these studies, there are many other facts, even apparent in these studies themselves, which cannot be explained in these terms. Thus Cowan et al. (1969) have shown that conditioning of behaviours appropriate to a higher level of development is more effective than the reverse case. Similar results have been obtained by Rosenthal and Zimmerman (1972) and Kuhn (1972), who also showed that conditioning in the reverse direction is weak. J. P. Cook (1974) and Cook and Murray (1975) found no effect at all when the model's behaviours were at a lower level of development than the subject's own.

Similar findings have been reported from workers outside the modelling tradition. Silverman and Stone (1972) and Silverman and Geiringer (1973) have shown that conservers who interacted with non-conservers did not change, whereas the non-conservers tended to progress. F. B. Murray (1972) used a scale of cognitive level based on several conservation tests, and found that children who were, according to this scale, more advanced than their partners nevertheless benefited from interaction with them. Our own experiments, with their detailed clinical investigations of children's operational structures, fully confirm these findings which cannot be explained by the theory of social learning. Processes of imitation do not allow us to understand why models with less advanced behaviour are not imitated, nor why, when imitation does take place (at least in the domain of moral judgment) its effects are less both in the short and the long term (Sternlieb and Youniss, 1975). Furthermore, imitation is an inadequate explanation for the appearance of novel behaviours, as described by F. B. Murray (1972), or as occurred in our own experiments, whether these were produced by more advanced subjects interacting with less advanced ones unable to offer them examples of advanced behaviours, or by non-conservers who acquired their behaviours through interacting with more advanced subjects, but who produced novel arguments in justifying these behaviours.

Where, then, can the explanation of all these results be found? It would seem more appropriate to look more closely at the conditions under which the behaviour changes which interest us occur, in other words at the conditions which bring about change in cognitive structures. This has been done by studies within the framework of equilibration theory.

Following the approach made by Rest *et al*. (1969) and Turiel (1969) to the experimental study of moral development within an equilibration theory framework, Kuhn (1972) attempted to show in a similar fashion that the social model is a source of *cognitive* change for the subject, but that the model does not provide a *form* of thought for the subject to imitate, rather *stimulates* the development of the child in the natural direction of development. Such an account predicts that the effectiveness of the model will increase with the optimization of the gap between the model's and the subject's developmental level: the gap should be small enough so that the difference in behaviours corresponds to the acquisition the child has to make, and large enough so that the contradiction between the two sets of behaviours creates a cognitive disequilibration in the subject. Then it is the process of internal reorganization thereby set in motion which brings about operational change. This re-structuring, which seeks a state of cognitive balance, can only lead to a more advanced stage of development. It is this conceptualization which allows Silverman and Geiringer (1973) to explain why, following an interaction between conservers and nonconservers, the latter progress and the former do not regress, Kuhn has shown that exposure to a model at the developmental stage immediately above the subject's is more effective than when the developmental gap is as large as two stages. She has also shown that a less advanced or similar model hardly affects the subject, and uses arguments similar to those of Silverman and Geiringer to explain this. Our experiment on the conservation of number (Chapter 4) also revealed the problem of the gap between partners' levels, since the results indicated that nonconservers of the least advanced sub-levels (NCg and NCo) were not sensitive to interaction with conservers. We also put forward hypotheses about the difference between the subject's initial behaviour and the behaviour to be acquired, in pointing out the different effects of the subject's initial competence (see also J. P. Murray, 1974). Sensitivity to conflict has as its prerequisite the ability to understand the question at issue in an exchange. However, does this imply, as Silverman and Geiringer state, that it is necessary for the model to be more advanced than the subject, and that the only possible effect of a less advanced model would be to leave the subject unchanged, or even to cause regression in the subject? Their position is based on the assumption that imitation plays an important role, and so does not account for the progress shown after interaction with a less advanced subject. Our interpretation is that the cognitive disequilibrium created in the subject is not due to imitation, but to the conflict between different points of view. If the developmental gap between the two partners is too great, there is the risk that the subject will not be aware of any conflict, or will not understand the nature of the conflict. If the partners are at the same developmental level, or if the other is less advanced, the subject can only benefit from the interaction if there is conflict, i.e. if the difference in centrations and the nature of the collective task call for reorganization of the coordination between the partners. Experiments using tasks of this type have probably not been done by the authors discussed above, which is why they are not aware of effects of the type we showed in Chapter 5, following interaction with a less advanced or a similar partner.

The same interpretation was made by Mugny and Doise (1978) in a recent experiment. Using the same paradigm as an experiment reported in Chapter 2 (see also Doise *et al.*, 1974) Mugny gave subjects an individual pre-test on spatial relations, then asked them, in pairs, to carry out a joint task requiring the coordination of perspectives. They were then given a post-test similar to the pre-test. The pre- and post-tests allowed a tripartite classification of subjects: those who acted without compensating for changes in the frame of reference (NC); those who made partial compensations (PC); and those who made full compensations (FC). They looked at four types of collective situation, according to the composition of pairs, as follows:

(1) interaction between an NC and another NC
(2) interaction between an NC and a PC
(3) interaction between a PC and another PC
(4) interaction between an NC and an FC

It should be noted that, by definition, the FC subjects cannot show further progression, and it was verified that they did not regress. The objects of interest were the NC and PC subjects. The results showed that, for the least advanced subjects (NC) interaction with a more advanced partner was more profitable than with a similar partner if, and only if, the developmental gap between the two was not too great. In other words, NC subjects benefited from interaction with PC partners, but hardly at all from interaction with FC or other NC partners. In contrast, the more advanced (PC) subjects seemed to benefit from a collective session with partners at the same level as themselves, and still more from a session with FC partners. The cognitive advance stimulated in this experiment was not directly related to the partner's level. For some subjects (PC) an NC partner was most effective, while for others (NC) it was, conversely, interaction with a PC partner which was most effective. For both categories of subject, it was a situation which confronted them with a different viewpoint from their own which was most stimulating. The results show once more then, that it is neither necessary nor sufficient to be exposed to a correct model in order to progress; and that the principal characteristic of a beneficial social interaction is that it opposes different viewpoints which are at an optimum degree of divergence. The cause of the resulting conflict is not, directly, the developmental gap between the partners, but the differing centrations which arise from the developmental gap.

THE INTERACTIONIST AND CONSTRUCTIVIST APPROACH: THE ROLE OF
COGNITIVE CONFLICT IN SOCIAL INTERACTIONS

The experiment by Mugny and Doise described above corroborates our own interpretation of the research we have presented, and this allows us to break out of the restrictive interpretation imposed by some theories of equilibration. Their experiment illustrates an interactionist and constructivist view of development which considers the genesis of cognitive structures as resulting, not from the passive appropriation by the subject of external behaviours, but from an active re-structuring by the child of its own representation of reality. This re-structuring takes place in a quite specific manner during the course of inter-individual coordinations. While imitation, as a process of assimilation, may eventually explain certain instances of development, it is important to emphasize that social interaction does not merely offer a kind of "intellectual nourishment" to assimilate, but rather stimulates an activity of *accommodation*, and it is this which creates new development. If children were fashioned in the image of the behaviours which occur in their social environment, the presentation of less developed models, or interaction with them, should bring about regression; on the contrary, however, we have shown experimentally that in certain cases children are impermeable to such influence, and, more remarkably, they can even draw profit from it in terms of cognitive development.

This type of analysis suggest a re-interpretation of results which are presented as arising from a learning by imitation or "modelling" effect.

In fact the behaviours of a cognitively more advanced model cannot be directly *assimilated* by a child, since they correspond—by definition—to a mental structuring which is different and more complex than the child's own. While some experiments succeed in producing this assimilation in so far as the behaviours of the more advanced model are successfully imitated, it must be understood that this assimilation—and the ability to imitate which it brings about—can only result from a cognitive re-organization produced by the subject's own activity in accommodating. According to Piaget (1975, p. 25) every regulation is a reaction to a disturbance, and genetic psychology has demonstrated the role of cognitive conflict which creates disequilibriums that the child actively seeks to correct. Thus Piaget (ibid., p. 45), referring to the work of Inhelder *et al.* (1974), emphasized how this research confirms "the theoretical analysis and the fundamental notions (in particular the relations between assimilation and accommodation)" by showing "that the most productive factors in acquisition (are) the disturbances brought about by conflict . . ." But what is the origin of the cognitive conflict brought about by the presentation of a model? It is not in the disturbing effect of resistance by material

objects to the subject's actions, nor in the feedback from these actions; nor is it, at least at the start, in the internal conflict among the subject's schemas or sub-systems of schemas. The child in such an experiment experiences a conflict between the behaviours which he or she would have deployed in relation to the task, and the behaviours observed. If we analyse the experimenter's request to the child to observe the model, in the context of the social relations experienced within the experiment, it is clear that it signifies that the subject is placed in a situation of *confrontation* between their own reactions and those of the model. It is this conflictual aspect of observing a model which, in so far as the subject is at an opportune stage of development (we have seen the differential effect of the subject's initial developmental level)* triggers off the mechanisms of cognitive re-organization which lead to the progress observed.

In one of his early experiments, following Smedslund's (1966) hypothesis concerning the role of conflict in communication, F. B. Murray (1972, p. 4) interprets the cognitive progress induced by interaction among children as indicating that social conflict or interaction are important mediators of mental growth. But in the report of a more recent experiment (Botvin and Murray, 1975), he tends to reduce the effect of conflict in communication to a "modelling effect". This is no doubt due to the fact that his experiments do not focus specifically on the conflict of which he writes, or do not envisage different types of conflict. We have already indicated why it seems to us better to adopt the opposite approach, and to consider the effect of imitating a model, in so far as it has been operationalized in the research cited, as a particular instance of the effects of cognitive conflict in social interaction.

While discussing the results of our own experiments, we advanced the hypothesis that cognitive conflict in social interaction would be more likely to bring about development in the subject if it was "salient" to the subject. This salience should be facilitated by certain types of interaction (for example, in the "constellations" in experiment II where, not one, but two partners represented conserving behaviours);

* " . . . the same experimental arrangement will generate conflicts only at certain given levels of the structure under consideration. In other words, it is not disturbing in itself or in any absolute sense, but on the contrary is conceived as a disturbance, or not so conceived, according to the elements already acquired, or not acquired, of the structure in course of formation." (Piaget, 1975, p. 45.)

and masked by other interfering elements (perhaps tied to the nature of the task which may be too difficult, or may arouse evaluative judgments of the subject's behaviour by the partner; in general, the emotiveness of the exchange may be too strong). An observation made independently by Marion *et al.* (1974, p. 95) is relevant here: "interactions among participants increase when a cognitive conflict is felt by all".

The notion of cognitive conflict in social interaction allows us, then, to re-interpret the results from different traditions of research on learning in social situations, and to situate them all within the framework of an interactionist and constructivist conception of development.

SOCIAL INTERACTION: A CAUSAL FACTOR IN DEVELOPMENT

Commenting on our work and that of our colleagues (Perret-Clermont *et al.*, 1976) in the light of its psychosociological approach to development, Piaget (1976, p. 226) pointed out two problems: (1) that of the source or the originating mechanism of operations as well as their structure; (2) that of the facility or rapidity of the growth of operations.

Where does our object of study lie in relation to these two problems? Point (1) is not our object of study. This statement will be explained more fully, but first of all it must be emphasized that point (2) is not our object of study, either. We are not concerned with the problem of the formative mechanism of operations, the elucidation of which has been one of Piaget's greatest contributions to psychology. Piaget describes this mechanism in great detail in his work on the equilibration of cognitive structures, where he stresses that this is "an indispensable process in development, and a process whose manifestations differ from stage to stage in the direction of a better equilibrium both in its qualitative structure and in its range of application . . ." (Piaget, 1975, p. 23). These facts are established, and if, as Piaget suggested a long time ago, "general coordinations are the same, whether they occur in inter- or in intra-individual actions", it would seem that this can be explained, as he himself proposes, by their common origin in biological regulatory mechanisms: "In other words, the operational structure has a general, or universal, and therefore biopsychosociological nature, and it is for this reason that it is fundamentally logical" (Piaget, 1976, p. 226).

For our part, we have not specifically sought to discover this identity at a given moment in the development of the child, simultaneously in the cognitive and the social domains. That there is an isomorphism at a certain level between "operations" and "cooperations", and that these provide "alimentation" for each other, does not of itself mean that social interaction does not play any other role at other stages of mental development. Therefore, we have not looked at whether the forms which social interaction takes at a given time (monologue or dialogue, cooperation or "co-action" in a forced or hierarchical relationship) influences the forms of thought. We limited ourselves to the investigation of the development of operational thinking, and the effects which can be produced on this of *certain types* of inter-individual coordination or confrontation. It should be noted, however, that most of the interaction types we observed were of a "cooperative" nature, although their impacts on cognitive development differed. It should also be noted that effects of social interaction were found in relatively young children: in the experiment on the conservation of number (Chapter 4) and in that on drawing (Chapter 5) the children were only 4–5 years old, and were hardly at the threshold of the stage of concrete operations. They therefore did not yet possess mastery of the operations whose structure is isomorphic with that of "cooperative" exchanges (see Piaget, 1965, pp. 143–171 on this subject). The notion of "the stage of concrete operations" is in fact too general to take account of the different parameters which our experiments demonstrated the relevance of. Consider, for instance, the role of the subject's level of development in relation to the precise concept called upon by the task, the nature of the specific prerequisites for a given social interaction, and the effect of the types of divergence between points of view. Specific consideration of these different parameters should allow us to avoid certain difficulties which have also arisen in other studies on cognitive and social development. Thus, for example, the debate on childhood "egocentrism" and the processes of decentration (Aebli, 1966; Huttenlocher and Presson, 1973: Eiser, 1974; Chaplin and Keller, 1974; Hoy, 1974; 1975; Borke, 1975) can be avoided by using less general concepts in order to define levels of both cognitive and social behaviour.

Returning now to problem (2). On this subject, Piaget writes that "it seems established, therefore, that the factor of exchange (or, here, of communication) generates the power for cognitive work" (1976, p. 226). This point has certainly been established repeatedly in the experiments we have reported and cited here, and recent developments in our work concerning the relevant mechanisms permit us to go further with this interpretation. Our results indicate that, while collective exchange can certainly facilitate cognitive work and the formation of operations, *cognitive conflict in social situations*, in certain conditions, and at a particular stage in the development of the child, can actually bring this about directly. Of course, cognitive conflict of this kind does not create the *forms* of operations, but it brings about the disequilibriums which make cognitive elaboration necessary, and in this way cognitive conflict confers a special role on the social factor as one among other factors leading to mental growth. Social-cognitive conflict may be figuratively likened to the catalyst in a chemical reaction: it is not present at all in the final product, but it is nevertheless indispensable if the reaction is to take place.

Considering the problem of the subject's awareness of the contradiction, Piaget (1974b, pp. 161–162) writes on the one hand that this occurs when the subject is capable of carrying out the task (we have dealt with this problem in relation to the role of the subject's initial developmental level in our experiments), and on the other hand that the occurrence of awareness "is much easier between a prediction and a new external datum which inflicts a denial . . . " because "in this case the negation has not had to be constructed, but is imposed from outside by the new event which only needs to be located within a widened frame of reference. All this constitutes merely a problem which is more or less easy to solve, and not an awareness of contradiction". Elsewhere, Piaget (1975, p. 21) reports that "the only cases where negation is precocious are those where the subject has not had to construct it, because it has been imposed from outside: for example a factual denial following a false prediction (or a refusal in the case of a conflict with an opposed will)". We would be tempted to underline "or a refusal" here, because this seems to be the most frequent type of denial experienced by the child in daily life, and in the educational situations of the types known in our society. Although it is plausible that the subject may sometimes, during the course of the epistemic quest, be alone when confronted with some physical event external to self-action or to the results of self-action, this theoretical debate can be pursued by posing two questions. Would the subject persist in this quest if it were not for the incitement of social relations and inter-individual exchange (which bear on content tied to the cultural context) which occur in everyday life? Furthermore, is a distinction valid which is sometimes made between the "physical" and the "social" environments? Is the child ever confronted with the physical in the total absence of the social? In any case, this certainly never happens in experimental situations.

Piaget himself (1965, p. 155) has denounced "the artificiality which considers the individual, and the individual's relations with the physical environment, as a closed system". Is it possible to imagine that, in the absence of any social situations, the child would be sufficiently sensitive to internal cognitive disequilibrium to attempt to construct, alone, the intellectual instruments which would permit him or her to adapt to the environment (which first of all imposes itself in biological terms)? In attempting to answer this question, we meet the question of the role of *exchanges* in the rise of civilization, and therefore in the development of all systems of understanding, and all fields of knowledge.

Rooted in biological structures, put to work by the individual, intelligence itself also appears to be, in essence, the fruit of community.

NEW PERSPECTIVES: TOWARDS A GENETIC SOCIAL PSYCHOLOGY

For Piaget (1966, p. 249) "there are many unnecessary problems arising from the fact that some have committed themselves from the outset to a dichotomy 'individual or society', while forgetting that there is a relational perspective according to which there exist only interactions, which can be globally studied either sociologically or ontogenetically during the course of individual development. Just as, in contemporary biology, ontogenesis and phylogenesis are linked together by dialectical circuits or spirals, so a close collaboration between psychologists and sociologists in questions of development would be profitable to both disciplines". The experimental investigations we have carried out with a psychosociological approach to development seem to us to come within this perspective. But this effort to relate the individual and the collective still needs to be continued on the more specifically sociological level.

Smedslund (1966, p. 159) "pleads in favour of a change in the framework" informing genetic psychology research "in the direction of an explicit psychosociological formulation". This is only just beginning. We will not repeat here the many questions Smedslund raises, the answers to which would contribute "to a deeper understanding of the mechanisms and of the content of cognitive development" and of learning. Smedslund points out that this is not a matter of a simple "change of programme offering the promise of immediate simplification of problems", but rather one which will show the potential contribution of social psychology to genetic psychology.

From the opposite direction, genetic psychology offers psychosociology a solid base of knowledge at one of the poles of its object of study: the individual; it also offers the method of the genetic approach, which permits the study of social behaviours, like individual behaviours, in the course of their development. This would oblige psychosociology to construct a conceptualization of problems which would take account, not only of the different types of social interaction and the functioning of groups, of the nature of the task and its representations, and of the impact of these processes on the collective production (see Moscovici and Paicheler, 1973, on this subject) but also of the level of development of the concepts in each participant as a variable affecting all these processes, the performance of the group, and also their effects on the individual level.

" . . . If genetic psychology can render any service to sociology, it is precisely in helping it to differentiate between the types of social interaction affecting the individual . . . " (Piaget, 1951, p. 37).

A sociological perspective

THE EMPIRICAL DATA

Our first experiment on the conservation of liquid took place in schools in the centre of a city. The following year, physical and administrative reasons obliged us to carry out the second experiment on the same subject in a school situated in a city suburb. At that time, we noticed that the proportion of children in the first and second year of first school who were conserving on pre-test differed as between the village and the suburban children. There were more conservers among the suburban children.*

---

* Piaget himself also noticed this at an early stage in his research, since his book "Le Jugement Moral Chez L'Enfant" (1932) contains the footnote on p. 28: "it is important to take this opportunity to point out (what we have not sufficiently stressed in earlier work) that most of our research has been done with children from the poor areas of Geneva. In other environments, the mean ages would almost certainly have been different".

Did the ages of the two samples of children differ? The dates of birth that we obtained from the class registers, and data from the Geneva Statistical Yearbook for Education (Sociological Research Service, 1974) showed that this was not the case. More precisely, these same sources of information confirmed that children of different socio-occupational origins, who were unequally represented in the two samples numerically, were nevertheless of similar ages in the same classes across the two samples, and that the system of allocation to class according to age on entry into compulsory education had had little effect in this respect.

The results of these comparisons were only clearly seen at the time that the results of the second experiment were being analysed, which led us to re-analyse the second set of results with the inclusion of a new (and therefore *post hoc*) variable: the "socio-occupational origin" of the subject.*

Since the data available to us concerning the occupation of fathers (or respondents) were only coarsely specified, we had to be content to use the three categories of social origin defined by the Sociological Research Service of Geneva:

Class A: Manual workers, skilled manual workers, public employees, etc.

Class B: Qualified employees, small businessmen, farmers, middle management, etc.

Class C: The professions, senior management, directors.

Although this classification is very coarse, its only disadvantage for us is that it may lead to underestimation of differences between social environments.

Re-analysis of Data from Experiment II, introducing the Variable of Social Class

Table 29 shows the results of the conservation of liquid pre-test according to the social class of subjects.† It will be seen that the proportion of non-conservers is lower in class C (4 out of 16) than in the other social

---

* "socio-occupational origin" refers to the social class corresponding to the father's or respondent's occupation.
† We had no data concerning respondent's occupation for 9 out of the 100 children in the experiment. This was usually because the family had recently moved into the area. Consequently Table 29 includes only 91 subjects.

TABLE 29

Subjects' levels on pre-test in experiment II (conservation of liquids) according to social class of origin

| | Pre-test level | | | | |
	NC	I	C	Total	% of NC
Social class A	21	5	15	41	51%
Social class B	15	4	15	34	44%
Social class C	4	0	12	16	25%
Totals	40	9	42	91	

environments (36 out of 75). The proportion is slightly less in class B (15 out of 34) than in class A (21 out of 41).

This finding is not new. We have already mentioned several studies in Chapter 1 which have shown the same inequality of performance across children from different social environments, not only on the classic tests, but also on operational tests.

After the pre-test, the non-conserving children were assigned to one of the conditions specified in the experimental design. The various contingencies attendant upon running the experimental sessions prevented us from proceeding further with all the non-conservers, but it is possible to verify that this omission was not inadvertently a systematic one: the non-conservers who completed the experiment were of the same age and social class distribution as those who did not continue after the pre-test. Recall that it was conditions I and II which were most likely to stimulate cognitive progress. This is seen in Table 30, which shows the progress made by all subjects for whom we were able to obtain socio-occupational data.

TABLE 30

Progress made by NC subjects in experiment II (conservation of liquids) by post-test 1, according to experimental conditions

	Progress	No progress	Total[a]
Experimental conditions I and II (1 NC + 2 C or 2 NC + 1 C)	8	8	16
Experimental condition III (3 NC) and control condition (no interaction)	2	15	17

[a] Exact probability: $p = 0.021$.

TABLE 31

Distribution of subjects from different social environments across the conditions of experiment II, and their progress by post-test 1

	Experimental conditions				Control condition		Total
	I and II		III				
	Progress	None	Progress	None	Progress	None	
Social class A	5	2	0	3	1	3	14
Social class B	3	3	0	5	1	3	15
Social class C	0	3	0	0	0	1	4
Total	8	8	0	8	2	7	33

Table 31 shows the distribution of children from different social environments across the experimental and control conditions, and their subsequent progress. It will be seen that subjects from class C only progress in conditions I and II, which is interesting since these were the conditions most likely to induce cognitive conflict. The 3 out of 6 subjects from class B, and 5 out of 7 from class A had made progress by the post-test. In spite of the small number of subjects, which was due to the fact that we had not initially intended to carry out a social class analysis, this result is surprising. In conditions I and II, the proportions of subjects who progress differ according to social origin in such a way that the gap between them which was evident on pre-test has

TABLE 32

Childrens' level on pre-test, conservation of number (experiment III) according to social class of origin

	Level on pre-test			
	NCg + NCo	NCc + NC4	I + C	Total
Social class A	7	18	27	52
Social class B	10	23	33	66
Social class C	1	5	16	22
Total	18	46	76	140

disappeared by the time of the post-test. (See Table 32 for an illustration of this differential progress according to social class origin.) Given the precision of the theoretical framework by which the childrens' cognitive levels were determined, it seems unlikely that these results are due to chance. Even so, we checked to see whether similar trends were to be found in the following experiment.

Re-analysis of Data from Experiment III (Conservation of Number) introducing the Variable of Social Class

The data from this experiment were also re-analysed *a posteriori*. Table 33 gives the results on the conservation of number pre-test for 140 children. Performances differ according to social class. For the next analysis, we removed the less advanced subjects (NCg and NCo) because we had found that they did not reach the level of development permitting them to benefit from the social interaction in conditions (a)

TABLE 33
Illustration of "differential progress" according to social class of origin, experiment II (conservation of liquid)

By way of illustration, let us suppose the outcome if *all* non-conservers on pre-test had been placed in experimental conditions I and II
On pre-test
51·22% of the non-conservers in class A
44·11% of the non-conservers in class B
25%   of the non-conservers in class C

Following the interaction sessions (conditions I and II): Levels of progress
71·4% for the non-conservers in class A
50%   for the non-conservers in class B
0   for the non-conservers in class C

If all subjects underwent experimental conditions I and II, and if the observed tendencies were maintained, this would reduce the number of non-conservers so that the following post-test results would be obtained:
14·64% of the non-conservers in class A
22·05% of the non-conservers in class B
25%   of the non-conservers in class C
This amounts to the disappearance of the pre-test gap between social classes

and (b). Among the remaining subjects, the non-conservers (NCc and NC4) constituted 40% of the sample from social class A, 41·07% from class B, and 23·81% from class C. These data are of the same order of magnitude as those in the preceding experiment.

After the pre-test in this experiment, the non-conservers were separated into three groups according to the experimental conditions. It was shown (see Table 34) that conditions (a) and (b) were most likely to induce progress, which is explained by the fact that these were the only conditions which placed subjects with different viewpoints together.

TABLE 34

Non-conservers' (NCo and NC4) progress in experiment III
(conservation of number): post-test scores according to
experimental condition

	Progress	No progress	Total[a]
Conditions (a) and (b)			
(1 NC+ 1 C, or 1 NC+ 1 I)	8	14	22
Condition (c) (2 NC)	0	10	10
Total	8	24	32

[a] Exact probability: $p = 0.034$.

TABLE 35

Distribution of subjects from different social environments across the experimental
conditions of experiment III, and their progress by post-test

	Experimental conditions				
	(a) and (b)		(c)		
	Progress	None	Progress	None	Total
Social class A	3	5	0	6	14
Social class B	5	7	0	4	16
Social class C	0	2	0	0	2
Total	8	14	0	10	32

Table 35 shows how NCc and NC4 subjects were distributed in the
different experimental conditions, and indicates their progress as
measured on post-test. It will be seen that, in this experiment also, no
child from social class C progressed, whereas there was development in
the subjects from the other classes: 3 out of 8 children from class A, and
5 out of 12 from class B. The pattern is the same as that in the preceding
experiment: the gap between social classes which was apparent on
pre-test has disappeared by the time of the post-test (here of course we
are only concerned with sub-levels NCc and NC4 since the interaction
in the experiment called for an initial level of development at least equal
to NCc).

INTERPRETATION OF THESE TRENDS

Suppose that the trends we have found in experiments II and III were
to be confirmed by a new investigation which showed their nature more
precisely—how then should they be interpreted?

Other research, for example, that undertaken within the framework of "compensatory education" which we have already discussed in Chapter 1, has supposed that the gap between the performance of children from different social backgrounds can in part, be "compensated for" by appropriate teaching.However, the teaching methods which have been tried in these studies have generally not had a significant effect on these inequalities. Our experiments, in contrast, have produced situations in which the inequalities seem to have completely disappeared.

It should be noted, following the demonstrations made by Campbell and Erlebacher (1970) and Campbell and Boruch (1975), that the effectiveness of compensatory teaching programmes is often underestimated, particularly by evaluation studies which do not make proper use of statistical regression techniques.

Nevertheless, it seems to us that precautions at the level of statistical techniques would not be sufficient in themselves to reduce the inequalities to the same degree that we have observed in our experiments. Why should our approach have been more successful?

In seeking for an explanation, our first considerations were methodological ones. Our method of evaluation of performance allowed us to avoid a frequent theoretical confusion between the notion of an individual's characteristic *aptitude** and that of *mastery* resulting from an intervention having a clear effect. This also allowed us to take into account the sequential structure of the acquisition of behaviours, and removed the necessity to postulate that the degree of development attained by the subjects would vary in a continuous fashion in a population. Such a postulation would have been already a doubtful presupposition on which to base the pre-test, but in the case of the post-test, the contradition with the experimental aim would have been even clearer, since the aim was, like that required of any educational intervention, to bring about specific learning in *all* the children. In assessing subjects' developmental levels within the framework of a theory of stages, we had to take acount, on the one hand, of the developmental prerequisites that all educational interventions presuppose, and on the other hand of the ceilings (or plateaux) that the acquisition of a concept or a behaviour implies. These features of our approach, together with the fact that it was based on precise knowledge

---

* The concept of aptitude is unsatisfactory in itself, remaining so after the early debates on the difference between "aptitude", "capacity" and "faculty". Is it possible that this is too broad a concept to permit theoretical advance?

of the learning processes involved (and could therefore avoid the problems that Campbell (1974, p. 37) has pointed out concerning the definition and evaluation of experimental aims)* perhaps made our method especially suitable for a comparative study of subjects from different social groups.

In other words, the experimental or educational treatment (in our case, the social interactions) never represents the sole correct combination of circumstances for the learning or development concerned to take place in and be observed (consider the question of developmental prerequisites, for instance). Furthermore, the theory and the research method must be flexible enough to take account of the wide range of combinations of circumstances which may be relevant.

The results of our experiments demonstrate two points, the necessity for an adequate methodology, and the role of social interactions in development. With proper regard given to both these factors, it is possible to obtain and record equivalent performances from all children, regardless of their social origin. This possibility indicates the potentialities of improving research by more effectively integrating the different levels: the methodological, the psychosociogenetic and the educational.

This analysis suggests also a possible re-interpretation of the results of an experiment carried out by Varnava-Skouras (1973) with disadvantaged children, in which the effects of a language programme and an operational programme on cognitive learning were compared. The operational programme was far superior, showing a very clear effect. Varnava-Skouras attributes this to the nature of the tasks and the materials she had designed. The source of the operational progress observed was said to be the subject's interaction with a physical environment structured in such a way that intellectual conflicts would be engendered ("conflicts of schemas" of the kind described by Inhelder *et al*). However, in describing the experimental procedure, Varnava-Skouras points out, without taking this point up again in her interpretation of the results, that the children were always placed in situations in which they had to play *together* with the materials provided. In other words, the children were in social interaction situations.

* Consider the following problem, for example: Is it acceptable to evaluate an educational programme using items which the children have been trained to answer in the course of the programme? Thoroughgoing training has not in fact been found to have any effect in the domain we are concerned with, thus we not subject to this particular criticism.

Were the materials effective because of the way in which they had been designed, or because the experimental situation provided the opportunity for cognitive conflict to take place among the children? It would appear that Varnava-Skouras' approach was similar to ours in two ways: she used a method of performance evaluation based on a theory of developmental stages, and she accorded an important place to social interaction among subjects—without, however, explicitly treating this as a factor. Her success, where so many educational experiments have failed, may equally well be explained by such factors.

Finally, since we have made reference to certain results of research within the compensatory education framework, we would like to pursue this theoretical analysis in commenting further on the psychological, sociological and educational aspects of this type of research.

In the light of the experiments which we have carried out or analysed, and the theoretical and methodological problems which have been raised by our attempt to articulate the psychological and the social; in the light also of the success of educational experiments like those of Cecchini et al. (discussed in Chapter 1) which were based on educational methods taking account of the child's own activity and rhythm of development, and which, most importantly, intensified social interactions among pupils, it seems to us that the weight of all these results leads to the need for a reformulation of the possible role of an "adequate education", and to the abandonment of the expression "compensatory education".

In fact, the practices which are still current in infant schools arise from a method of collective teaching* which addresses itself simultaneously to all the children in a class through the medium of presentations (a method which is very similar to the "presentations of models" which have been studied experimentally). It is difficult for such an approach to capture all the children's attention, interest and therefore activity (a factor whose importance for the development of every child is well known), but it is even less possible for it to accommodate to individual differences in level of development. According to our analysis of the results of "modelling effect" experiments, this type of intervention can only affect a child's mental development in so far as it succeeds in creating cognitive conflict between the child's point of view and that of

---

* It should be pointed out here that experiments have been in progress for some time in the attempt to find an alternative to this type of teaching (particularly in relation to the new mathematics).

the model. This can only be achieved by very precisely adapting the presentation to the child's current level of development, and it is just this type of adaptation which the class teaching method cannot provide. It should be noticed, however, that the existence of such adaptation, in a context in which teaching is individualized, is the sign of a real communication between the child and the teacher which permits social interaction on the cognitive level. But is not the same thing facilitated by interactions among children, which, as we have seen, are the source of development? Any educational practice aiming at the individualization of teaching should at the same time be founded on the intensification of social interactions among children, and we have already seen the advantages, in this case, of placing together children of different developmental levels.

Since, then, the current methods of infant school teaching are addressed to children as a collectivity, and use techniques such as presentation, they create a kind of social vacuum in the pupil-teacher relationship, since they do not offer the possibility of communication, and therefore deprive the child of social interactions of a *cognitive* order bearing on the *content* of the teaching. Nevertheless, we are bound to point out that these methods have attained a measure of success with children from certain social groups. Even so, there is the possibility that these children's families systematically compensate for the inadequacies of communication inherent in these teaching methods. Would not the solution be to integrate the content presented in school lessons into social interactions, rather than for certain types of parent to concern themselves with seeking out joint family activities which correspond to those experienced by the child in school, or with questioning the child about what has been done or said in class? While the effectiveness of such strategies may not always be consciously known to the parents who adopt them, it is nevertheless true that they are accompanied by very specific anxiety that they should not lose touch with what happens to their children in school. This is revealed in parents' reactions to efforts to discontinue homework (which represents a source of information about the content of school work for parents, and also an opportunity to check that the child is "keeping up") and also in parents' fears when innovatory programmes are introduced, such as the new mathematics, which mean that they will not be able to follow their children's progress in the unfamiliar subject.

Our interpretation of the possible role of an adequate education is, then, a moderately optimistic one. While it is not the function, nor is it within the capabilities of the school to compensate alone for the inequalities of society (see the critiques of sociologists on this subject, especially Bernstein, 1973) it nevertheless seems to us to be possible, and urgently necessary, to find ways of intervening more successfully in those of its functions which consist in giving all children, regardless of social origin, basic knowledge and techniques. We would like to hypothesize that, if the school were to base its teaching methods on theories which take account of *all* the factors in child development (including the role of social interaction) it would at least manage to fulfil its elementary teaching function without having to be supported by the family.

Why certain types of family are more successful than others in compensating for the school's deficiency is also a problem for the psychosociology of education, but it seems to be largely independent of the problem with which we are concerned here.

7

Future Research

Many questions have been raised by the research we have reported, which need careful consideration. Conclusions are impossible without a further series of experimental investigations together with theoretical research within the new framework of a genetic social psychology.

The interpretation of the facts we have reported, and the hypotheses to which they give rise, call for verification. As we have already indicated in citing their research, some of our colleagues are undertaking this, in parallel with our own current research. What new lines of exploration have emerged from this work?

The interest has become apparent of re-examining the classic social psychological question of the links which exist between the structure of groups and their performance, by placing it in a genetic perspective. Two new findings have led to this recommendation: firstly the observation that collective performances are superior *at the developmental stage during which the concept concerned is being elaborated*, an observation which allows us to step outside the terms of the current debate comparing individual, with group productions; and secondly, the demonstration of the benefit to the individual following collective action. The interest of joint activity does not lie solely in its superiority over individual performance, but as much in the opportunity which it provides for social interactions which can be fruitful for the cognitive development of the participants. We should therefore consider the effects of different networks of communication, and also the nature and role of the experimental task from this point of view. Doise and Mugny (1975) have shown that the absence of opportunity for verbal communication impairs collective performances at certain stages of development. Experimental tasks need to be evaluated in terms of their complexity in relation to the developmental level of coordination between subjects that they require, but they probably also need to be differentiated according to whether they facilitate intellectual confrontation, or instead lead to emotional conflicts which mask any cognitive conflict.

Here we come close to the problem pointed out by Haroche and

Pêcheux (1972) concerning the subject's relationship with the content of the task, and we have ourselves elsewhere looked at the role played by the significance which the subject attributes to the content of a task (Doise *et al.*, 1976). We should further study the course and the impact of the processes presupposed in these investigations, by observing them in the setting of particular social interactions, and evaluating their effect on the intellectual development of subjects.

The question would then be raised of the impact of the *nature* of the social relations entered into by the partners to any social interaction on the development of knowledge. Piaget (1958–1960), has already approached this question in his proposal to distinguish between the "collective representations" transmitted under the pressure of authority or tradition from the "scientific knowledge" which is the fruit of the subject's own active reconstruction, permitted by a situation of intellectual exchange among equals. What is meant by this idea of "equals"? We have seen that it is not necessary for partners in an exchange to be at the same level of development; and that children can benefit from social interactions with adults. The problem is this: Do the social relationships among the members of a collective situation distort the nature of the cognitive exchange? Using techniques derived from social categorization studies, we can approach this question by looking at the effects of subjects' representations of their partners, on both the course of the interaction and the succeeding individual cognitive changes.

In such attempts to articulate psychological with social processes, it is important to remember that experimentation itself is always inserted into a network of pre-existing social relations. Only sociological analysis can take proper account of this. Chapter 6 is no more than a first attempt in this direction; the results obtained need to be verified by new research which would be sociologically more sophisticated.*

In further studies of the psychology of intelligence, we should envisage not solely the effect of inter-individual coordination on *judgment* behaviour, or on *performance* as an index of development, as we did in most of the research we have reported, but also the impact of different types of social interaction, and in particular of partners' strategies, on the *strategy* which the subject adopts in order to carry out the task; in other words, how are inter-individual and intra-individual coordinations articulated?

* We have in fact attempted this in new experiments in different social contexts (Mugny *et al.*, 1979).

Our work is currently concerned with only one point in development: the beginning of the stage of concrete operations. If we adopt a genetic perspective, we must consider the role of social interactions throughout development, from the sensory-motor period to the stage of hypothetico-deductive thinking—even to the level of the elaboration of scientific knowledge: what is the role of cognitive conflict between researchers who are constantly either criticizing or defending theories and results? With a longitudinal approach, it would be possible, for a given concept, to specify the prerequisites and the social interactions necessary for each level of its construction by the subject. Our research on the conservation of number has shown which are the prerequisite conditions which permit the child to benefit from a given social interaction, but it was only possible to postulate that, if these conditions are fulfilled, it will only be thanks to previous social interactions. If this dependency could be systematically demonstrated, it would extend our knowledge of how the mechanisms of development are activated.

An understanding of this process of activation would be of great interest to the teacher, one of whose functions is to discover the methods of intervention which are most likely to facilitate, or even induce, cognitive development in children. As Hutmacher writes (1976, p. 13): "practice* is not conceived out of piecemeal recipes, but presupposes a coherent system of schemas and representations, knowledge and know-how which are able to generate the appropriate strategy at any moment and in any situation".

At the end of Chapter 6, we underlined the need, if teaching methods are to be adequate for all children, for them to be founded on a theoretical basis which takes simultaneous account of all factors in development, including the role of certain types of social interaction. This amounts to a vast field of research, which can only be embarked upon with the close cooperation of teachers who have practical knowledge of the problems of technical, material and temporal organization involved in dealing with a class of young children. Yet we feel that our

---

* Hutmacher is referring here to practice in the treatment and prevention of social deviance, but he stresses that the point is relevant in other domains. Furthermore it seems to us, that the problem of school failure is closely analogous to that of social deviance, if only because of the necessity which it reveals of relating psychological and sociological factors. For the same reasons, it also calls for interdisciplinary collaboration at the level of fundamental research. In both cases, it is only theoretical frameworks which can articulate the different levels of analysis and investigation pursued by the social sciences which are likely to lead to coherent practice.

research can already contribute, at least at the level of conceptualization (the "representations and knowledge" that Hutmacher refers to) to understanding the cognitive processes involved in interactions between teacher and pupil, or among pupils, and to the evaluation of their impact on individual learning.

It should be understood that our aim is not to bring theoretical frameworks to bear on the "intrinsic" evaluation of teaching methods, except perhaps in the first instance when this could prove useful in imagining alternatives, and aspects previously ignored. Rather, it is to go beyond the simple theoretical justification of certain teaching practices (whether they are new or old) in order to find out what conditions must be met, what processes must be brought about, for educational intervention to be productive. This is therefore a matter of being able to verify that intervention is productive in the sense desired, with the use of technically adequate means (we have mentioned the problem of methods of measurement in Chapter 6). The observations resulting from such evaluation should then either suggest adjustments at the level of practice, or raise new questions for researchers, who, as in the classic experimental situation, are faced with effects which must be explained even if this means changing the original theory. Attempted applications of genetic psychology have rarely taken this form, in fact.

This approach, which we have described elsewhere (Perret-Clermont, 1976, 1978) as a continuation of the interests which motivated our previous work, seems an appropriate one for the study of reciprocal teaching and group work in school.

Gartner *et al.* (1971) have reported several experiments which demonstrate the "tutor effect", or the personal benefit which a child can derive from teaching another child. But these authors evaluate the effect at the level of the motivation and socialization of the "tutor" child, without having the means to deal explicitly with the gains of *both* partners on the *intellectual* level. Allen and Feldman (1973) have found the same effect at the level of school performance: so-called "less gifted" children had better performances after acting as "tutors" to other children, than if they had done their work individually. Such experiments need to be refined: can this method of teaching be recommended regardless of the material to be taught, and of the pre-existing knowledge of the children? The first results of work in progress with teachers indicate that children aged 9–10 years, who act as tutors to each other in turn, are able to learn in this way to apply correctly the rules of grammar, even when later, they are given individual exercises. Analysis of these interactions suggests that learning can only begin if there is transmission from one child who has already acquired at least partial knowledge of the rule. But from the moment when the child has attained a certain level, it seems that they can draw benefit from acting as tutor to another child, regardless of the other child's level of development; for the "pupil" to benefit, however, the tutor must already possess some knowledge of the rule to be mastered by both of them. These results are awaiting confirmation from work which is now in progress. The question arises whether it is necessary to attribute such specific roles as "tutor" and "pupil" to children, which only transpose the classic teaching relationship, and whether it might be sufficient to create a cooperative situation. In the experiment we have just cited, it was the case that children who had the reputation of being "clever" refused to be tutored by children who were known as less bright than themselves. This problem relates to that of the representation of partners, which we have mentioned before. In fact, all of our previous experiments showed that cognitive learning can take place in circumstances of social interaction where the teaching aim is not made explicit, and may remain unrecognized by the subjects.

This leads us to place the tutor effect, and reciprocal teaching, together in the more general context of group work. There are some clarifications which need to be brought to the arguments surrounding this issue.

There often seems to be confusion between the *performance* of groups and individual *learning and development* when this type of activity is being evaluated. Also, there is often a problem concerning the interpretation to be placed on the existence of an isomorphism between the structure of concrete operations and the form of social relations in cooperation (in the sense that Piaget gives to these terms). This isomorphism has led some psychologists to speak of the incapacity of the pre-operational child (6–7 years old) to cooperate with peers, and therefore to deflect the interest of teachers away from group activities for children younger than this. Our research, however, has shown the importance of social interaction among very young children (note that 2 of our experiments were with 4–5-year-old children). We have also shown that, for a task to have educational value, it is not sufficient for it merely to engage children in joint activity; there must also be confrontation between different points of view. Are all the activites described as "cooperation" by research workers such as to induce real inter-individual coordinations which are the source of cognitive conflict? This question can only be answered by the systematic observation which remains to be done.

As far as the teacher-pupil relationship is concerned, we need to find out how the teacher can induce thinking in the child. This question relates to others we have raised previously concerning the effect of different types of social relations. Does the teacher's authority necessarily inhibit the child from constructing knowledge autonomously? Would it be possible, in some cases, for the teacher to make use of authority, not to impose an idea, but to make the child see that different viewpoints exist? This would mean that the child would carry out a real cognitive restructuring, instead of merely adopting a "belief". But what are the psycho-social contexts in which the child can distinguish between that which is the result of reasoning in the teacher, and that which depends on the application of norms which the teacher is seeking to induce respect for?

It seems plausible to suggest that this discrimination would be easier for pupils whose social and family environment appeals to norms which are similar to those of the teacher (concerning behaviour, discipline, language, styles of communication, the exercise of authority) which would mean that the social interaction in which they engage with this teaching adult is more cognitively stimulating for them.

These future possibilities for study are too numerous for us to be able to "conclude" our work properly at this point. It is therefore offered in its present provisional state, in the hope that we will receive the comments, criticisms and exchanges which bring about the restructuring required for progress, and in the certainty that the size of the task involved is greater than any one person can comprehend, and so calls for cooperation with other researchers, educators and teachers.

References

Aebli, H. (1966). "Egocentrism" (Piaget) not a phase of mental development but a "substitute solution" for an insoluble task. Report delivered at the XVIIIth International Congress of Psychology, Moscow, 1966.

Allen, V. L. and Feldman, R. S. (1973). Learning through tutoring: low-achieving children as tutors. *Journal of experimental Education* **42**, 1–5.

Bandura, A. (1971a). "Social Learning Theory." General Learning Press, New York.

Bandura, A. (1971b). "Theories of Modeling." Atherton Press, New York.

Bandura, A. and McDonald, F. J. (1963). Influence of social reinforcement and the behaviour of models in shaping children's moral judgments. *Journal of abnormal and social Psychology* **67**, 274–281.

Bernstein, B. (1961). Social structure, language and learning. *Educational Research* **3**, 1963–176.

Bernstein, B. (1973). A critique of the concept of compensatory education. *In* "Class, Codes and Control." Vol. I, pp. 214–226. Paladin, St. Albans, Herts.

Borke, H. (1975). Piaget's mountain revisited: changes in the egocentric landscape. *Developmental Psychology* **II** (2), 240–243.

Botvin, G. J. and Murray, F. B. (1975). The efficacy of peer modeling and social conflict in the acquisition of conservation. *Child Development* **46** (3), 796–799.

Bovet, M. (1968). Etudes interculturelles du développement intellectuel. *Revue suisse de Psychologie* **27**, 189–199.

Bovet, M. and Othenin–Girard, C. (1975). Etude piagétienne de quelques notions spatio-temporelles dans un milieu africain. *International Journal of Psychology* **10** (1), 1–17.

Bruner, J. S., Olver, R. R., Greenfield, P. M. (1966). "Studies in cognitive growth." J. Wiley, New York.

Campbell, D. T. (1975). Assessing the impact of planned social change. *In* "Social Research and Public Policies." (G. M. Lyons, Ed.) (The Dartmouth OECD Conference), The Public Affairs Center, University Press of New England, Hanover, New-Hampshire.

Campbell, D. T. and Boruch, R. F. (1975). Making the case for randomized assignment to treatments by considering the alternatives: six ways in which quasi-experimental evaluation in compensatory education tends to underestimate effects. *In* "Evaluation and Experiment." (C. A. Bennet and A. A. Lumsdaine, Eds) Academic Press, New York.

Campbell, D. T. and Erlebacher, A. E. (1970). How regression artefacts in quasi-experimental evaluation can mistakenly make compensatory education look harmful. *In* "Compensatory Education: A national debate." Vol. 3: Disadvantaged Child. (J. Hellmuth, Ed.) Brunner Mazel, New York.

Cecchini, M. and Piperno, F. (In press). Livello di aspirazione, età e classe sociale. I.P./C.N.R., Rapporto technico. *Archiva di Psicologia Neurologia Psicologia*.

Cecchini, M. and Tonucci, F. (1973). "Méthode pédagogique et développement du langage—quelques problèmes." Mimeo, Istituto di Psicologia, C.N.R., Rome. Avril, 1973.

Cecchini, M., Tonucci, F., Piṇto, M. A. and Dubs, E. (1972). "Teacher training, pedagogical method and intellectual development." Mimeo, Istituto di Psicologia, C.N.R., Rome.

Chaplin, M. V. and Keller, M. R. (1974). Decentering and social interaction. *Journal of Genetic Psychology* **124,** 269–275.

Ciutat Montserrat, A. and Udina, Abello M. (1974). Funcion de la escuela en la genesis de la nocion de cantidades continuas. *Annuario de Psicologia*, Departamento de Psicologia, Universidad de Barcelona **10,** 119–133.

Coleman, J. S. (1966). Equality of educational opportunity. US Government Printing Office, Washington, D.C.

Coll Salvador, C., Coll Ventura, C. and Miras Mestres, M. (1974). Genesis de la clasificacion y medio socioeconomico. Genesis de la seriacion y medios socioeconomicos. *Annuario de Psicologia*, Departamento de psicologia, Universidad de Barcelona **10,** 53–99.

Conférence des ministres de l'éducation des Etats d'Europe, membres de l'Unesco sur l'accès à l'enseignement supérieur, 1967. Accès à l'enseignement supérieur en Europe. Etudes et documents comparatifs. Rapport de la conférence Vienne. 20–25 novembre, 1967.

Cook, H. and Murray, F. B. (1975). "The acquisition of conservation through the observation of conserving models." Mimeo, Istituto di Psicologia, C.N.R., Rome.

Cowan, P. A., Langer, J., Heavenrich, J. and Nathanson, M. (1969). Social learning and Piaget's cognitive theory of moral development. *Journal of Personality and social Psychology* **11** (3), 261–274.

Cox, M. V. (1975). The other observer in a perspective task. *British Journal of educational Psychology* **43** (1), 83–85.

C.R.E.S.A.S. (1974). *Pourquoi les echecs scolaires dans les premières années de la scolarité?* Recherches sur les rôles respectifs des caractéristiques individuelles des enfants, de leur origine sociale et de l'institution scolaire. *Recherches Pédagogiques* No. 68. INRDP, Paris, 1974.

Dami, C. (1975). "Stratégies cognitives dans les jeux compétitifs à deux. "Doctoral thesis, Mimeo, Genève.

Department of Education and Science: Central Advisory Council for Education (England) (1967). "Children and Their Primary Schools" (Plowden Report). HM Stationery Office, London.

Deschamps, J. C. and Doise, W. (1974). "Attribution intersexes dans des conditions de catégorisation simple et de catégorisations croisées." Mimeo, Faculté de Psychologie et des Sciences de l'Education, Genève.

Deschamps, J. C., Doise, W., Meyer, G. and Sinclair, A. (1976). Le sociocentrisme selon Piaget et la différentiation catégorielle. *Archives de Psychologie* **44** (171), 31–43.

De Vries, R. and Kamii, C. (1974). "Why group games? A Piagetian perspective." (Paper to be edited by D. Sponseller in a monograph on play). Mimeo, 1974.

Doise, W. (1973). La structuration cognitive des décisions individuelles et collectives d'adultes et d'enfants. *Revue de Psychologie et des Sciences de l'Education* **8,** 133–146.

Doise, W. (1976a). "L'articulation Psychosociologique et les Relations entre Groupes." De Boeck, Bruxelles.

Doise, W. (1976b). Interaction sociale et développement cognitif. French translation of a chapter to appear in "Die Psychologie des 20. Jahrhunderts." Kindler Verlag, Zürich.

Doise, W. and Mugny, G. (1975). Recherches socio-génétiques sur la coordination d'actions interdépendantes *Revue Suisse de Psychologie* **34,** 160–174.

Doise, W., Mugny, G. and Perret-Clermont, A. N. (1974). Ricerce preliminari sulla sociogenesi delle strutture cognitive. *Lavoro educativo* **1** (1).

Doise, W., Mugny, G. and Perret-Clermont, A. N. (1975). Social interaction and the development of cognitive operations. *European Journal of Social Psychology* **5** (3), 367–383.

Doise, W., Meyer, G. and Perret-Clermont, A. N. (1976). Etude psycho-sociologique des représentations d'élèves en fin de scolarité obligatoire. *Cahiers de la Section des Sciences de l'Education* **2** (Enseignement et vie sociale), 15–27. (The pagination cited in the text is that of a previous mimeoed version.)

Douglas, J. W. B. (1964). "The Home and the School." MacGibbon & Kee, London.

Eells, K., Davis, A., Havighurst, R. J. (1951). "Intelligence and Cultural Differences." University of Chicago Press.

Eiser, C. (1974). Recognition and inference in coordination of perspectives. *British Journal of educational Psychology* **44,** 309.

Ferreiro, E. (1971). "Les Relations Temporelles dans le Langage de L'Enfant." Librairie Droz, Genève.

Finney, D. J., Latscha, R., Bennett, B. M. and Hsu, P. (1963). "Tables for Testing Significance in a 2 × 2 Contingency Table." Cambridge University Press, Cambridge.

Flavell, J. H. (1967). Role-taking and communication skills in children. *In* "The Young Child." (W. Hartup and N. Smothergill, Eds) National Association for the Education of Young Children, Washington D.C.

Flavell, J. H., Botkin, P. T., Fry, C. L., Wright, J. W. and Jarvis, P. E. (1968). "The Development of Role-taking and Communication Skills in Children." J. Wiley, New York.

Gartner, A., Kohler, M. C. and Riessman, F. (1971). "Children Teach Children: Learning by Teaching." Harper and Row, New York.

Garvey, C. (1974). Some properties of social play. *Merill Palmer Quarterly of Behavior and Development* **20** (3).

Garvey, C. and Hogan, R. (1973). Social speech and social interaction: egocentrism revisited. *Child Development* **44,** 528–562.

Girod, R. (en collaboration avec) Rouiller, J. F. (1963). "Milieu Social et Orientation de la carrière des Adolescents." Centre de recherches de la Faculté des sciences économiques et sociales de l'Université de Genève, Section de sociologie, Genève.

Glassco, J., Milgram, N. A. and Youniss, J. (1970). The stability of training effects on intentionality of moral judgment in children. *Journal of Personality and social Psychology* **14,** 360–365.

Goldschmid, M. and Bentler, P. M. (1968). Dimensions and measurement of conservation. *Child Development* **39,** 787–802.

Goldschmid, M. and Bentler, P. M. (1968). "Manual: Concept assessment kit, conservation." Educational and Industrial Testing Service, San Diego.

Gonvers, J. P. (1974). "Barrières Sociales et Sélection Scolaire." Thesis submitted to the University of Lansanne.

Greco, P. (1962). Quantité et qualité, nouvelles recherches sur la correspondance terme-à-terme à la conservation des ensembles. *In* "Structures Numériques Elementaires." (P. Gréco and A. Morf, Eds) Etude d'épistémologie génétique, Vol. XIII, P.U.F., pp. 1–70.

Greco, P. and Piaget, J. (1959). "Apprentissage et Connaissance." Etudes d'épistémologie génétique, Vol. VII, P.U.F.

Haan, N., Smith, M. and Block, J. (1968). Moral reasoning of young adults: political-social behavior, family background, and personality correlates. *Journal of Personality and social Psychology* **10**, 183–201.

Haramein, A. (1965). "Perturbations Scolaires." Delachaux et Niestlé, Neuchâtel.

Haroche, C. and Pêcheux, M. (1972). Facteurs socio-économiques et résolutions de problèmes. *Bulletin du C.E.R.P.* **21**, 101–117.

Hollos, M. (1975). Logical operations and role-taking abilities in two cultures: Norway and Hungary. *Child Development* **46** (3), 638–649.

Hollos, M. and Cowan, P. A. (1973). Social isolation and cognitive development: Logical operations and role-taking abilities in three Norwegian social settings. *Child Development* **44**, 630–641.

Hoy, E. A. (1974). Predicting another's visual perspective: A unitary skill? *Developmental Psychology* **10**, 462.

Hoy, E. A. (1975). The measurement of egocentrism in children's communication. *Developmental Psychology* **11** (3), 392.

Hunt, J. (1968). Environment, development and scholastic achievement. *In* "Social Class, Race and Psychological Development." (M. Deutsch, I. Katz and A. R. Jensen, Eds) Holt & Rinehart, New York.

Hutmacher, I. (1976). Déviance et maladie: invitation à la collaboration interdisciplinaire. *Revue suisse de sociologie* **1**, 5–14.

Huttenlocher J. and Presson, C. (1973). Mental rotation and the perspective problem. *Cognitive Psychology* **4**, 277–299.

Inhelder, B., Sinclair, H. and Bovet, M. (1974). "Apprentissage et structures de la connaissance." P.U.F., Paris.

Jencks, C. (1972). "Inequality. A reassesment of the effect of family and schooling in America." Basic Books, New York and London.

Kagan, J. (1971). "Personality Development." Harcourt Brace Jovanovich Inc., New York.

Kamii, C. (1972). How to choose group games. *In* "Piaget for Early Education." Book 3 (R. De Vries and C. Kamii, Eds).

Kamii, C. and De Vries, R. (1974). "La theorie de Piaget et l'éducation préscolaire." Mimeo. (Later appeared in *Cahiers de la section des sciences de l'éducation* (1975) **1**).

Katz, I. (1973). *In* "Psychology and Race." (P. Watson, Ed.) pp. 156–266. Penguin Education, Harmondsworth.

Kohlberg, L. (1969). Stage and sequence: the cognitive developmental approach to socialization. *In* "Handbook of Socialization Theory and Research." (D. A. Goslin, Ed.) pp. 347–480. Rand McNally, Chicago.

Kuhn, D. (1972). Mechanisms of change in the development of cognitive structures. *Child Development* **43**, 833–844.

Labov, W. (1972a). The logic of Non-Standard English. *In* "Language and Social Context." (P. P. Giglioli, Ed.) pp. 179–215. Penguin Education, Harmondsworth.

Labov, W. (1972b). The study of language in its social context. *In* "Language and Social Context." (P. P. Giglioli, Ed.) pp. 283–307. Penguin Education, Harmondsworth.

Latscha, R. (1953). Tests of significance in a 2×2 contingency table: extension of Finney's table. *Biometrika* **40**, 74–86.

Lautrey, J. (1974). Niveau socio-économique et structuration de l'environnement familial. *Psychologie Française* **19**, (1–2).

Lefebvre–Pinard, M. (1976). Les expériences de Genève sur l'apprentissage: un dossier peu convaincant (même pour un piagétien). *Canadian Psychological Review. Psychologie Canadienne* **17** (2), 103–109.

Lefebvre, M. and Pinard, A. (1972). Apprentissage de la conservation des quantités par une méthode de conflit cognitif. *Revue canadienne des Sciences du Comportement* **4**, 1–12.

Lefebvre, M. and Pinard, A. (1974). Influence du niveau initial de sensibilité au conflit sur l'apprentissage de la conservation des quantités par une méthode de conflit cognitif. *Revue Canadienne des Sciences du Comportement* **6**, 398–413.

Little, A. and Smith, G. (1971). "Stratégies de Compensation." OCDE. Paris, 1971.

Lorge, I and Solomon, H. (1955). Two models of group behavior in the solution of Eureka-type problems. *Psychometrika* **20**, 139–148.

McManis, D. L. (1974). Effects of peer-models vs adult-models and social reinforcement on intentionality of children's moral judgments. *Journal of Psychology* **87**, 159–170.

Maitland, K. A. and Goldman, J. R. (1974). Moral judgment as a function of peer group interaction. *Journal of Personality and Psychology* **30**, 699–704.

Marion, A., Desjardins, C. and Breaute, M. (1974). Conditions expérimentales et développement intellectuel de l'enfant de 5–6 ans dans le domaine numérique. *In* "Pourquoi les échecs dans les premières années de la scolarité? Recherches Pédagogiques." (C.R.E.S.A.S., Ed) No. 68. INRDP, Paris.

Masangkay, Z. S., McCluske, K. A., McIntyre, C. W., Simsknig, J., Vaughn, B. E. and Flavell, J. H. (1974). Early development of inferences about visual percepts of others. *Child Development* **45** (2), 357.

Miller, S. A. (1973). Contradiction, surprise and cognitive change: the effects of disconfirmation of belief on conservers and non-conservers. *Journal of experimental Child Psychology* **15**, 47–62.

Miller, S. A. and Brownell, C. A. (1975). Peers, persuasion, and Piaget: dyadic interaction between conservers and non-conservers. *Child Development* **46**, 992–997.

Moessinger, P. (1974). Etude génétique d'échange. *Cahiers de Psychologie* **17**, 119–123.

Moscovici, S. and Faucheux, C. (1972). Social influence, conformity bias and the study of active minorities. *In* "Advances in Experimental Social Psychology." (L. Bertowitz, Ed.) Vol. 6. pp. 149–202. Academic Press, New York and London.

Moscovici, S. and Paicheler, G. (1973). Travail, individu et groupe. *In* "Introduction à la psychologie sociale." (S. Moscovici, Ed.) Vol. II, pp. 9–44. Larousse.

Mounoud, P. (1970). "Structuration de l'Instrument chez l'Enfant." Delachaux et Niestlé, Neuchâtel.

Mugny, G. (1975). Bedeutung der Konsistenz bei der Beeinflussung durch eine konkordante oder diskordante, minderheitliche Kommunikation bei sozialen Beurteilungsobjekten. *Zeitschrift für Sozialpsychologie* **6** (4), 324–332.

Mugny, G. and Doise, W. (1978). Socio-cognitive conflict and structuration of individual and collective performances. *European Journal of Social Psychology* **8** (2), 181–192.

Mugny, G., Doise, W. and Perret–Clermont, A.-N. (1976). Conflit de centrations et progrès cognitif. *Bulletin de Psychologie* **29** (**321**, 4–7), 199–204.

Mugny, G., Perret–Clermont, A.-N. and Doise, W. (1979). Interpersonal coordinations and sociological differences in cognitive development. *In* "Progress in Applied Social Psychology." (G. M. Stephenson and J. H. Davis, Eds) Vol. 1. Wiley, New York.

Murray, F. B. (1972). Acquisition of conservation through social interaction. *Developmental Psychology* **6**, 1–6.

Murray, J. P. (1974). Social learning and cognitive development: modeling effects on children's understanding of conservation. *British Journal of Psychology* **65** (1), 151–160.

Nielsen, R. (1951). "Le Développement de la Sociabilité chez l'Enfant." Delachaux & Niestlé, Neuchâtel.

Nuttin, J. M. (1972). Changement d'attitude et role playing. *In* "Introduction à la Psychologie Sociale." Vol. I, pp. 13–58. (S. Moscovici, Ed.) Larousse.

Paicheler, G. (1974). Normes et changements d'attitudes. De la modification des attitudes envers les femmes. Doctoral thesis, Ecole Pratique des Hautes Etudes, Paris, (Roneo).

Pazienti, M., Dubs, E. and Cecchini, M. (1972). "Influenza della classe sociale, dell' ambiente sociale e del metodo pedagogico nell 'acquisizione del linguaggio scritto alla fine della seconda elementare." Mimeo, Istituto di Psicologia, C.N.R. Rome. Novembre, 1972.

Perrenoud, P. (1970). "Stratification Socio-Culturelle et Réussite Scolaire. Les Défaillances de l'Explication Causale." Librairie Droz, Genève.

Perrenoud, P. (1974). Education compensatrice et reproduction des classes sociales. Esquisse d'une sociologie politique de la démocratisation de l'enseignement, SRS, Genève. "Symposium de recherche éducationelle sur les handicapés socio-culturels", Gand, 24–28 september, 1973).

Perret–Clermont, A. N. (1976). Vers une approche des relations entre l'enfant, l'école et la vie sociale à travers l'étude de la communication, *Cahiers de la Section des Sciences de l'Education* Université de Genève **2**, 3–13.

Perret–Clermont, A. N. (1978). Processos psicossociologícos e insucesso escolar. *Análise Psicológica* Lisbonne, **2** (1), 69–81.

Perret–Clermont, A. N. (1978). Psychologie sociale expérimentale, recherche pédagogique et pratique éducative. *Cahiers de la Sections des Sciences de l'Education* Université de Genève **6,** 21–48.

Perret–Clermont, A. N., Mugny, G. and Doise, W. (1976). Une approche psycho-sociologique du développement cognitif. *Archives de Psychologie* **44** (171), 135–144.

Piaget, J. (1924). "Le Jugement et le Raisonnement chez l'Enfant." Delachaux and Niestlé, Neuchâtel. (English edition 1928) "Judgment and Reasoning in the child." Harcourt-Brace, New York.)

Piaget, J. (1947). "Le Langage et la Pensée chez l'Enfant." Delachaux and Niestlé, Neuchâtel and Paris. (1st edition 1923) (English edition 1926 "The Language and Thought of the Child." Harcourt-Brace, New York.)

Piaget, J. (1951). Pensée égocentrique et pensée socio-centrique. *Cahiers Internationaux de Sociologie* **10**, 34–49.

Piaget, J. (1956). "La Psychologie de l'Intelligence." Armand Colin, Paris. (Ist edition 1947) (English edition 1950 "Psychology of Intelligence." Harcourt-Brace and World, New York.)

Piaget, J. (1958–1960). Problèmes de la psycho-sociologie de l'enfance. *In* "Traîté de Sociologie." (G. Gurvitch, Ed.) Vol. II, pp. 229–254. P.U.F., Paris. p. 229–254.

Piaget, J. (1965). "Etudes Sociologiques." Librairie Droz, Genève.

Piaget. J. (1966). La psychologie, les relations interdisciplinaires et le système des sciences. *Bulletin de Psychologie* **254,** 242–254.

Piaget, J. (1967). "Biologie et connaissance." Gallimard, Paris. ("Biology and knowledge–University of Chicago Press, 1971").

Piaget, J. (1969). "Psychologie et pédagogie." Denoël, Paris.

Piaget, J. (1972). Intellectual evolution from adolescence to adulthood. *Human Development* **15**, 1–12.

Piaget, J. (1973). "Le Jugement Moral chez l'Enfant." P.U.F., Paris. (1st edition 1932) (English edition 1948 "The Moral Judgment of the Child." Free Press, Glen Coe, Illinois.)

Piaget, J. (1974a). "Adaptation Vitale et Psychologie de l'Intelligence." Sélection organique et phénocopie. Hermann, Paris.

Piaget, J. (1974b). "Recherches sur la Contradiction." Etudes d'Epistémologie génétique, Vol. XXXII, P.U.F., Paris.

Piaget, J. (1975). "L'équilibration des Structures Cognitives." Problème central du développement. Etudes d'Epistémologie génétique, Vol. XXXIII, P.U.F., Paris.

Piaget, J. (1976). "Postface." *Archives de Psychologie* **44** (171), 223–228.

Piaget, J. and Inhelder, B. (1941). "Le Développement des Quantités chez l'Enfant." Delachaux et Niestlé, Neuchâtel and Paris. (Later editions under the title "Le Développement des Quantités physiques chez l'Enfant".)

Piaget, J. and Inhelder, B. (1948). "La Représentation de L'Espace chez l'Enfant." P.U.F., Paris. (English edition 1956 "The Child's Conception of Space." Routledge and Kegan Paul, London.)

Piaget, J. and Inhelder, B. (1959). "La Genèse des Structures Logiques Elementaires." Delachaux and Niestlé, Neuchâtel. (English edition 1969 "The Early Growth of Logic in the Child." Norton, New York.)

Piaget, J. and Inhelder, B. (1967). "La Psychologie de l'Enfant." P.U.F., Paris, (1st edition 1967).

Piaget, J. and Szimenska, A. (1941). "La Genèse du Nombre." Delachaux and Niestlé, Neuchâte land Paris. (English edition 1952 "The Child's Conception of Number." Routledge and Kegan Paul, London.)

Piaget, J. Inhelder, B. and Szeminska, A. (1973). "La Géométrie Spontanée de l'Enfant." P.U.F., Paris. (1st edition 1948) (English edition 1960 "The Child's Conception of Geometry." Basic Books, New York.)

Rest, J., Turiel, E. and Kohlberg, L. (1969). Level of moral development as a determinant of preference and comprehension of moral judgments made by others. *Journal of Personality* **37**, 225–252.

Rose, S. A. (1973). Acquiescence and conservation. *Child Development* **44**, 811–814.

Rosenthal, T. L. and Zimmerman, B. J. (1972). Modeling by exemplification and interaction in training conservation. *Developmental Psychology* **6**, 392–401.

Rubin, K. H. (1974). The relationship between spatial and communicative egocentrism in children and young and old adults. *Journal of genetic Psychology* **125**, 295–301.

Selman, R. (1971). The relation of role-taking to the development of moral judgment in children. *Child Development* **42**, 79–91.

Service de la Recherche Sociologique (1974). "Annuaire Statistique de l'Education." Département de l'Instruction Publique, Genève.

Siches, E. and Vives, M. (1974). Funcion de la escuela in la genesis de la nocion de conservacion de cantidades discretas. *Anuarios de Psicologia* Departamento de Psicologia, Universidad de Barcelona **10**, 103–133.

Silverman, I. W. and Geiringer, E. (1973). Dyadic interaction and conservation induction: a test of Piaget's equilibration model. *Child Development* **44**, 815–820.

Silverman, I. W. and Stone, J. (1972). Modifying cognitive functioning through participation in a problem-solving group. *Journal of educational Psychology* **63**, 603–608.

Sinclair, H. (1967). "Langage et Opérations." Dunod, Paris.

Smedslund, J. (1966). Les origines sociales de la décentration. *In* "Psychologie et Epistémologie Génétiques. Thèmes Piagétiens." (F. Bresson, M. de Montmolin, eds) pp. 159–167. Dunod, Paris.

Smedslund, J. (1969). Psychological diagnostics. *Psychological Bulletin* **71**, (3), 237–248.
Sternlieb, J. L. and Youniss, J. (1975). Moral judgments one year after intentional or consequence modeling. *Journal of Personality and social Psychology* **31** (5), 895–897.
Tort, M. (1974). "Le Quotient Intellectuel." Cahiers Libres. pp. 266–267, Maspero, Paris.
Trevarthen, C., Hubley, P. and Sheeran, L. (1975). Les activités innées du nourrisson. *La Recherche* **56**, 447–458.
Turiel, E. (1966). An experimental test of the sequentiality of the developmental stages in the child's moral judgments. *Journal of Personality and social Psychology* **3**, 611–618.
Turiel, E. (1969). Developmental processes in the child's moral thinking. *In* "New Directions in Developmental Psychology." (P. H. Mussen, Langer, J. and E. M. Covington, Eds) Holt, Rinehart & Winston, New York.
Turnure, C. (1975). Cognitive development and role-taking ability in boys and girls from 7 to 12. *Developmental Psychology* **2** (2), 202–209.
Varnava–Skouras, E. (1973). "Les Apprentissages Cognitifs chez des Enfants de Milieux Défavorisés. Comparaison des effets d'un programme opératoire et d'un programme linguistique." Doctoral Thesis, University of Paris-Nanterre. Mimeo.
Vial, M., Stambak, M. and Burgviere, E. (1974). Caractéristiques psychologiques individuelles, origine sociale et échecs scolaires. *In* "Pourquoi les Echecs Scolaires dans les Premières Années de la Scolarité?" Recherches pédagogiques **68**, INRDP, Paris.
Villaronda, P., Fernandez, C. and Serra, B. (1974). Funcion de la escuela en la genesis de la clasificacion: 1. Cuantificacion de la inclusion. 2. Dicotomias. *Anuarios de Psicologia*, Departamento de Psicologia, Universidad de Barcelona **10**, 137–151.
Vinh–Bang (1966). La méthode clinique. *In* "Psychologie et Epistémologie génétiques. Thèmes piagétiens." (F. Bresson, M. de Montmolin, Eds) Dunod, Paris.
Waghorn, L. and Sullivan, E. (1970). The exploration of transition rules in conservation of quantity (substance) using film mediated modeling. *Acta Psychologica* **32**, 65–80.
Whitheman, M. and Deutsch, M. (1968). Social disadvantages as related to intellectual and language development. *In* "Social Class, Race, and Psychological Development." (M. Deutsch, I. Katz and A. R. Jensen, Eds) Holt, New York.
Zimmerman, B. J. and Lanaro, P. (1974). Acquiring and retaining conservation of length through modeling and reversibility cues. *Merrill-Palmer Quarterly of Behavior and Development* **20** (3), 145–161.
Zimmerman, B. J. and Rosenthal, T. L. (1972). Observation, repetition and ethnic background in concept attainment and generalization. *Child Development* **43**, 605–613.
Zimmerman, B. J. and Rosenthal, T. L. (1974). Conceptual generalization and retention by young children. Age, modeling and feedback effects. *Journal of genetic Psychology* **125**, 233.

Subject Index

European Monographs in Social Psychology

Series Editor: HENRI TAJFEL

E. A. CARSWELL and R. ROMMETVEIT
Social Contexts of Messages, 1971

J. ISRAEL and H. TAJFEL
The Context of Social Psychology: A Critical Assessment, 1972

J. R. EISER and W. STROEBE
Categorization and Social Judgement, 1972

M. VON CRANACH and I. VINE
Social Communication and Movement, 1973

CLAUDINE HERZLICH
Health and Illness: A Social Psychological Analysis, 1973

J. M. NUTTIN, JR. (and Annie Beckers)
The Illusion of Attitude Change: Towards a Response Contagion Theory of Persuasion, 1975

H. GILES and P. F. POWESLAND
Speech Style and Social Evaluation, 1975

J. CHADWICK-JONES
Social Exchange Theory: Its Structure and Influence in Social Psychology, 1976

M. BILLIG
Social Psychology and Intergroup Relations, 1976

S. MOSCOVICI
Social Influence and Social Change, 1976

R. SANDELL
Linguistic Style and Persuasion, 1977

H. GILES
Language, Ethnicity and Intergroup Relations, 1977

A. HEEN WOLD
Decoding Oral Language, 1978

H. TAJFEL
Differentiation between Social Groups: Studies in the Social Psychology of Intergroup
    Relations, 1978

M. BILLIG
Fascists: A Social Psychological View of the National Front, 1978

C. P. WILSON
Jokes: Form, Content, Use and Function, 1979

J. P. FORGAS
Social Episodes: The Study of Interaction Routines, 1979

R. A. HINDE
Towards Understanding Relationships, 1979

In preparation

B. A. GEBER and S. P. NEWMAN
Soweto's Children: The Development of Attitudes, 1980

S. H. NG
The Social Psychology of Power, 1980